CONDI

THE

CONDOLEEZZA RICE STORY

CONDI

THE
CONDOLEEZZA RICE
STORY

NEW UPDATED EDITION

Antonia Felix

Newmarket Press • New York

This book is published in the United States of America.

New updated edition

ISBN 1-55704-675-1

Designed by MaryJane DiMassi

Manufactured in the United States of America.

*To Maria Yeliseyeva,
my Russian sister*

"HENRY, SORRY TO TELL YOU THIS,
BUT IT'S NO LONGER A FRATERNITY."

—*Newly appointed
Secretary of State Madeleine Albright
to Henry Kissinger, 1997*

CONTENTS

ACKNOWLEDGMENTS

There are many people to thank for their vital and generous contributions to this book. I am grateful to Clara Bailey Rice of Palo Alto, California, for taking the time to speak to me about her stepdaughter. My heart goes out to all the warm, gracious, and considerate people who made my research in Birmingham so enlightening and productive, including Miss Juliemma Smith for her wonderful conversations and guided tour of Birmingham's Westminster Presbyterian Church and Titusville, as well as to Westminster's Reverend William Jones and Annette Cooper. Special thanks to my other Birmingham guide, Pam King, who conducted a fascinating tour and generously shared her expertise of the city's history. It was also a pleasure and an honor to receive a civil rights tour from distinguished University of Alabama Professor Jack Davis, whom I also thank for the literary football analogy sources. I also thank Birmingham ladies Margaret Cheatham and Shirley Epps for their words, their time, and their efforts. I am deeply indebted to Deborah Carson for her enormously important input. It was a great pleasure to meet one of Condi's oldest friends.

My deep appreciation goes to Rebecca Laurie of the University of Denver's Communication Department for her diligent work in tracking down a vast amount of information for me. Thank you, Professor Karen Feste at the University of Denver, for your generous interview. And warm thanks to all the Rice family friends in Denver: Darcy Taylor, Russ and Margaret Wehner, and Reverend Richard Hutchison, as well as Condoleezza's former teachers at St. Mary's, Sister Sylvia Pautler, and Therese Saracino.

Most of what I learned about Condoleezza's graduate work at Notre Dame I owe to the generosity of her former professor there, Dr. George Brinkley. I wish him a wonderful continued retirement.

Many thanks to Paul Brest, president of the Hewlett Foundation, and John Raisian, director of the Hoover Institution, for taking the time for interviews. I am also grateful to Professors George Barth and John Ferejohn of Stanford University for their insightful comments. It was great talking to Condoleezza's former workout coach at Stanford, Mark Wateska, and I appreciate the thoughtful correspondence I received from Professor Gail Lapidus, Robby Laitos, Jim Copland, and Jason Gailie. Thanks to Professor Albert Cannella for providing key insights about women's paths to corporate boards. And thank you, Dmitri Gerasamenko, for sharing your compelling personal stories about Russian urban life.

This project would not have been possible without the excellent research work of Sandra Upson at Stanford and Shannon Berning at Newmarket Press. I also extend warmest thanks to Keith Hollaman, my editor, and Esther Margolis, the president of Newmarket, for their enthusiasm and support and for creating such an author-friendly publishing house. Your patience and kindness is deeply appreciated. And, as always, love to my husband Stanford for all his support, encouragement, and late-night readings.

The input of those mentioned, as well as information gleaned from scores of previously published interviews and articles by and about Dr. Condoleezza Rice, has allowed me to present the first biography of one of America's most prominent foreign policy officials—and perhaps one of the most famous black women in the world. Dr. Rice has made history by being named the first female national security advisor and the second black person to hold that post (General Colin Powell was the first), and delving into her life story has been an inspiring and highly informative experience. I have been inspired by the Rice/Ray family legacy and how Dr. Rice carries that inheritance into the world with her own brand of passion and commitment. I have been informed about the realities of growing up black in Birmingham in the 1950s and 1960s and the differing types of black experience during that struggle. And I have also been stimulated by insights into the inner workings of academia, policy making, corporate boards, and other areas that are covered in Dr. Rice's life story.

My intent has been to focus on Dr. Rice's family, childhood, education, and career path rather than to construct a commentary on her political and policy views. It has been my goal to create a comprehensive portrait of the person who has the president's ear perhaps more than anyone else in the White House—a black woman who has risen to the top in a field traditionally dominated by white men and who has experienced firsthand some of the nation's darkest and brightest moments.

PRELUDE

WHEN Condoleezza Rice was ten years old, her parents took her on a trip to Washington, D.C. For John and Angelena Rice, whom Condoleezza has described as "education evangelists," the nation's capital was the ultimate vacation destination—so much history to discover, so many museums to explore, so much to inspire a young mind. Strolling along Pennsylvania Avenue, they stopped to peer through the gate in front of the White House. Condoleezza stared quietly at the pillared façade. The trio stood in silence until the girl turned to her father and said, "Daddy, I'm barred out of there now because of the color of my skin. But one day, I'll be in that house."

Not only was she a precocious child, but prophetic, too. Twenty-five years later she was working fourteen-hour days as President George H. W. Bush's top advisor on the Soviet Union, helping write U.S. policy through the unification of Germany and the end of the Cold War. Eleven years after her two-year stint in that administration, she reentered the White House as President George W. Bush's national security advisor.

During George W.'s presidential campaign, Jay Nordlinger predicted in the *National Review* that whatever post Condoleezza Rice received in the administration she would be "rock-star big"—a household name. She has not yet appeared on any billboards in Times Square, but her celebrity status is on the rise. This became most evident after September 11, 2001, when she was appointed one of the primary White House spokespeople on the war on terrorism. Her visibility has also been enhanced by ritual appearances on the Sunday Washington talk shows and through lengthy profiles in magazines such as *Vogue, George* (now defunct), and *O: The Oprah Magazine.* And in some parts of the country, she has been a star for quite some time. In East Palo Alto, California, for example, where she cofounded an after-school academy for children from underfunded school districts, she is a local hero. And in the field of Soviet studies, her chosen specialty since first hearing a lecture on Stalin as a junior in college, she is a nationally renowned expert and scholar.

Condoleezza Rice has two passions in her life: music and Russia. This book explores her family's musical roots, which formed both her name and her goal of becoming a concert pianist. That part of her story took a sudden detour in her teen years when she decided she did not have what it takes to enter the very small ranks of the concert world. She made a sharp turn when she heard a charismatic professor (the father of former Secretary of State Madeleine Albright) lecture on the Soviet Union, and entered that oddly familiar and captivating territory, never to turn back.

From her childhood in Birmingham, Alabama, which in the 1950s and 1960s was the most segregated city in the South and a focal point of the Civil Rights movement, to her ascension to one of the most powerful posts in government, Condoleezza Rice's story is founded on a compelling family legacy. She is a proud daughter of the Rices and the Rays, two lineages devoted to education and achievement. She is also very much her father's daughter, a preacher's child devoted to the same causes, solidified with the same strength of character, and supported by the same faith.

This story follows Condi's journey into the highest ranks of a field dominated by men, in which her colleagues describe her style as firm but friendly. "She is, all agree, an immensely appealing person," stated the *National Review*, "poised, gracious, humbly smart, still markedly Southern after all these years in other parts." Several people interviewed for this book remarked on her exuberance, noting that she is an extremely content person who draws from a deep well. "Condi is one of those happy-go-lucky kinds of people," said her University of Denver Professor Karen Feste. "She doesn't have an unhappy side to her; at least I've never seen it." In describing herself, Condi explains the source of her outlook. "I'm a really religious person," she said, "and I don't believe that I was put on this earth to be sour, so I'm eternally optimistic about things." She does not hide her achievements, but at the same time does not overestimate herself. "I think I'm above average," she said, "but not much more. When you've been a professor and provost at Stanford, you know what real genius is. I've seen genius, and I'm not it."

President George W. Bush would probably disagree. His father came to admire Condi during his administration when she worked for his national security advisor Brent Scowcroft, recognizing her formidable intelligence and loyalty. George H. quickly brought her into the Bush fold, treating her like family. She has been George W.'s friend since his first weeks as governor of Texas and his top foreign policy advisor since his presidential campaign. As national security advisor, she is also his top referee in delivering the often powerfully divided opinions of the secretary of defense, secretary of state, and other members of the National Security Council to the president's desk.

If her life were mapped in sonata form, Condoleezza Rice could well be in the development phase, each theme gathering momentum in an upward arch toward their peak moment. At the pinnacle, her interwoven motifs will burst out in one dramatic, triumphant declaration. To some, this peak lies before her as first woman president of the United States. Others envision her as governor of California or as a U.S. senator from that state. But for now, she is one of the president's top advisors and closest confidants, whether they are in the White House, at Camp David, or at the Bush ranch in Crawford, Texas.

ONE

Coaching the Candidate

> "The presidency is not just the President. It's a whole team of people who are going to get things done."
> —*Condoleezza Rice, 1999*

TO everyone in her inner circle, she is known as Condi, a name that trips off the tongue more easily than her full given name. Her mother, a pianist and organist, fashioned Condoleezza (kahn-dah-LEE-za) from the Italian term *con dolcezza*, which in a score of music instructs the performer to play "with sweetness." There is a tradition of Italian names on both sides of Condi's family—Theresa, Angelena, Angela, Genoa, Alto—and the unusual spin that the Rices put on her name was fitting for the distinctive individual she would become. In raising Condoleezza, John and Angelena Rice followed the direction inherent in her name, always heaping kindness upon her in their zealous efforts to educate, inspire, and motivate her to excel. Condi's rock-solid foundation of love and positive influence underlies every step she has taken, including her entry into an office just down the hall from the president of the United States.

The president has always called her Condi, while her staff members call her Dr. Rice. She appears to have escaped the president's penchant for nicknames, even though most of his associates as well as press people have been dubbed with one. Even heads of state are not immune—as his friendship with Russian President Vladimir Putin warmed in early 2002, George W. dubbed him "Pootie-Poot."

Condoleezza's foray into the Bushes' inner circle was launched at a dinner at Stanford University in 1987, when a few remarks she made changed the course of her career. Along with other members of the political science faculty, she attended an event at which President Gerald R. Ford's national security advisor, Brent Scowcroft, made a speech. During the dinner afterward, which was attended by many of the top foreign policy minds in the country, Scowcroft found the conversation "dreary" until a young political science professor named Dr. Rice spoke up. "Here was this slip of a girl," he recalled. "Boy, she held her own. I said, 'That's someone I've got to get to know.'" From her comments, Scowcroft realized that she possessed a profound understanding of Soviet ideology that matched his own brand of political realism. "She saw where we could cooperate and where not," he recalled.

Scowcroft was so bowled over by Rice that she immediately came to mind when he became national security advisor in the first Bush administration. Immediately after the election in 1988, Scowcroft began selecting the staff that would join him in the White House. "One of my first phone calls was to Condi Rice," he said. Based on her scholarly expertise of the Soviet Union, he appointed her director of Soviet affairs at the National Security Council. Not only did she gain the respect of her colleagues in this post, she quickly became a personal friend of both President and Barbara Bush.

Just as his son would do a decade later, the elder George Bush relied upon Condi to tutor him on Soviet military and political history. During his term, in which the Berlin Wall fell and the Soviet Union dismantled, he forthrightly credited her for keeping him up to speed on the subject, telling one head of state that she "tells me everything I know about the Soviet Union." After Bush I's term was over, Condi returned to her teaching job at Stanford. She remained friendly with George and Barbara, and was often invited to their Houston home and their summerhouse in Kennebunkport, Maine.

She met frequently with the former president as part of what Barbara called the "book group," at times consisting of Condi, Scowcroft, and Bush, to help write a book about major global events that occurred during Bush's administration. The work was begun during Bush's first year out of office and included the input of many people. Condi made lengthy visits to Houston and Kennebunkport throughout 1997 to help Bush with the book.

The final product, *A World Transformed*, was published in 1998 and covers events that occurred from 1989 to 1991, including the fall of the Berlin Wall, the collapse of the Soviet Union and end of the Cold War, and the Gulf War. In the introduction, Bush and Scowcroft state, "Some of the most dramatic and epochal events of the twentieth century took place during the short period of 1989 to 1991 . . . did we see what was coming when we entered office? No, we did not, nor could we have planned it. . . . Yet, in only three years—historically only a moment—the Cold War was over." Bush credits Condi for contributing extensively to the book by helping the authors scope out its content, refreshing their memories of particular details, and sharing research she had done for *Germany Unified and Europe Transformed*, a book she co-wrote with Philip Zelikow in 1995.

During a visit with George and Barbara Bush in Houston in 1995, George asked Condi to make a call on his son in Austin before going home. George W. was settling in as the newly elected governor—his first political office (in 1978, he had made an unsuccessful bid for a state congressional seat). Perhaps George Sr. felt that Condi could be an asset to his son down the road should his political aspirations grow beyond the state of Texas. Or maybe he wanted to introduce them because they share an obsession for sports and carry their steely self-discipline into their workout routines, a trademark of the athletic and competitive Bush clan. Such a common thread would be a strong foundation for friendship and create a context in which they could discuss politics and world affairs. Whatever his reasons, George suggested Condi meet the new governor, and she agreed.

The governor and Condi hit it off immediately, bonding like any two sports fanatics. George W. was still a co-owner of the Texas Rangers, and they chatted about baseball as they looked over George's signed-baseball collection, lovingly arranged in a set of glass display cases. Condi wowed George with stories about Willie Mays, who was a student in one of her mother's classes at Fairfield Industrial High School in Birmingham—real-life stories about Mays that probably only a handful of people have ever heard. For a baseball fan, it just doesn't get any better than that. "Governor Bush was very impressed," Condi recalled.

During that visit, George W. gained not only Condi's friendship but her respect as well. "He's really smart—and he's also disciplined, which I admire," she said. "He's tough, calm and even-keeled . . . [and] he also has a great sense of humor." George Senior's instincts about Condi and George W. were on target; the two had a chemistry that created a bond of friendship, loyalty, and respect. As a result, Condi would figure large in the next step of his political career.

During one mini-vacation with the Bush clan at Kennebunkport in the summer of 1998, George W. and Condi had a series of intense conversations about pressing global issues of the day. The governor was considering a run for the presidency, and he knew that his friend could give him clear, straightforward summaries of complex issues. Neither of them were the type to relax and chat while sipping ice tea on the porch, so they hammered out their discussions while running side-by-side on the treadmill, whacking balls on the tennis court, or fishing. Condi didn't actually fish—she left that to George W. and his father. She isn't even fond of the water, but in this case she went along. "I don't get seasick," she said, "but I also don't like the water very much and I most certainly don't fish. I let President and Governor Bush fish and I sat and talked. We talked a lot about the state of the American armed forces and ballistic missile defense." All the while, George W. fired questions such as, "What about relations with Russia, what about relations with China? [And] what about the state of the military?"

This grueling exchange marked the beginning of Condi's long-term relationship with George W. as his closest foreign policy advisor.

In late 1999, when George W.'s campaign began to take shape, he enlisted Condi as his primary tutor on foreign policy. She had stepped down from her job as provost of Stanford University and had been contemplating a variety of options at the time. She figured she could keep exploring those options while coaching the candidate on foreign affairs.

When Condi started out on the campaign, she assumed it would be part-time and, apart from her tutoring sessions, limited to a few appearances here and there. Her friend, Deborah Carson, who had worked on Clinton's campaign in 1992, soon set her straight. "When we talked about it, she thought she would just be giving a few speeches on national security," Deborah said. "Condi told me, 'I'm not really going to be part of the campaign.' She thought they'd just fly her out and she'd give a few speeches on national security! I said, 'Well, wait a minute, you don't know campaigns. You're going to be at every chicken dinner—it's not going to happen right away, but as that thing gets going, they're going to pull you in. You're not going to be talking about national security, you're going to talk about whatever they need you to talk about at the time.' And so as the campaign progressed, we were talking and she said, 'You know, you were right.'"

Not only did Condi take charge of George W.'s foreign policy advisory group and work with him as his main tutor, she eventually got called out to make other appearances not related to foreign policy. The campaign needed her as a woman—to help get the female vote—and as a black person—to emphasize the candidate's intent to place minorities in his new administration.

From early on in the campaign, it was obvious that Condi had the candidate's ear and had the closest affinity to him. They shared an obsession for fitness and sports, and it appeared that only she could temper the complexities of foreign policy with the clarity Bush appreciated. And perhaps most importantly, they had chemistry. "I like to be around her," the governor said. "She's fun to be with. I like lighthearted people, not people who take themselves so seriously that they are hard to be around. Besides, she's really smart!" He revealed the depths of their working relationship when he described Condi as "a close confidant and a good soul." And from the start, the admiration was mutual. "I've respected him from the first time we talked," said Condi, "because he has the kind of intellect that goes straight to the point. You can get a bunch of academics in a room and they can talk for three hours and never actually get to the point."

George W.'s cadre of foreign policy advisors included eminent veterans of previous administrations (including his father's) such as Richard Armitage, Robert Zoellick, Paul Wolfowitz, Robert Blackwill, and Richard Perle. As coordinator of the group, Condi caught George W.'s bug for nicknaming and set out to find a label for the group. She chose the name of her hometown's most famous mascot, Vulcan, the Roman god who created thunderbolts and hammered metal into tools for the gods, loomed over Birmingham, Alabama, when Condi was a child. The colossal statue, which stood on the crest of Red Mountain, had been built by the steel town for an exhibit at the 1904 St. Louis World's Fair. When Vulcan returned to his hometown he was placed on top of the mountain, far enough from view so that his scantily clad physique wouldn't offend anyone. The Jaycees even gave him a job, placing a neon torch in his left hand that normally glowed green but switched to bright red whenever a fatal traffic accident occurred in the city.

"I grew up right there in Birmingham with Vulcan," said Condi. "I remember as a little girl that it was red if there was an accident or green if everything was clear."

The candidate's foreign policy advisory group was committed to forging the candidate's grasp of world affairs and proving to the world that he was presidential material. Condi, who has a fondness for football metaphors, described herself as a "quarterback" for the Vulcans. "I don't try to do it all myself," she said. "Like a quarterback, I can hand off or throw downfield." She fielded this key position because George W. valued her ability to decipher complex policy issues into easy-to-digest, nuts-and-bolts language. He described her as someone who "can explain to me foreign policy matters in a way I can understand."

Whether Condi's talent for clarity is natural or has been gleaned from years of teaching political science to undergraduates, it is one of her most highly respected qualities in Washington. "She has an extraordinary ability to be clear," one European diplomat in Washington stated in a *Vogue* profile of Rice. "Her powers of exposition on a very wide range of complicated topics are extraordinarily strong." That point was also made by Philip Zelikow, a former colleague who worked with Condi in the first Bush administration. "One of the things that is appealing to Bush is that she can be very down to earth in cutting right to the heart of matters," he said. "People in the foreign policy world are generally not good at that."

In her role as director of Bush's foreign policy advisory team, Rice took the lead in what has traditionally been an all-male domain. She was not intimidated; rather, she approached the job with the confidence of past experience—having served in the elder Bush's administration—and with a sense of control gleaned from years of teaching at Stanford. "She is a novel commodity," observed Ivo Daalder, a former National Security Council member. "Here is a highly accomplished African-American woman . . . being part of what is and always has been [a] boys' club."

Part of Condi's responsibilities with the Vulcans involved working with Paul Wolfowitz to set up intensive half-day training seminars for George W. that covered defense, weapons proliferation, Europe, and other topics. The chemistry between Condi and George W. allowed this process to run smoothly, and she remarked that they had a similar approach to confronting the material. When the press questioned the governor about his lack of experience in foreign affairs, he assured them that he had strong resources behind him. "I may not be able to tell you exactly the nuance of the East Timorian situation, but I'll ask people who've had experience, like Condi Rice, Paul Wolfowitz, or Dick Cheney. I am smart enough to know what I don't know, and I have good judgment about who will either be telling me the truth, or has got some agenda that is not the right agenda."

Condi strenuously backed the governor during these press sessions. She explained that any executive, including a governor, is accustomed to facing issues about which he or she has minimal previous experience. Gathering information and making important decisions on items as they come up is a natural part of the territory, even for a president in training. Condi's executive experience came from her role as provost at Stanford, the number-two post just beneath the president, responsible for the $1.5 billion budget and administrative decisions. George's executive experience came from his years in the oil industry in West Texas, as a managing partner of a very profitable baseball team, and as governor of Texas. "As an executive," said Condi, "you're always asked to make important decisions about which your knowledge base is relatively slim. Someone might ask me to support a million-dollar physics telescope. I don't know a lot about that, but I can ask hard questions and get a sense about whether it's important, and prioritize it against other issues."

When the press pointed out the candidate's inability to name heads of state and his slips in vocabulary, Condi dismissed the attacks as a "parlor game" played by Washington pundits. She stressed the experience he had gained in both business and politics and reminded them that every president relies upon a team of advisors and experts. "Governor Bush has not spent the last ten years of his life at Council on Foreign Relations meetings," she said. "He's spent the last ten years of his life building a business and being governor of a state."

She also had to discuss her own limitations and admitted that the candidate was not the only one with much to learn. Condi's career as a Soviet scholar gave her vast insight into that part of the world but little background in the political histories of other regions. She did not have a strong grasp of America's policies in Asia, Africa, Latin America, or other non-European nations, and had to undergo her own crash course in those areas. "I've been pressed to understand parts of the world that have not been part of my scope," she said. "I'm really a Europeanist."

Because George W. did not like to read prepared manuals about policy or national security, Condoleezza had to devise a more interpersonal approach to his tutoring sessions. She set up question-and-answer roundtables for him and the advisors. Another of her primary tasks was drafting a clear-cut nuclear weapons policy for the candidate. The Vulcans worked for a year on this issue at specially arranged policy retreats, and their efforts culminated in Bush's nuclear policy speech delivered on May 23, 2000.

The speech was Condoleezza's baby. In addition to reviewing it with the Vulcans, she sought feedback from her former White House boss Brent Scowcroft, former Secretaries of State Henry Kissinger and George P. Shultz, General Colin Powell, and others. Once she felt the content was as precise as possible, she spent hour after hour going over every line with Bush. A crucial part of her job was to ensure that he understood every facet of the policy and the background of every issue contained in the speech. Condoleezza and Paul Wolfowitz created a companion document containing questions and answers about topics in the speech for Bush's study. But George W. didn't like to work in isolation, reading and integrating facts on his own, so they scheduled verbal question-and-answer sessions.

The heart of the nuclear policy speech recommended reducing America's nuclear arsenal; removing more weapons from high-alert, "hair-trigger" status; and immediately building a missile defense system. "America must build effective missile defenses," Bush stated, "based on the best available options, at the earliest possible date. Our missile defense must be designed to protect all fifty states—and our friends and allies and deployed forces overseas—from missile attacks by rogue nations, or accidental launches." The Vulcans' policy stressed the need to erase the Cold War mind-set and face facts about new types of threats. "The Cold War era is history," Bush continued in the speech. "Our nation must recognize new threats, not fixate on old ones. On the issue of nuclear weapons, the United States has an opportunity to lead to a safer world—both to defend against nuclear threats and reduce nuclear tensions."

As the campaign progressed, George W. and Condi's smooth-running, efficient working style solidified their friendship and further enhanced their respect for each other. As a result, George W. felt confident about bringing Condi into other areas of the campaign. Just as her friend Deborah predicted, she was called upon to make appearances that she had not anticipated. Most of these involved the "W is for Women" program. A major goal of the Bush campaign was to lure women voters from the Democratic party, and the "W is for Women" tour featured George W.'s mother, Barbara; his wife, Laura; and Richard Cheney's wife, Lynne. Condi joined the troupe in mid-October 2000 as the trip wound through Michigan, Pennsylvania, and Wisconsin.

"W is for Women" was one part of a calculated move to undo what previous Republican campaigns and National Conventions had done—create a gender gap between the parties. Barbara Bush and her group sought to portray George W. as the face of a new and improved Republican party committed to education and women's health—a far cry from the angry, warrior-like tone of the pro-gun, anti-abortion, macho-white-male party of past GOP conventions. Things would be different, Barbara Bush stressed, because George W. is comfortable with tough and capable women. "He's always been surrounded by strong, smart women," Barbara said at a stop in Blue Bell, Pennsylvania. "Sometimes by choice, sometimes by birth."

The "W is for Women" theme was also in full force at the Republican National Convention in Philadelphia, where keynote speakers included Laura Bush, Elizabeth Dole, Lynne Cheney, and Condoleezza Rice. In her speech, laced with personal anecdotes, Condi talked about her family's proud legacy of college education, her father's decision to join the Republican Party, and the integrity of the candidate she had come to know well.

"George W. Bush, the George W. Bush that I know," she said, "is a man of uncommonly good judgment. He is focused and consistent. He believes that we Americans are at our best when we exercise power without fanfare and arrogance. He speaks plainly and with a positive spirit."

Throughout the campaign, political commentators discussed where Condoleezza Rice would be placed in the new Bush administration. The two positions mentioned most often were national security advisor and secretary of state. When asked about this herself, Condi always deflected the debate and said that her dream job was to be commissioner of the National Football League. She wasn't joking. "Anybody who really knows me knows that that's absolutely true," she told one interviewer, "and that if the NFL job comes up, the governor is on his own." With a football coach for a father, she had learned more about football by age ten than most fans discover in a lifetime. She loves to talk about football and to describe where it fits in the bigger picture as a vital part of the culture. "I actually think football, with all due respect to baseball, is a kind of national pastime that brings people together across social lines, across racial lines. And I think it's an important American institution." On another level, she is fascinated with the comparisons between military and football history. "Military history has swung back and forth between advantage to the offense and advantage to the defense," she explained. "Football has that kind of pattern, too."

Like other women in Bush's inner political circle, including his long-time advisor Karen Hughes, Condi is a strong personality who is fully capable of holding her own in a male-dominated field. Although Colin Powell has remarked that she was "raised first and foremost to be a lady," Condi cannot be stereotyped as a Southern belle who depends upon her Southern charm to smooth over difficult situations. In an article written in the last weeks of the campaign, *The New York Times*' Elaine Sciolino wrote that members of the foreign-policy team did not dare speak a word to reporters without getting Condi's permission first. "'You make me sound like a tyrant!' she exclaimed, then added with a smile, 'We are disciplined, we are disciplined.'"

Her former boss Brent Scowcroft has remarked that while Condi is on the whole a pleasant person, she also has a tough side. "She's got this quiet demeanor," he said, but anyone who "thought they could push her around learned you could only try that once. She's tough as nails." In the same article, former CIA Chief Robert Gates recalled a dramatic moment during Condi's first post at the White House as a director of the national security staff. An official from the treasury department attempted to undermine her authority, and "with a smile on her face she sliced and diced him," said Gates. "He was a walking dead man after that."

Paul Brest, a friend of Condi's who was dean of Stanford Law School when she was provost of the university, describes her as "both very upbeat and very down to business. You have a sense that she's having fun with what she does as long as other people are behaving themselves. The only time I have ever seen her be curt, because she's an extremely gracious person, is when somebody was rude or clearly out of line. When somebody's out of line with Condi, she lets them know very quickly."

Being a woman in the high echelons of foreign policy is unique in itself, but being single added an even rarer dimension to Condi's role as George W.'s top foreign policy tutor during his presidential campaign. During her two-year stint in the first Bush administration, she elicited hordes of marriage proposals, and rumor had it in the White House that she had talked about returning to Stanford because she wanted to settle down and get married. Now, like then, her high profile job brings her plenty of attention from the opposite sex, but as of yet she has not found her soul mate.

There's still a possibility that the right proposal will come along one day, of course. She was engaged once (as we will see in Chapter Five) and has dated several famous men, including NFL football players. Her football boyfriends brought her into another uniquely American inner circle—NFL wives (and girlfriends)—a group that socializes and sits together at the games. But other than her one close call with marriage, she has not made long-term plans with any of her boyfriends. "I am a very deeply religious person," she said in October 2001, "and I have assumed that if I'm meant to get married that God is going to find somebody that I can live with." (Condi's single status allows her to devote all of her energy to her job, something that undoubtedly crossed the president's mind in mid-2002 when Karen Hughes resigned and returned with her family to Dallas. Without a husband or children vying for her energies and attention, Condi is perhaps more apt to stay with the job.)

Shortly after the thirty-three-day post-election debacle of 2000, Bush began announcing his choices for senior staff positions. On December 18, he held a press conference to name three positions: White House counsel (Al Gonzales), counselor to the president (Karen Hughes), and national security advisor—Condoleezza Rice. "Dr. Rice is not only a brilliant person," he told the press, "she is an experienced person. She is a good manager. I trust her judgment. America will find that she is a wise person,

and I'm so honored [she is] joining the administration."
George W. asked Condi to make a few remarks, which included the following:

> This is an extraordinary time for America because
> our values are being affirmed, and it's important to
> always remember what those values are at home.
> And I grew up in Birmingham, Alabama. I did not
> go to integrated schools until I was in tenth grade
> and we moved to Denver, Colorado. And there's
> very often a lot said about whether we've made any
> progress as one America. I think that you will see in
> the presidency of George W. Bush recognition of
> how important it is that we continue the last 30-
> plus years of progress toward one America; that he
> will have an administration that is inclusive, an ad-
> ministration that is bipartisan, and perhaps most
> importantly, an administration that affirms that
> united we stand and divided we fall, and I'm very
> proud to have a chance to be a part of it.

On Bush's first official day of business in the White
House, January 22, 2001, he led a swearing-in ceremony
for senior members of his staff in the East Room of the
White House. With Bush's Senior Advisor Karl Rove
(whom George W. calls "Boy Genius") at her right, Condi
raised her right hand and said:

> I, Condoleezza Rice, do solemnly swear that I will
> support and defend the Constitution of the United
> States against all enemies, foreign and domestic;
> that I will bear true faith and allegiance to the same;
> that I take this obligation freely, without any mental
> reservation or purpose of evasion; and that I will
> well and faithfully discharge the duties of the office
> on which I am about to enter. So help me God.

One journal expressed the behind-the-scenes work of the national security advisor as part of the system that molds the president as much as it allows him to shape policy. "Advisors such as Rice and Kissinger must not only be prominent personalities," stated an editorial in *New Presence*, "but also have the ability to integrate diverse outlooks and approaches and—when the situation calls for it—to step back and allow the fruits of their labor to become the property of those whom they serve. Simply put, the American president is a collective and collectively created person."

The weighty issues discussed by the NSA and the president demand that the two people have an enormously trusting relationship. By referring to Condi as a "close confidant," entrusting her to teach him about world affairs, consistently asking for her opinion in addition to the views she's collected, and sending her out on crucial assignments, it's evident that George W. is as trusting of Rice as his father was of his NSA, Brent Scowcroft.

In a letter the senior Bush wrote to Scowcroft after a NATO meeting in May, 1989, he revealed how heavily he relied upon his advice and support. "I will remember the sound advice you have given me. Thanks for your key role. Thanks for being at my side. Thanks for being my trusted friend." In a footnote in his memoir, Bush further indicated his reliance upon Scowcroft. "I always suspected Brent would have preferred to have been secretary of defense, but I needed him at my side in the White House." George W. feels the same way about Condi Rice.

Condi may have preferred to manage the National Football League after the campaign, but she agreed to stay by George W.'s side instead. Happily for the president-elect, Paul Tagliabue held onto his job as commissioner of the NFL and the subject never came up. For Condi, the NFL office on Park Avenue in New York would have to remain a fantasy. In the meantime, she was about to step into a role that has been described as "one of the single most important positions in the American government."

TWO

An American Legacy

"The multiethnic part [of American society] does not work without another important value: belief in upward mobility. The core of that has always been the ability to level the playing field through education. Unless education is provided to all . . . that part of the dream will be lost."

—*Condoleezza Rice*

SCENE: *Civil War-era Alabama, on a plantation near Clinton in Greene County. Behind the main house, hundreds of acres of cotton rise from the dark clay soil that gives the region its name, the Black Belt. As darkness falls, a sense of urgency permeates the buildings. Inside the master's house, slave house servants search for places to hide the silver and other valuables. Outside, male slaves scramble to hide stores of food. For the past week, word has spread like wildfire through the county that Union soldiers are nearby, sacking homes and stealing everything in sight. Battles over the Tennessee River Valley, just 150 miles to the north, have rumbled for months as both sides fight to claim control of the superhighway of the South. From time to time, stories of atrocities inflicted upon families and slaves by the federal troops filtered through the slave quarters and the main house. A young woman, Julia, daughter of the white plantation owner and one of his black house slaves, follows her*

*father's orders and rounds up the family's horses, moving them
from the barn to a hiding place that only she knows . . .*

It could be the opening moments in a film version of
Condi's story, introducing great-grandmother Julia Head
Rice—a child born into slavery on a Greene County plantation. Her successful feat in hiding the homestead's
horses from Union soldiers has been handed down in the
Rice family lore. Condi's second cousin, Constance
"Connie" Rice, has remarked that the slaves in their family ancestry were primarily house slaves, not field slaves,
which gave them more opportunity. Julia's mother was
such a slave, exposed to privilege and determined to pass
along as much of it as possible to her children. She had
learned how to read and write, and her desire to better
herself became a hallmark of the Rice family legacy. Each
generation of the line would carry a zeal for education.

After the war Julia married John Wesley Rice, a former slave from South Carolina who had also learned how
to read and write. They worked as tenant farmers in
Eutaw, Alabama, and although neither of them had gone
to school, they instilled an appreciation for learning in
their nine children and raised them as Methodists. If
they practiced like the vast majority of blacks in the
South at the time, they were members of one of the
black Methodist churches. These congregations made
up the largest black religious group in the South after the
war, offering an established system of Christian worship
that was already firmly established in the North. De-
nominations such as the African Methodist Episcopal
(AME) church, founded in 1816, formed new churches
in all the Southern states, as did the African Methodist
Episcopal Zion Church (AMEZ). Southern black ministers also formed their own denomination, the Colored

(later "Christian") Methodist Episcopal Church. These churches felt a large responsibility toward helping freed slaves adjust to a new American life, and education was their major theme. Theophilus Gould Steward, an AME minister from 1864 to 1914, stressed the value of education for America's black people in his book, *Fifty Years in the Gospel Ministry*:

> Knowledge must be acquired; knowledge of words and things. Every fact acquired arouses new thoughts; the mind expands; the faculties are strengthened and the progress is onward to manhood. "Wisdom is strength" says Solomon; "Knowledge is power" says Bacon . . . .Barbarous peoples have been civilized, the waste country made the home of a mighty nation, the oppressed elevated, by infusing into them the power of education. England grew to its present stage of wealth and power through the diffusion of education among its population. America sprang up to its prodigious wealth and greatness by the use of the school house. And education, diffused among our people in this state and others, is the thing needed to change their condition.

One of Julia and John's sons, John, Jr., heard the call and decided to leave the farm and go to college. In her speech at the Republican National Convention, Condi talked about him—Granddaddy Rice. "Around 1918," she said, "he decided he was going to get book-learning. And so, he asked, in the language of the day, where a colored man could go to college. He was told about little Stillman College, a school about fifty miles away. So Granddaddy saved up his cotton for tuition and he went off to Tuscaloosa."

Stillman was founded by a group of white Presbyterian ministers in 1874 as a school for training black ministers. It was named for the head of the founding group, Dr. Charles Allen Stillman. Twenty-five years later—well before the time John Rice arrived—the school expanded its scope to include other major courses of study as well. The Stillman Institute was not yet a degree-granting institution, and it would not become a four-year college until 1949, but it was one of the few institutions of higher learning available to blacks in Alabama.

When John's supply of cotton ran out after his first year, he had nothing else to sell to pay for his tuition. Condi explained the turn of events that allowed him to continue his education. "My grandfather asked how those other boys were staying in school," she said, "and he was told that they had what was called a scholarship. And they said, if you wanted to be a Presbyterian minister, then you can have one, too." John responded as if this had been his idea all along, telling the administrators that becoming a minister was just what he had had in mind.

Condi's grandfather finished the program and was ordained a Presbyterian minister. "My family has been Presbyterian and well educated ever since," she said.

John, whom the family began to call "Uncle Doc," was a minister by profession but equally committed to helping black youth get a college education. After serving his first congregation in Baton Rouge, Louisiana, the church sent him to oversee a Presbyterian mission in Birmingham, close to his home turf. Under Reverend Rice's leadership, this small congregation eventually became Westminster Presbyterian Church. One of his top priorities was encouraging the congregation to help the young men and women go to college, and in many cases, to his alma mater, Stillman. He was zealous in his commitment and, when it came to seeing that the students got every opportunity to finish their programs, fearless in his approach. Stillman's policy did not allow a student to take final exams if his tuition was not paid. Every year there were a few students from Rice's flock who had not paid, and every year he boarded a bus to make the sixty-mile trip to the campus in Tuscaloosa. One student whom he helped, Evelyn Glover, recalled those yearly treks to the stately president's residence on campus. "I can see him even now, walking stern and erect to the president's door," she said. "You did not see that back then—a black man at a white man's front door. And they'd let him in! And whatever he said, it worked, because I never knew a student he helped who didn't have an opportunity to make those exams, and I know our parents didn't have the money."

Condi's grandfather had married by the time he began preaching in Baton Rouge, and his son, also named John Wesley Rice, was born in that city. John nurtured his son's deep faith and instilled in him a keen drive to excel, which culminated in a seminary education, graduate degree, and several university posts. He became another powerful force in Birmingham's black community, encouraging young people to rise above the limits that segregation and racism attempted to place on them. "He really was a person who believed that even if Birmingham was, at the time, a place of limited horizons for black children, it should still be a place of unlimited dreams," said Condi. "It is because of people like my father . . . that Birmingham's children were not sacrificed to the limited horizons."

Strong parallels run between Condi's paternal and maternal ancestry, such as a commitment to self-reliance and education. Her maternal great-grandfather was a white slave owner who bore a son and two daughters with a black house slave. Like Condi's paternal great-great-grandmother, this woman came from an educated family and was a favored servant in the household. She had high aspirations for her children, and her two daughters (Condi's great aunts) graduated as nurses from one of the South's landmark institutions—Booker T. Washington's Tuskegee Institute.

Washington, who based his educational philosophy on his experiences as a student and teacher at the Hampton Institute in Virginia, began to provide vocational and teacher training for blacks at the institute in 1881. A cornerstone of the school was Washington's mission to develop moral character and high standards of etiquette and cleanliness in his students. This "civilizing agent," according to Washington, rounded out a total education for blacks that would help them return to their communities with both practical skills and social refinement. By combining classroom instruction with hands-on training—often through jobs that helped cover tuition—Washington strove to increase black students' "habits of thrift, . . . love of work, ownership of property, [and] bank accounts."

Condi's great aunts were among the first to graduate from the Tuskegee Institute, and they became the first nurses in the Ray family. Their brother, Albert Robinson Ray III (Condi's grandfather), was a proud and devoted father who refused to let segregation or prejudice define his self-worth or that of his children. He left home at thirteen and began working in the mines. Later, when his family began to grow, he began building homes and worked hard enough to become one of the more well-off blacks in the community. "Albert Ray," said Condi, "worked three jobs as a mining contractor, a blacksmith and on Saturdays he built houses." The Rays were one of the few black families in Birmingham to own a car. Albert was determined that none of his children would work in the mines as he did and, with his wife, Mattie Lula, worked hard to put all five of his children through college. "When the Great Depression came," said Condi, "they had been so frugal that they bought their home outright with money saved in a mattress."

Condi's maternal grandparents shielded their children from Jim Crow statutes that materialized in greater Birmingham in everything from "colored" latrines and water fountains to city buses. One of the Ray children, Alto (Condi's uncle), recalled that his father would ask him and his siblings to wait until they got home to go to the bathroom or get a drink rather than use one of the segregated public services. "As a matter of fact," he said, "I never got on a bus, a segregated bus, in my life."

Alabama was particularly detailed in its Black Codes, the state and city statutes that defined segregation in the Jim Crow era. (The term Jim Crow was derived from a character in blackface minstrel shows; a character originated by a white actor named, ironically, Thomas "Daddy" Rice.) Jim Crow was not only a system of legal statutes but a way of life that encompassed an unwritten standard of behavior between blacks and whites. These standards were based on a belief that blacks were intellectually and culturally inferior to whites, a conviction that pervaded Southern society and was preached from church pulpits to university classrooms. Jim Crow included a host of social taboos: a black man could not offer his hand to shake hands with a white man; he could not offer his hand to a white woman or he risked being accused of rape; if whites and blacks ate together, the whites would be served first; black couples could not kiss or show affection for each other in public; white drivers always had the right-of-way at intersections; whites did not address blacks with the titles Mr., Mrs., or Miss, but called them by their first names—conversely, blacks had to use such courtesy names when speaking to whites; a black person always rode in the back seat of a car driven by a white person (or in the back of a truck); and so on. These were the social norms. The Black Codes translated these norms into law, and Southern cities such as Birmingham were dotted with signs in all types of public places, from restaurants to train stations, that pointed out separate facilities for blacks and whites.

By 1914, every Southern state had passed Black Codes. Those specific to Alabama included:

- Nurses: No person or corporation shall require any white female nurse to nurse in wards or rooms in hospitals, either public or private, in which Negro men are placed.
- Buses: All passenger stations in this state operated by any motor transportation company shall have separate waiting rooms or space and separate ticket windows for white and colored races.
- Railroads: The conductor of each passenger train is authorized and required to assign each passenger to the car or the division of the car, when it is divided by a partition, designated for the race to which such passenger belongs.
- Restaurants: It shall be unlawful to conduct a restaurant or other place for the serving of food in the city, at which white and colored people are served in the same room, unless such white and colored persons are effectively separated by a solid

partition extending from the floor upward to a distance of seven feet or higher, and unless a separate entrance from the street is provided for each compartment.

- Pool and Billiard Rooms: It shall be unlawful for a Negro and white person to play together or in company with each other at any game of pool or billiards.
- Toilet Facilities, Male: Every employer of white or Negro males shall provide for such white or Negro males reasonably accessible and separate toilet facilities.

Condi's grandfather and grandmother Ray insulated their children as much as possible from these aspects of society. They forbade their children, for instance, from working as hired help in white homes to supplement the family income. Cooking and cleaning for white families was routine for other black Birmingham children in the 1930s and 1940s, but not for the Rays. Condi and her cousins grew up hearing grandfather Ray's watchwords, his guiding principle for them all: "Always remember you're a Ray!"

Reflecting upon both sets of grandparents, Condi remarked that they had freed themselves from the society around them. "They had broken the code," she said. "They had figured out how to make an extraordinarily comfortable and fulfilling life despite the circumstances. They did not feel that they were captives." Addressing young Birmingham readers in an editorial in the *Birmingham News*, she wrote, "If you take the time to learn from these 'ordinary people' you will reject the most pernicious idea of our time—that somehow life is harder for you and for me than it was for our forefathers. . . . Men and women who refused to be denied have changed their circumstances time and time again throughout history and almost magically—those personal triumphs have propelled their country forward." Condi's second cousin, Connie Rice, added, "Our grandfathers had this indomitable outlook. It went: Racism is the way of the world, but it's got nothing to do with your mission, which is to be the best damned whatever-you're-going-to-be in the world. Life was a regimen: Read a book a day. Religion, religion, religion."

One of Albert and Mattie Ray's daughters, Angelena, was a serious piano student who went to college to obtain a degree in education. She then taught music and science at Fairfield Industrial High School in Fairfield, a predominately black, tidy southwest suburb of Birmingham set on a hill overlooking the steel mills.

While teaching at Fairfield Industrial, Angelena met a young Presbyterian minister who was also teaching at the school to supplement his minister's salary (as most ministers did in those days). John Wesley Rice was also the head coach of the basketball team and assistant coach of the football team. When he wasn't at the church or Fairfield High, he was working as a guidance counselor at Ullman High School in downtown Birmingham.

John was born in Baton Rouge on November 3, 1923, to John Wesley Rice and Theresa Hardnett Rice, and he and his sister, Angela Theresa, grew up attending the public schools in that city. After graduating from high school, he enrolled in his father's alma mater, Stillman College in Tuscaloosa, but transferred to another Presbyterian-based black college Johnson C. Smith University in Charlotte, North Carolina. This historic school was founded in 1867 by two Presbyterian ministers and began as a small high school and Bible institute. By the early

1920s it had grown into a four-year liberal arts college and seminary and was renamed after one of its benefactors.

After receiving his bachelor's degree at Smith, John spent two more years working on a master of divinity degree, which he completed in 1948 at age twenty-four. He led his first congregation in Baton Rouge before moving to Birmingham to take over his father's ministry at Westminster Presbyterian Church in 1951. When he arrived, the church had completed its new, red brick building on South Sixth Avenue.

John's sister, Angela Theresa Rice Love (Condi's aunt), left Louisiana to attend the University of Wisconsin, where she received a Ph.D. in English Literature. She specialized in Victorian literature and was a professor at Southern Illinois University Edwardsville, where she received the Outstanding Faculty Award in 1989. Her book, a study of Dickens entitled *Charles Dickens and the Seven Deadly Sins*, was published by Interstate Press in 1979. One of her colleagues, Professor Betty Richardson, recalled that before coming to Illinois, Theresa spent a great deal of time building the curriculums of black schools in the South—struggling to win budgets for programs and foregoing her own academic advancement in the process. "Dr. Love was absolutely committed to African-American studies and dedicated to her students," said Betty. "She is a woman whose total career deserves nothing but the highest respect. She was in the South creating curriculum for black schools when it was not fashionable to do so."

When John and Angelena met, they discovered they shared a deep faith, a love for teaching, and a commitment to their own professional development. They both had aspirations for graduate school and for helping the youth of Titusville, and they both wanted to have a family. They

were married in the early 1950s. Angelena has been described as a petite, light-skinned beauty who was nearly
inseparable from her sister, Mattie (named after her
mother). Friends called them the twins because they
dressed alike and did everything together. "Angelena was
very beautiful, very elegant," said her sister-in-law, Connie Ray, and Condi has said that her mother always
dressed beautifully.

John and Angelena's marriage brought together two
family lineages that believed strongly in religion and
achievement through education. Condi, described by one
political journal as "the very picture of American over-
achievement," recognizes that she is the product of a
family legacy that has always made education a priority.
With three generations of college-educated family members, including preachers, teachers, and lawyers, the bar
has always been set high. "So I should have turned out
the way I did," she told the *Financial Times*.

"I don't know too many American families, period,
who can claim that not only are their parents college-
educated, but their grandparents are college-educated
and all their cousins and aunts and uncles are college-
educated," said Coit Blacker, a Stanford professor and
friend of Condi. Upon hearing that Condi grew up in
Birmingham, many assume that her childhood was de-
prived and underprivileged and that she did not see the
light of opportunity until the Civil Rights movement
began to bear fruit. But that is not Condi's story. As she
has often repeated, it is not a matter of America's civil
rights struggle but of her own family legacy.

With the birth of Condi, John and Angelena funneled
all the family support, strength, pride, faith in God, and
sense of responsibility that had shaped their lives into
their child. "They wanted the world," said Connie Rice.

"They wanted Rice to be free of any kind of shackles, mentally or physically, and they wanted her to own the world. And to give a child that kind of entitlement, you have to love her to death and make her believe that she can fly."

THREE

Twice as Good

"My parents had me absolutely convinced that . . . you may not be able to have a hamburger at Woolworth's but you can be president of the United States."

—*Condoleezza Rice*

CONDI was born on a Sunday morning while her father was leading the eleven o'clock service at Westminster, a fitting time for a child of deeply religious parents to enter the world. The congregation often glanced over at the empty organ bench that morning, wondering how Angelena was doing and offering silent prayers that all would go well. They knew that Reverend Rice wanted a son—a football-, baseball-, and basketball-playing boy with whom he could share all the joys of sports. But if it was a girl, that would be wonderful, too— whatever the Lord delivered. On November 14, 1954, Angelena gave birth to a girl, and she named her Condoleezza. John simply named her his "Little Star," and he continued to call her that for the rest of his life.

John Rice preached at Westminster Presbyterian for eleven years, making the church Condi's second home. When she was born, the Rices still lived in the pastor's quarters, a set of rooms in the church building. Later, the church built a parsonage about eight blocks south at 929 Center Way, and the Rices moved in. The small, brick house sat on the corner of a brand-new, tidy block in a newly developed section of Titusville, one of Birmingham's black middle-class neighborhoods. The area would continue to grow, encroaching into the lush forest with block after block of attractive, well-landscaped homes. Because Condi's house was so close to the church, she spent most of her time in this small, protected enclave of friends and family.

This close-knit community of Birmingham's black teachers, preachers, and other middle-class citizens was a parallel world in which the Rices sheltered Condi from the harsh realities of segregated Birmingham. All the parents in their neighborhood dedicated themselves to nurturing strong, self-confident children. "They simply ignored, ignored the larger culture that said you're second class, you're black, you don't count, you have no power," said Connie Rice, Condi's second cousin. But that was just one element of the type of parenting that Condi received. John and Angelena showered their daughter with love, attention, praise, and exposure to all the elements of Western culture—music, ballet, foreign language, athletics, and the great books. "I had parents who gave me every conceivable opportunity," she said. "They also believed in achievement." When Condi was born, Angelena devoted herself to her intellectual and artistic development. With piano lessons and a full schedule of training in other subjects, Condi gained self-discipline long before she started attending school. "It was a very controlled environment with little kids' clubs and ballet lessons and youth group and church every Sunday," Condi said. "The discipline comes from that."

Music had always been at the center of Angelena's life, and she was determined to give her daughter every opportunity to become a professional musician. From the first days of her life, Condi was immersed in church and classical music, listening to the piano, the organ, and the choir. Her relatives recall that she was an early reader, but Condi has remarked that she learned how to read music before learning to read books.

Condi was the fourth pianist in her mother's line. "My mother played, my grandmother and my great-grandmother all played piano," she said. When Angelena went back to work, Condi spent each weekday at her grandmother Mattie Ray's house. Hour after hour the piano students marched in, and Condi was fascinated with the sounds they made and all the attention her grandmother gave them. Little Condi would walk up to the piano and bang on the keys, trying to copy her grandmother's playing. Mattie felt that there was more to Condi's interest than simple curiosity, and she wanted to explore it. "So she said to my mother, let's teach her to play," Condi said. "I was only about three. My mother thought I might be a little young, but my grandmother wanted to try it and as a result I learned to play very, very young."

Angelena could not have been happier. She had always planned to immerse her daughter in music, like her own mother and grandmother had done with her, and was thrilled to discover that Condi was already attracted to the piano on her own. "Condi's always been so focused, ever since she was really, really young," said her mother's sister, Genoa Ray McPhatter, who was a school principal in Chesapeake, Virginia. "She would practice her piano at a certain time without anyone having to remind her." Angelena set Condi upon the fast track immediately, not only with piano lessons but also by accelerating her education.

Because Condi could read fluently by age five, Angelena wanted to start her in school that year. The principal of the local black elementary school said that she was too young, however, so Angelena took a leave of absence from Fairfield High for one year and stayed home to homeschool Condi—it just didn't make sense that her perfectly capable child should be forced to waste a year of learning. Down the road, Condi was so advanced that she skipped the first and seventh grades.

Condi's year of homeschooling was regimented and intense. Juliemma Smith, a long-time family friend, said that Angelena organized Condi's day as if she were in a regular classroom, but her lessons were more rigorous. "They didn't play," she said. "They had classes, then lunch time and back to classes." Juliemma, who taught at Davis Elementary and helped John with the church youth fellowship, recalled seeing a reading machine at the house. "Condi learned how to read books quickly with a speed-reading machine. I had heard that President Kennedy used one, but I had never seen one before. That was also the first time I heard of homeschooling. Angelena and John were just interested in Condi maturing and getting the best of everything. It paid off."

Angelena also wanted Condi to have every chance to develop into a first-rate pianist, which meant she would need a sharp memory as well as excellent technique. Mother and daughter spent long hours together exploring the worlds of music and language and art, both at home and on trips into the city. And Condi adored her for it. "My mother was stunningly beautiful," she said. "She was tremendously talented. . . . I remember how much exposure she gave me to the arts. I remember when I was six she bought me this recording of *Aida*."

Angelena's unflagging guidance of Condi's musical training from a very early age is typical of parents who have produced world-class musicians. Many of the great pianists had, like Condi, at least one musically trained parent who nurtured their talents early and was devoted to the child's training. Van Cliburn, for example, began taking piano lessons from his mother at age three and studied with her until he entered Juilliard at age seventeen. Earl Wild heard classical music in the home from the day he was born and also began taking lessons from his mother at age three. Claudio Arrau began lessons with his mother as a toddler and read music before he read words. Clara Haskil, Alicia de Larrocha, Glenn Gould, and Arthur Rubinstein (one of Condi's favorite pianists) each received very early encouragement. Duke Ellington also started piano lessons as a child, and even though he often complained that he would rather be out playing baseball, his parents made him stick with it.

The benefits of a family background in music, dedicated parents, an exceptional aptitude that is recognized early (often at age three), a deep feeling for music, and prodigious raw talent have been the prerequisites for most great performers. Condi possessed all of them.

Angelena knew that her daughter was exceptional in many areas, as did the rest of the family. "My sister always knew that Condoleezza was a different child," said Genoa Ray. To confirm their notion that she was gifted, the Rices took Condi to Southern University in Baton Rouge for psychological testing. The results were undoubtedly impressive because Angelena told the family, "I knew my baby was a genius!"

The first song Condi learned to play on the piano was

"What a Friend We Have in Jesus," and shortly afterward she began "accompanying" her mother at church by sitting beside her on the organ bench. At age four, she mastered a handful of pieces and gave her first recital. The intense focus on piano cut into her playtime, as did the other projects Angelena set up for her. Condi spent more time indoors—practicing piano and French—than did most of the other girls on the block. Two girls who lived across the street remembered "waiting for what seemed like hours for her to finish her latest Beethoven or Mozart and come outside." When she did come out to play hopscotch or jump rope or play school, it wasn't usually for long. "[She] wasn't an outdoors child, running in the neighborhood," recalled Ann Downing, one of Angelena's neighbors and a member of her church. "She played with her parents, her family more or less," she said. Angelena and John lived to fill Condi's waking hours with productive, enriching experiences; to pour as much knowledge and culture into her young, impressive mind as possible. This dedication was based on love as much as on their longstanding family standards of achievement.

A specific incident sheds light on the depth of Angelena's devotion. Mrs. Downing dropped in one day while Angelena was ironing the tiny lace edges of Condi's anklet socks. "What in the world are you doing?" she asked. "I just love her so much," replied Angelena. Mrs. Downing then remarked that with so much love, she should have another child. "I can't take this love from Condi," she said. John Rice held an equal amount of reverence for his daughter and felt an equal obligation to give her every opportunity. One member of John's congregation recalled him saying, "Condi doesn't belong to us. She belongs to God."

By the time she began elementary school, Condi was already a serious music student and more ready to get down to business than most of her classmates. One day, while the other students were noisily blowing on their plastic flutophones and generally raising a ruckus, Condi raised her voice above the din and said to her teacher, "I'm waiting for my instructions. And would you please write the music down for me?" She was accustomed to paying attention, behaving well, and keeping an orderly routine. She acted mature because that was the way she was treated at home. "John and Angelena were the perfect parents," said Moses Brewer, a friend of Condi's from the University of Denver. "They never talked to her like she was a child, which is why she was mature beyond her years." Some of her schoolmates took this maturity and perfectionism, as well as her dainty manners and habit of walking nearly on her tiptoes, as a sign of being prissy. But Condi got bored in situations where time was being wasted. And after seven years of piano, she got bored with that, too.

"I remember when I was about ten I really wanted to quit playing the piano," she said. "I had been a child prodigy, now I was ten, there were lots of kids who could play the piano at ten." For Condi, the uniqueness of being "the cute little piano prodigy" was over and she was ready to move on to something else. "[But] my mother said you're not old enough or good enough to make that decision, and she was right."

Instead, she enrolled in a local conservatory and took her playing to a new level. At age ten, she entered the Birmingham Southern Conservatory of Music, which had recently opened its doors to black students. "I think I was the first black student to go to that newly integrated conservatory," she said, "and I began to compete in piano at that point." The conservatory also introduced her to the basics of flute and violin, which rounded out her private study of ballet and French. And in her spare time, Condi tackled a carefully selected pile of books—always the best literature for her age group. One of the downsides of her attentive mother's efforts was that books were always an assignment, never a relaxing way to escape. "I grew up in a family in which my parents put me into every book club," she said. "So I never developed the fine art of recreational reading."

Another way Angelena sought to expand Condi's horizons was to enroll her in different public schools, exposing her to a variety of social and educational experiences. At every school—as well as in all of her extracurricular activities—she was told to go beyond what was expected of her, always hand in work that was above average, always rise to the top. This was the unwritten yet firm law of Titusville families: to raise children who were "twice as good" as white kids to gain an equal footing and "three times as good" to surpass them. This was the driving force behind the high, uncompromising standards that the Rays and the Rices expected of their children. By encouraging them to always be far above average, they gave them the best shot at competing at an equal level when they left the secure enclave of Titusville and their families. "It wasn't as if someone said, 'You have to be twice as good' and 'Isn't that a pity' or 'Isn't that wrong,'" Condi said. "It was just, 'You have to be twice as good.'"

"My parents were very strategic," she explained. "I was going to be so well prepared, and I was going to do all of these things that were revered in white society so well, that I would be armored somehow from racism. I would be able to confront white society on its own terms." Children who asked their parents about racist comments they overheard or about Jim Crow codes they observed on a rare trip to another part of Birmingham were told not to worry about it: "It's not your problem."

Condi's mother refused to play by the Jim Crow rules, and Condi witnessed several episodes, usually on shopping trips, in which Angelena stood her ground. One confrontation took place at a downtown department store, where Angelena and Condi were browsing through girls' dresses. Condi picked one that she wanted to try on, and the two walked toward a "whites only" dressing room. A white salesperson blocked their path and took the dress out of Condi's hand. "She'll have to try it on in there," she told Angelena, pointing to a storage room. Without batting an eye, Angelena told the woman that her daughter would be allowed to try on her dress in a real dressing room or she would go and spend her money elsewhere. Angelena was composed, firm, and resolved. Aware that the elegantly dressed black woman before her would not stand down, the clerk decided that her commission was worth more than a public incident, and she ushered them into a dressing room as far from view as possible. "I remember the woman standing there guarding the door, worried to death she was going to lose her job," said Condi.

A painful memory of many black Birmingham children was not being able to go to the circus when it came to town or visit the local amusement park, Kiddieland. One of Condi's aunts recalled how upset her niece became when she learned she couldn't visit the Alabama State Fair that was advertised all over the radio and the television once a year, tempting children with visions of petting zoos and carnival rides. "She just could not understand" why she could not go to the fair whenever she wanted, said Connie Ray. But for the most part, Condi's parents shielded her from such disappointments, especially Kiddieland. With its Ferris wheels, carousel, cotton-candy stands, bumper cars, and other bright attractions, the whites-only park was a constant reminder that the city was divided in two. On one day each year, the park opened its gates to blacks, but the Rices never went. John and Angelena tried to keep Kiddieland out of Condi's mind entirely, and it appeared to work. "I don't remember being distressed," she said. Besides, John and Angelena took her to Coney Island in Brooklyn one summer while John was taking summer courses at Columbia. John tried to downplay Kiddieland to all the kids who felt disappointed over not being able to go. Condi recalled that her father told one child, "You don't want to go to Kiddieland. We'll go to Disneyland."

Condi's parents taught her about the greater opportunities that lie beyond Birmingham, the rewards that awaited her for her hard work and high goals. "My parents had to try to explain why we wouldn't go to the circus," she said, "why we had to drive all the way to Washington, D.C., before we could stay in a hotel. And they had to explain why I could not have a hamburger in a restaurant but I could be president anyway, which was the way they chose to handle the situation."

John Rice played a role in many young lives in Titusville. He had a hearty laugh, jovial outlook, imposing presence, and tireless commitment to the community. According to Condi's second cousin Connie Rice, John was somewhat of an anomaly in his stoic line. "The Rices were kind of joyless except for Condi's dad," she said. His outgoing, positive outlook endeared him to the young people who came to him for guidance at school, church, and at the fellowship center he founded.

The after-school and weekend fellowship was actually a mini-academy, a place where students could study after school with teachers John brought in from the black high schools, learn how to play chess, and analyze famous works of art through field trips to museums. He also organized sports teams and set up parent-approved co-ed dances on the weekends. "He was a big man," said Margaret Cheatham, one of the teachers who came in to tutor kids in math, algebra, and geometry. "They were amazed to see him play basketball."

Reverend William Jones, the current pastor at Westminster Presbyterian in Birmingham, noted that John spearheaded another important organization at the church, a Boy Scout troop. He put tremendous energy, discipline, and leadership into it, which was proven by the fact that two of his scouts ascended to the highest rank. "John's scouts made up one of the strongest troops in Birmingham, if not the strongest," said Reverend Jones. "They had so many accomplishments, including making two Eagle Scouts. Some troops never make one in their history, but there were two from that troop. That takes years of education and commitment from the boys and from the leadership." Only 4 percent of all Boy Scouts become Eagle Scouts, a process that involves many hours of community service as well as learning skills that lead to merit badges.

To say that John Rice was a tireless youth leader and educator is an understatement. In addition to his ministry, teaching and counseling jobs, coaching duties, and youth fellowship activities, he was also very active in the larger community. He helped set up the first Head Start center in Birmingham soon after the program was launched in Washington in 1965. He helped black youth find part-time and summer jobs as a staff member at the

Birmingham Youth Opportunity Center located downtown. He was the first black person to work on that state agency staff.

As a high school guidance counselor, John had many opportunities to talk to kids about colleges and the steps necessary to be accepted into them. He tutored students for standardized tests and pressed them to take stock of their dreams and turn them into reality. He had a gift for offering both practical advice and emotional inspiration, cheering each student on to think big, dream big, and follow through. The principal of Ullman High, where John was a guidance counselor, was the uncle of Alma Powell, wife of Secretary of State Colin Powell. Her father was also a principal at another school, and she recalled that they often spoke about the Reverend John Wesley Rice as "this fine young man they were so lucky to have in Birmingham." The kids called him "Rev," and his daughter was crazy about him. The two were very close.

Condi learned to love football like other little girls love horses or books. "My dad was a football coach when I was born," she said, "and I was supposed to be his all-American linebacker. He wanted a boy in the worst way. So when he had a girl, he decided he had to teach me everything about football." Starting at age four, Condi cuddled up with her father on Sunday afternoons to watch games on TV while he gave detailed commentary on the rules, the plays, the strategies, and the conferences. And being a girl did not sideline her from the sport—every year on the day after Thanksgiving they stopped talking and played their own "Rice Bowl" in the backyard. She loved the turf battles, the drama—and the guys. "When I grow up I'm going to marry a professional football player!" she said to the mother of one of her grade-school friends.

John also spent quality time with Condi going over current events and talking about how they fit into history. "It was music with my mother, and sports and history with my father," Condi said. When she was still a preschooler, she would often call her neighbor Juliemma Smith to talk about the latest stories in the newspaper. "Condi was always interested in politics because as a little girl she used to call me and say things like, 'Did you see what Bull Connor did today?' She was just a little girl and she did that all the time. I would have to read the newspaper thoroughly because I wouldn't know what she was going to talk about." (Eugene "Bull" Connor was Birmingham's brutally racist city commissioner.)

Both John and Angelena had summers off from teaching, and most years they packed up their Dodge for long road trips. These outings usually involved stopping along the way to visit a college campus or two. The Rices couldn't resist strolling through a famous university or college—a wondrous, tree-lined shrine of American opportunity. "We almost always stopped on college campuses," said Condi. "Other kids visited Yellowstone National Park. I visited college campuses. I remember us driving 100 miles out of the way to visit Ohio State in Columbus."

During several summers, both John and Angelena took graduate courses at the University of Denver, and John earned his master's degree in education there in 1969. Angelena took classes on and off for twenty years, from 1961 to 1982, and received her master of arts in education in 1982. When she and John were in class all day during those Denver summers, they wanted Condi to be doing something productive and supervised. The solution was the skating rink. "Figure skating was high-priced child care," Condi said, but she loved it. She spent several hours each day developing her skills, focusing on one thing that, like piano, brought gratifying results. Years of ballet gave her the grace, refinement, and strength of a good skater, and she also enjoyed the structure of training. Later, she would intensify her commitment and enter competitive programs. Even though she never reached the level she had hoped to achieve, skating had positive side effects that stayed with Condi for the rest of her life.

Summers in Denver were an ideal escape from the Alabama heat—and from the violence that had turned Condi's hometown into "Bombingham." As blacks gradually began to move into white neighborhoods, the Ku Klux Klan retaliated by bombing their homes. One of the Rices' friends, attorney Arthur Shores, was among those black families who relocated to a predominantly white area and paid the price. On August 21 and September 4, 1963, vigilantes bombed and nearly destroyed his home as they had others in the neighborhood by then known as Dynamite Hill. Condi and her parents brought food and clothes over to the Shores after their house was bombed.

The Birmingham bombings were also motivated by federal court orders to integrate Birmingham's schools, orders that Governor George Wallace himself vowed to fight in his famous campaign slogan to "stand in the schoolhouse door." From the capitol in Montgomery the governor urged citizens to resist desegregation, and his speeches fueled the violence. Like all the children in her church and her neighborhood, Condi was frightened by stories about the explosions and remembers 1963 as "the year of all the bombings." She said that "Arthur Shores was a friend, [and] here was a period when the movement turned violent." Shores had been the target of this kind of violence for decades as a defender of black rights in

Birmingham. For many years he was the only black attorney in Alabama, and his cases often involved the city's unconstitutional zoning codes. Back in 1949, his efforts on behalf of a black family who wanted to move into a traditionally white neighborhood resulted in bombs being placed in his office and his home. He found them before they were ignited, but when he brought them to the police and the FBI, neither organization helped him. The bombings of his home in 1963 were more of the same.

Shores and others knew that going to the police didn't help because the police department itself played a role in the bombings. "The police would show up and tell everybody to get off the streets," said Birmingham historian Pam King. "They'd clear the streets and the Klan would come through and throw the bombs. They weren't looking out for the safety of the citizens, they were just trying to clear the way for the Klu Klux Klan to come through and bomb." When a firebomb landed in the Rices' neighborhood—a dud that didn't go off—John Rice took it to the police and requested an investigation, but they would not conduct an inquiry.

With the bombings that summer came marauding groups of armed white vigilantes called "nightriders" who drove through black neighborhoods shooting and setting fires. Condi's father and other neighborhood men guarded their streets at night to keep the nightriders away from their homes. Armed with shotguns, they formed night-long patrols. The memory of her father out on patrol forms Condi's opposition to gun control today. Had those guns been registered, she argues, Bull Connor would have had a legal right to take them away, thereby removing one of the black community's only means of defense. "I have a sort of pure Second Amendment view of the right to bear arms," Condi said in 2001.

For black people in Birmingham, especially the children, 1963 was a terrifying year. "Those terrible events burned into my consciousness," said Condi. "I missed many days at my segregated school because of the frequent bomb threats. Some solace to me was the piano and what a world of joy it brought me." She added that blacks from all walks of life came together to help each other, which strengthened the cause. "The bonding together of the black community was inspiring," she said. "We all helped each other. Class differences in the black community had no meaning. We were all bonded together." In the city-within-a-city that was black Birmingham, class differences ran deep. Middle-class black families set up rigid social boundaries to ensure they would not lose the place they had worked so hard to achieve. "It's too hard to get there and the fall back is too long," said historian Pam King. "It's too precious, too hard to get in, and too easy to fall out." Many sent their daughters to college before their sons, knowing that black women stood a better chance of making it because they did not present as much of a threat to white society. They also left some of the black neighborhoods of Birmingham for the suburbs, just as whites have done all over the nation, taking their money and resources with them. "When integration occurred, places like the Fourth Avenue District [Birmingham's all-black business and entertainment district] and black neighborhoods collapsed because the blacks moved out, moved to other places," said Pam King. "We don't talk about black flight much, but it's the same phenomenon; blacks have moved out to the suburbs just like the white middle class."

Several weeks before "the year of all the bombings," Condi worried about a different type of bomb threat. In

October 1962, the newspapers and evening news reported the day-by-day developments in the Cuban Missile Crisis. Condi was seven years old and she discussed the story with her parents. Somehow, the news reports that came into her living room—with maps showing the projected routes of the missiles—felt like a closer threat than the bombings going on in her own city. Her father could protect her from greater Birmingham, but could he protect her from Fidel Castro and his nuclear warheads? "We all lived within range," she said. "The Southeast was it—you'd see these red arrows coming at Birmingham. And I remember thinking that was something that maybe my father couldn't handle."

The Rices were also friends of Reverend Fred Shuttlesworth, an icon of the movement in Birmingham with whom Reverend Martin Luther King, Jr., teamed up when he became active there. When Alabama outlawed the National Association for the Advancement of Colored People (NAACP) in the state, Shuttlesworth founded the Alabama Christian Movement for Human Rights. One of the operations organized by Shuttlesworth and other civil rights leaders involved children's marches, which would bring renewed attention to the movement and also enlarge ranks that were becoming sorely depleted with the arrests of many black adult demonstrators. These protests were part of an ongoing plan called Project C, for "confrontation," that sought to tackle segregation through sit-ins, boycotts of white retail stores, mass marches, and Freedom Rides—the co-racial bus movement that rolled through Alabama and other Southern states.

A handful of students from Miles College—where Condi's mother received her degree—carried out peaceful "sit-in" protests at segregated lunch counters in

Birmingham in 1960. Their attempts were not immediately successful, however. "The white power structure put pressure on the president of Miles College to get these kids to stop," explained Jack Davis, an assistant professor of history at the University of Alabama-Birmingham. "And any time there was any sort of demonstration, Bull Connor clamped down and did everything he could to frustrate protests and maintain segregation. He was very much opposed to any talk of the retail stores downtown lifting their segregation policies."

Jack, who is white, remembered his father's conversations about the reactions of the business community in Birmingham during the Project C protests of the 1960s. "My father worked downtown in the heart of everything, and he remembered a lot of the pickets, rallies, and marches. He remembered how whites were so horrified by these demonstrations and how many of them were determined to maintain the status quo. But there were also those who realized that change was inevitable."

Thousands of school children participated in peaceful marches in May 1963, taking days off from school to protest the city's segregation laws. They did not foresee how dangerous their actions would become.

The city's power boss, Bull Connor, controlled both the police and fire departments and tried to put down the demonstrations. As a city commissioner, he did everything in his power to inflame racist sentiment among the white working class—and to keep segregation alive in Birmingham. He wrote some of the state legislation that tried to halt the Civil Rights movement in Alabama, for example, such as a bill outlawing the Freedom Rides. In his words, the Freedom Riders were agitators who were "challenging our way of life."

The marches showed no sign of waning in May 1963,

and Bull Connor commanded the police to use force to scatter the protesters. The dogs and fire hoses that had previously been pulled out as threat tactics were turned on the crowds. Powerful jets of water sent children rolling down the street and several people were bitten by the department's German shepherds. An article in the *Montgomery Advertiser* from early May described one scene from the first of May in a headline article entitled, "Dogs, Water Used to Halt Negro March":

> With firemen brandishing their hoses, a policeman with a loudspeaker warned the marchers, "Disperse or you'll get wet." The teen-agers, most of them 13 to 16, kept moving.
>
> Then the water hit them. Cowering, first with hands over their heads, then on their knees or clinging together with their arms around each other, they tried to hold their ground.
>
> A woman, Vivian Lowe, was bleeding from the nose. She said she was injured by a stream of water from the fire hoses. An unidentified girl suffered cuts about her eyes when struck by the stream of water. . . . another Negro, Henry Lee Shambry, 34, said he was bitten by two police dogs. One of his trouser legs was ripped nearly off and his underclothing was bloodstained.

Although John and Angelena Rice supported the goals of the Civil Rights movement, they did not agree with all of the tactics used in Birmingham. Boycotting a department store was one thing, but putting children in harm's way did not appeal to either of them. John did not condone the schoolchildren's marches because he believed that threatening children's safety was a step in the wrong direction. The students' marches were making news around the country and John's students wanted to know where he stood. He urged them to stay in school and fight with their minds.

"My father was not a march-in-the-street preacher," Condi said. "He saw no reason to put children at risk. He would never put his own child at risk." But as throng after throng of children and teenagers marched through the streets, John knew that the force of history was upon them and he wanted to give eight-year-old Condi a glimpse of what was happening. When the Rices' across-the-street neighbor children were arrested for marching in May 1963, John brought Condi to the state fairgrounds west of the city where the youth were being held, huddled beneath tents. In addition to his neighbors, many of the arrested kids were his students and he wanted to check on their safety. He strode through the hot crowd with Condi riding on his shoulders. Earlier in the day, they had watched demonstrations in the downtown business district from a safe distance a few blocks away.

Bull Connor's use of dogs and fire hoses against children was covered on national television that summer, bringing the escalating problems of Birmingham into sharp focus for millions of Americans. In May 1963, President Kennedy announced that it was time for the U.S. Congress "to act, to make a commitment it has not made in the century to the proposition that race has no place in American life or law." That month, his administration began drafting the Civil Rights Act.

A tragic event in the fall of 1963 brought Birmingham's battles to a new, horrifying level. On September 15, a Sunday morning, the sanctuary of the Sixteenth Street Baptist Church was full of worshipers, including many of Birmingham's prominent black families. Downstairs, the Sunday school classrooms along the east wall were bustling with children beginning their lessons. In

one room the children included four girls: Denise Mc-
Nair, eleven, and Carole Robertson, Cynthia Wesley,
and Addie Mae Collins, all fourteen. At 10:24 A.M., a dynamite bomb hit the building and blew a hole in the
wall of their room. All four girls were killed, buried beneath the rubble, and dozens of other children and
adults were injured.

The blast was felt throughout the city, including at
Westminster Presbyterian two miles away, where the
floor fluttered beneath Condi's feet. "I remember a sensation of something shaking, but just very slight," she
said. "And later people learned who had been killed in
the church." Denise McNair, the youngest girl killed in
the blast, was one of Condi's friends. They had attended
kindergarten together.

The Rices attended the funeral, and one image from
that day left a lasting impression in Condi's mind. "I remember more than anything the coffins," she said. "The
small coffins. And the sense that Birmingham wasn't a
very safe place." Two months shy of her ninth birthday,
Condi realized that hatred and bloodshed lie just outside
the haven her parents and community had so carefully
constructed. It was a brutal awakening.

Justice was slow in the four murders that made up the
deadliest act of the Civil Rights movement. In May 2002,
the last conviction was finally made. Bobby Cherry, age
seventy-one, was convicted of murder by a jury of nine
whites and three blacks. Before him, Thomas Blanton
had been convicted in 2001, and Robert Chambliss in
1977. The fourth Klansman involved in the murders,
Herman Cash, died before being charged.

For all of his efforts to protect his daughter and other
children in Birmingham from the ugliness of segregation,
John Rice could not always evade its effects himself. He

and Angelena could not, for example, take graduate classes at the University of Alabama, just blocks away from Titusville, because it did not accept black students. And voting for the pro-civil rights Democrats was impossible, as the Dixiecrats ruled the party with an iron fist in Alabama and were determined to "keep blacks in their place." (The Dixiecrats were formed in 1948 when a group of Democrats, led by Strom Thurmond of South Carolina, split off from the Democratic Party to oppose Truman's racial integration policies.) The Dixiecrats called the shots in Birmingham government, including the Democratic Party's voting process.

Blacks had won the right to vote with the passing of the fifteenth amendment in 1869, but the Southern states had developed several ways to circumvent the law. In the 1950s, Alabama was still enforcing various incarnations of the poll tax, a fee for voting that excluded many black people from the process. Other constraints were firmly in place when John Rice went to the polls in 1952. In a *Boston Globe* article, journalist Wil Haygood describes the scene that day:

> In 1952, John Rice himself went to vote in Birmingham. Stood there with his ministerial credentials and all his college learning. A man pointed to a jar. The jar was full of beans. The man told Reverend John Rice that if he could guess the number of beans in the jar, he could vote.

John had learned from a few Republicans in his congregation that the GOP did not use such tactics. He signed up for the Republican Party that day and never looked back. At the Republican National Convention, Condi shared this story about her father. "The first Republican that I knew was my father, John Rice, and he is still the Republican I admire most," she said. "My father joined our party because the Democrats in Jim Crow Alabama of 1952 would not register him to vote. The Republicans did. I want you to know that my father has never forgotten that day, and neither have I."

When President Lyndon Johnson signed the Civil Rights Act into law on July 2, 1964, the Rices watched the historic event on television. A couple of days later they went to a historically all-white restaurant in Birmingham for the first time. "The people there stopped eating for a couple of minutes," said Condi, but then the novelty wore off and everyone went about their business. The changes weren't so smooth everywhere, however. "A few weeks later we went through a drive-in," she said, "and when we drove away I bit into my hamburger—and it was all onions." Signing slain President Kennedy's bill into law made President Johnson "a revered figure" in the Rice household. Condi believes that an important part of the civil rights story also lies in the people who were ready to put the new laws into practice in their lives, the blacks who had prepared themselves through education. "The legal changes made a tremendous difference," she said, "but not in the absence of people who were already prepared to take advantage of them, and therefore took full advantage of them. You can't write them out of the story."

Condi is aware that her parents' approach to segregation—how they dealt with it and how they discussed it with her—and their uncompromising attitude about education made an enormous impact on her life. "I am so grateful to my parents for helping me through that period," she said of her childhood in Birmingham. "They explained to me carefully what was going on, and they did so without any bitterness. It was in the very air we breathed that education was the way out. . . . Among all my friends, the kids I grew up with, there was . . . no doubt in our minds that we would grow up and go to colleges—integrated colleges—just like other Americans."

In 1965, Condi's father took a job that launched him into a new phase of his career. As dean of students at Stillman College, he became part of the leadership of an institution that figured prominently in the Rice family legacy. This is where Condi's "Grandaddy Rice" came to get an education, lift himself out of the sharecroppers' fields, and rechart the family's journey in the church by training as a Presbyterian minister.

By the time John arrived as the new dean, Stillman had come a long way since its beginnings as "an institute for the training of Negro pastors" in 1876. In 1930, it added a women's nursing training school, and in 1953, became an accredited four-year college by the Southern Association of Colleges and Secondary Schools. Just four years before John arrived, the college had become a member of the United Negro College Fund, making it eligible for funds from the forty-college cooperative.

With this new job, the Rices moved to Tuscaloosa, less than sixty miles from Birmingham. They were still close enough to keep in close touch with relatives and friends, as the trip was a quick drive on newly completed Interstate 20. The position advanced John in his profession, moving him out of the world of secondary education. From that point on, he would continue to work with young people as part of his church and volunteer activities, but his academic work would involve young, college-age adults. His number-one pupil, his "Little Star," was growing up, too.

FOUR

Chopin, Shakespeare, or Soviets?

"I don't ever remember thinking I was
an exceptional student. I did think I
was a good pianist."

—*Condoleezza Rice*

AFTER working at Stillman College for three years,
John Rice received a new job offer that involved a
much bigger move for the family. This time the change of
locale would have a greater impact on Condi's life than
the family's initial move out of Birmingham, for not only
did they leave their family and friends in Alabama, they
left the South entirely. John's new job came about after
he completed his summer graduate courses at the University of Denver and received a master of arts in
education on June 10, 1969. That year the university offered him a position as assistant director of admissions,
and he soon began teaching as well.

From the start, John Rice worked in the academic as
well as the administrative halls of the university. He
began to coordinate and teach a class entitled "Black Experience in America," and over the years expanded the
scope of the course to include notable figures who held

sessions with students and gave formal presentations that were open to the public. The class discussed the black vote, the role of blacks in politics, and various cultural topics, and John invited national-level speakers to speak, including Howard Robinson, executive director of the Congressional Black Caucus, and Reverend Channing Phillips, the first black person to be nominated for the presidency of the United States. One seminar focused on blacks in popular culture and featured Gordon Parks, director and producer of *Shaft* and *Shaft's Big Score*, who led a discussion on "The Black Man in the Movies."

Condi recalled another speaker invited to the class, Fannie Lou Hamer, an icon of the Civil Rights movement known as the woman who was "sick and tired of being sick and tired." Fannie Lou first learned that she had the right to vote when she was forty-four years old. Volunteers from the Student Nonviolent Coordinating Committee (SNCC) were visiting her Mississippi town and encouraging blacks to register for the vote. Fannie Lou and a few others volunteered to go to the courthouse and register, but when they arrived, they were arrested, jailed, and severely beaten. Even though she continued to receive death threats after she returned home, Fannie Lou committed herself to the SNCC and traveled throughout the country speaking about the cause and helping people register. She eventually cofounded the Mississippi Freedom Democratic Party and alerted millions of Americans to the South's voting abuses via televised coverage of the Democratic National Convention in 1964.

"I will never forget meeting . . . Fannie Lou Hamer when I was a teenager," she said in her speech to the Stanford graduating class of 2002. "She was not sophisticated in the way we think of it, yet so compelling that I remember the power of her message even today. In 1964, Fannie Lou Hamer refused to listen to those who told her that a sharecropper with a sixth-grade education could not, or should not, launch a challenge that would dismantle the racist infrastructure of Mississippi's Democratic party. She did it anyway."

In 1974, after five years of teaching, John Rice's position was upgraded from instructor to adjunct history professor. Although this title still did not carry the perks of an assistant professorship, such as insurance benefits, a higher pay scale, or the opportunity to move toward a tenure-track position, it did not impede John's ability to do well for his family. He was covered by a benefits package through his administrative positions and, for him, the bonus of the teaching job was his ability to make an impact on the black studies program at the university. For the first time, he taught at the college level about issues that he had encountered first hand, from the segregation laws of the Jim Crow South to the demonstrations in Birmingham to the impact of education on forming black leaders. The day-to-day, frontline work he had done as a minister, counselor, and teacher in Birmingham became the material for teaching a new generation about what it meant to grow up black in the South.

John Rice held a variety of administrative positions at the university during the thirteen years he worked there. In addition to his job as assistant director of admissions, he became the assistant dean of the College of Arts and Sciences in 1969 and was promoted to associate dean in 1973. He served a brief stint as assistant vice chancellor for student affairs and in 1974 became vice chancellor of university resources.

As associate dean, John Rice helped turn the university into a black intellectual center. "DU is more aware of minority problems and is seemingly striving to do more about them than ever before," he said in 1972. "I feel we really have the ball rolling . . . toward making this school one of the few ones with real sense of the pluralism in American life." He announced a new dedication to finding additional black instructors and encouraging more black student participation in campus organizations. "I feel there is a total awareness of black culture on campus now," he continued, "and I hope to create a deeper understanding of it throughout the coming year."

Even more than the job security or the teaching opportunities, John and Angelena felt that the most attractive aspect of the university was its location. The move to Denver was a fundamentally positive change for their daughter.

For a black high school student like Condi in 1969, the 1,300-mile stretch between Tuscaloosa and Denver was nothing compared to the qualitative distance between them. Even the dramatic contrast in climate, from the wet and humid tropics of Alabama to the airy heights of Denver that receive an average of sixty inches of snow each year, was a milder shift than the change of overall sensibility between Tuscaloosa and Englewood, the cozy Denver suburb where Condi began high school. Englewood bordered South Denver, the neighborhood in which the Rices bought their house when they moved to the city. Condi enrolled in St. Mary's Academy, a private Catholic school and vastly different than any school she had attended in Alabama. At thirteen, she was in an integrated school for the first time.

St. Mary's Academy took pride in its rigorous academics, and as a sophomore, Condi was surrounded by older students who shared her sense of competitiveness. The school had been founded by the Sisters of Loretto in the mid-1800s to bring an education to frontier girls whose families had moved west in the gold rush. This religious order, among the first founded in America, was dedicated to educating children in the new territories. In 1864, three nuns from a Sisters of Loretto convent in Santa Fe were chosen to found the school and made the trip to Denver in a mule-drawn stagecoach. They set up St. Mary's in a large, two-story house, and in 1875, graduated its first high school senior, Miss Jessi Forshee—granting the first high school diploma west of the Mississippi. Since then both Catholic and non-Catholic families have sent their daughters there to receive a high-quality education and "polish" focusing on the arts and foreign languages, as well as standard academic subjects.

St. Mary's was just a few blocks away from the University of Denver, along the same boulevard, and over the years, it formed a tradition of educating daughters of university deans. Word spread that there was an excellent private school nearby that many university administrators had chosen for their daughters, and John Rice was no exception. "That seems to be how a lot of people found the school," said a former principal, "not by realtors but through people at the university. We had a tradition of bringing DU daughters down the street." Being Catholic was not a requirement, and the school drew girls of all faiths and creeds. Integration was slow in coming to the city, recalled the academy's Sister Sylvia Pautler. "In the 1940s a friend of mine, a nun who was the principal of an elementary school here, accepted an African-American student only to discover that the Archdiocese had a fit over it. For some reason, the student never enrolled. That was typical of the 1940s. But by the time Condi came, there was a whole bevy of black students."

When Condi entered St. Mary's in 1969, the school had

recently completed its new high school building, Bonfils Hall. The lower-grade schools were co-educational and the secondary level was an all-girls high school. Although integrated, St. Mary's—like schools all over Colorado—was primarily white. Of the seventy students in her class, Condi was one of just three blacks. Another dramatically new aspect that Condi had to digest in her first weeks was the fact that her academic prospects were called into question for the first time. During her first term, a school counselor told the Rices that Condi's standardized test scores showed that she was not college material—never mind her straight-A record or her long list of academic, musical, and athletic accomplishments. Condi was stunned, but her parents—immune to talk of limitation or failure—didn't flinch. They assured her that the assessment was wrong and that she should just ignore it. Not an easy task for a young woman with a vulnerable ego, accustomed to being on the top of the heap. But Condi trusted her parents and was distracted by the many good things about her new life in Denver. That combination helped her field the blow and move on. "All that I remember is focusing on the fact that I was going to wear a uniform for the first time," she said. "I probably was so excited to get to Denver, where I could skate year-round."

In the words of her second cousin Connie Rice, there was more to it than that. There was no space in Condi's psyche for negative influences to take hold. "Now once you got out into the larger world and you were hit with the first messages from the dominant culture . . . that you could not fly, that in fact you were stupid and you shouldn't be able to achieve, by that time it's too late, because you've got a fourteen-year-old who believes that she can be anything she wants to be." That belief was instilled by John and Angelena Rice, parents who set their child's self-esteem, self-respect, and self-confidence above all else. Looking back, Condi once remarked that a child without enormously supportive parents like hers might not have fared as well after an episode like the one she had in that counselor's office. A less secure child might have let the message get under her skin and begun to lower her sights. But Condi never for a moment forgot that she is a Rice and a Ray. Three generations of empowerment could not be squelched by one lone voice on one sparkling, autumn day at the start of a new school year when a bright student's hopes are highest.

The counselor's analysis did not appear to reach the teachers; at least it did not diminish their respect for her as one of the school's brightest students. "She was very self-possessed and mature," recalled Sister Pautler, Condi's religion teacher. "A lot of adolescent girls go through a tortured time, whether from lack of self-confidence or not being able to understand their maturation process or their family. But she didn't have any of that baggage; no self-doubt or confusion about growing up or about her family dynamics."

Therese Saracino, another of Condi's teachers, described the orderly and high-scholastic environment of St. Mary's, qualities that made it attractive to parents who were trying to shield their children from some of the chaos of the 1960s. "The Sisters of Loretto were an outstanding teaching order. They were the first order of sisters founded in America, and from day one their mission was to teach young Catholic women. St. Mary's was a wonderful environment. All of the Catholic schools had a reputation for good academics and strong discipline. The smallness of the school was an important draw for parents, and the fact that it was a safe place during the unrest of the '60s and fears of drugs and changing values."

Therese recalled that Condi's maturity made her unique among the girls at the school. "I was her math teacher, but I know that her interests went far more toward the verbal—English, social studies, history, and that sort of thing," she said. "Any of us who have raised children know that certain qualities are either there or not there. In the first place she was very, very poised. And she was beautiful even then, and charming, and her manners were impeccable, which is unusual for a sixteen- or seventeen-year-old. I cannot think of any instance that I was in contact with her that she wasn't a perfect lady. There was a core of her that revealed she knew what she wanted and was willing to make the sacrifices. I think in her mind they were not sacrifices, but things to do that were necessary to keep with her goals."

Condi continued her mission to be twice-as-good by taking on new challenges in Denver—primarily in sports. In addition to continued private piano study, she took up tennis and figure skating and entered both fields competitively. Her weekday routine now included getting up at 4:30 in the morning to go to the rink and practice her footwork, spins, edges, lunges, crossovers, toe loops, combination moves, and pair skating.

For all of her hours on the ice, piano still took center stage in Condi's life. She practiced as late as possible at the academy and was also able to use the university's practice rooms from time to time, but the Rices didn't want her to be out and about at all hours of the night. They solved the problem by taking out a loan to buy her a used Steinway grand so that she could practice at home as late as she wanted. Condi was awed by her parents' gesture. "That was a lot of money back then," said Condi's friend, Deborah Carson. "I remember her talking about it years later, the amazement still on her face when she told me that 'they paid *thirteen thousand dollars* for it.'" Every time she looked at it, the piano reminded Condi of the investment her parents were making in her music.

Condi breezed through her classes at St. Mary's and by the start of her senior year had already finished all the requirements for graduation. Her parents felt she should waste no time and leave the academy to start working on a bachelor's degree at the University of Denver. But the idea of abandoning high school, even for the best of reasons, did not sit well with Condoleezza. She couldn't bear the idea of not having a high school diploma, and she wanted to take part in graduation with her class. "It was the first time I ever really fought my parents on anything," she said, "I just had a sense that socially you're supposed to finish high school." So the Rice family formed a compromise: Condi would start college part-time while finishing up her senior year at St. Mary's. This created a grueling schedule in which she got up before sunrise to take figure skating lessons, then attended two morning classes at the university, followed by a full afternoon at St. Mary's.

It didn't take long for Condi to feel she'd moved light years beyond high school and that returning to the cozy grounds of St. Mary's was more of a nuisance than a necessity. She would much rather have stayed on campus all day and delved into activities with her new sorority sisters, but she kept to the plan anyway. She made heads turn at her senior prom when she waltzed into St. Mary's Academy on the arm of a college hockey player. Her date was something of a fish out of water among the high school kids. "Poor guy," she said. "He felt sort of out of place."

Attending high school and college at the same time is

almost a footnote to the musical accomplishments Condi made at age fifteen. She entered a young artist's competition and won, which allowed her to perform Mozart's Piano Concerto in D Minor with the Denver Symphony Orchestra.

Condi was sixteen when she got her diploma from St. Mary's and was thriving as a piano performance major at the University of Denver's Lamont School of Music. During her dual year as high school and college student, she studied the bulletins of many colleges and was certain that she would transfer to a different university after she was free of St. Mary's. One of her top choices was Juilliard, but her father did not want her to limit herself to a conservatory education. By putting all her resources into a performance-oriented degree, there would be little chance of going back to school to learn another profession if she changed her mind about a musical career down the road. "My father was fundamentally against it," Condi said. The issue didn't come up again because after two semesters at the University of Denver she was hooked and decided to stay for her entire bachelor's program. "At first I planned to attend for one year only and then transfer," she said in a university brochure in 1974. "But I stayed because I found that DU is small enough for people to care about what happens to you—yet not small enough to limit the scope of what you might want to study." She praised the school for giving opportunities to "all students—regardless of race or sex," but added that "when you're black and female you have to work twice as hard." She felt respected, validated, and challenged as a pianist at the university, and dreams of Juilliard faded beneath the heaps of dog-eared scores she rifled through every night at the family Steinway.

Condi's excellent grades and high school record paid

off when she started at the university. She was awarded an honors scholarship, which was renewed each year of her undergraduate program.

Condi would not find the university to be an oasis of unbiased thought, however. In one of her first classes she found herself in an immense lecture auditorium, one of a handful of blacks in a crowd of 250 students, listening to a professor preach about white superiority. The topic was William Shockley's theory of dysgenics, which stated that human evolution is on a backward track because populations with low IQs, namely black Americans, are reproducing more quickly than whites. Shockley's highly controversial ideas had gained national attention by the late 1960s, even though the majority of his scientific colleagues ridiculed and dismissed them. The widespread attention brought to his theories was due to his distinguished background as a Nobel-winning scientist who co-invented the transistor and spearheaded the invention of semiconductors and the computer age. Condi entered the university just as Shockley's ideas were being hotly debated on campuses throughout the country.

Shockley believed that art, literature, technology, linguistics—all the treasures of Western civilization—are products of the superior white intellect. What went through Condi's mind as the professor described and appeared to support Shockley's view of blacks as "genetically disadvantaged"? Rather than crouch down in her seat to avoid the onslaught, she sprang out of her chair and defended herself. "I'm the one who speaks French!" she said to the professor. "I'm the one who plays Beethoven. I'm better at your culture than you are. This can be taught!"

Not only was fifteen-year-old Condoleezza Rice living proof that radical social theorists like Shockley were wrong, she had the self-assurance to say so in front of hundreds of white students and her professor. She has not remarked on the professor's response, but has said that as she left the class she understood her parents' strategy for the first time. The Rices recognized that whites expected blacks to be intellectually inferior, and in order to offset that stereotype one had to be far above average. Their goal, from Condi's birth, was to ensure that she would be able to hold her own in every circumstance. "That had been my mother and father's strategy," she said. "You had to be better at their culture than they were. Recognize that you're always going to be judged more harshly. They made certain I was never going to be found wanting."

Undaunted by the freshman lecture, Condi continued her twice-as-good strategy and enrolled in honors courses, wrote for the school paper, worked four hours on her skating every morning, and practiced piano every night. She has admitted that she was less-than-perfect when it came to studying. "The truth is that I was a terrible procrastinator," she said, "so a lot of times I wasn't all that well prepared." Years after she was out of college she advised her own students to not do as she had done— cram for a test rather than gradually ingest the material over the semester. She told them about how she had handled one of her freshman classes at the University of Denver, "Great Religions of the World," and how she came to regret her negligence. "I did the reading at the last minute, passed the test, and immediately forgot everything," she said. "Fifteen years later I was in Japan, wandering around the temples, thinking, 'I once read something about this. I wish I could remember what it was.'"

Her long-held goal of becoming a professional pianist

provided a laser-like focus upon which everything else neatly revolved. But between her sophomore and junior year at the university, this well-constructed plan suddenly fell apart. That summer she attended the famous Aspen Musical Festival and ran into the stiffest competition she had ever faced. "I met eleven-year-olds who could play from sight what had taken me all year to learn" she said, "and I thought I'm maybe going to end up playing piano bar or playing at Nordstrom, but I'm not going to end up playing Carnegie Hall." If she could not be a career performer—appearing with symphony orchestras and playing Mozart and Beethoven on the world's eminent recital stages—she would not stay with the program. This change of heart had been coming for a time, but the Aspen experience clinched it for her.

"We both became disillusioned with piano," said Darcy Taylor, who studied at the Lamont School of Music with Condi. "Condi was extremely talented, but she decided it wasn't for her. We were all very good, but there are people who are just brilliant. There are not many people who get selected for concert work; there aren't that many positions. We had to realize that we'd be going into the teaching end of it, or the church music end of it, to be a choir director, for example; and we had to face up to the fact that we weren't good enough to cut it in the concert world. Like Condi, I wasn't willing to be second fiddle."

Darcy and Condi sometimes commiserated about the hard, cold reality of the music world. They found nothing glamorous about round after round of competing in front of distracted music professors. "We all entered several contests a year and had several major performances per year," Darcy said. "We all had to learn Beethoven, Bach and Chopin—Condi really liked Chopin—and these contests taught us a lot about the life a musician has lead. We talked about that a lot. You would work hard and then, during a jury or audition, the professors would rattle paper and talk to each other and interrupt you in the middle of your performance. Their comment to us was that this is what it's like in the real world, so get used to it. I didn't like that, and Condi felt the same way."

Condi could not envision herself teaching piano for the rest of her life, helping kids "murder Beethoven," as she put it. "I decided there had to be more to life than that," she said. She decided to drop her performance major. This change of plans was a painful dose of reality that went against much of what she had come to believe about herself. Her identity, which from earliest memory had been wrapped up in music, had been challenged at Aspen, and she was compelled to find another field that was equally challenging yet not as competitive. Some young people who lose their professional artistic dreams, such as ballet dancers who mature into un-ballerina-like figures, struggle for years with depression and feel too inadequate—or disinterested—to start over in something else. But Condi did not approach it that way. She resigned herself to the fact that she was "pretty good but not great," and immediately began to nose around for a new major. "Technically," she explained years later, "I can play most anything. But I'll never play it the way the truly great pianists do."

At this halfway point in her undergraduate program, Condi had to tell her parents that everything had changed. "I went on a mad search for a major," she said. "I went to my parents, who had spent a fortune and all of their time turning me into a pianist, and said, 'Mom and Dad, I'm changing my major.'" She couldn't tell them what it was; all she knew was that she no longer wanted to be a pianist. The three of them made one agreement—regardless of what her new major would be, she would still finish her B.A. in four years. During fall semester of her junior year she changed her major to "undeclared" and explored a few options like English and Government. She scratched English Literature because it was too conceptual—in her words, "squishy"—and not rigorous enough. She actually hated it, which is not surprising for someone whose early exposure to books was under the glaring light of a speed-reading machine.

Government studies also proved wanting. Classes in local and state administration, voting behavior, political parties, and the structure of government did not appear compelling or demanding enough to pique her interest. But at the start of spring semester she walked into a class that changed everything. The course was "Introduction to International Politics," the topic that day was Stalin, and the professor was Josef Korbel, former Central European diplomat and father of Madeleine Albright.

"It just clicked," she said. "I remember thinking, Russia is a place I want to know more about. It was like love. . . . I can't explain it—there was just an attraction." The challenge and mystique of Soviet studies was exactly the kind of challenge Condi was looking for. It was a specialized path in academia that fit her perfectly, requiring tough scholastic discipline and an aptitude for foreign languages. It was totally new territory that felt oddly familiar, and it ignited a passion that she had not felt for anything outside of music. She recalled feeling a hint of that engaging interest back in 1968, when she watched the news story of the Soviets invading Czechoslovakia. It hit her hard. "I can still feel the strong sense I had of remorse and regret that a brave people had been subdued," she said.

Dr. Korbel was impressed by her brightness and enthusiasm, and encouraged her to join the university's school of international relations, which he had founded. "I really adored him," she said. "I loved his course, and I loved him. He sort of picked me out as someone who might do this well." Condi immediately turned her sights onto the Soviet Union, immersing herself in "Soviet politics, Soviet everything."

With that introductory course, Condi knew she had found her place. Her parents were very surprised at her choice, but supported it. "Condi is the kind of person who is very sure of herself and makes excellent decisions," said her father. "But political science? Here's the time for fainting. Blacks didn't do political science."

Condi's fellow piano refugee, Darcy, ventured into business classes and at nineteen started up her own landscape design firm in Denver. Today her company is very successful, and she believes that both she and Condi found new ways to direct their creative energy. "Design is a way to have a create outlet and still use the expressive gifts I used in music," she said. "Condi, in taking all those foreign languages, is also using the brain power she needed as a musician, and the decision-making she does is also creative." Darcy remains grateful to Condi's father for all his guidance and support in helping her get scholarships at the university. "John Rice was friendly and outgoing, but also demanding at the same time," she recalled. "If he was going to stick his neck out for you, he wanted to make sure you really wanted it, worked hard for it, and didn't take it from someone else who also deserved it and needed it as much. He gave, but he also expected a lot. I thought that was wise. If you're going into college and trying to figure out what to do with your life, it's nice to have someone to prompt you to think and grow from what you're doing. He was a very smart man."

Condi signed up for political science and Russian language courses, but she did not close the door on music. Even though she was no longer working toward a career in piano, she remained a serious student of the instrument. "I found my passion in the study of Russia but, in fact, I continued to be passionate about music," she said. "I continued to work at it and to study for quite a long time." This aspect of her background puts her in the ranks of a small group of prominent government officials who started their college careers in music. Edward Heath, prime minister of Great Britain from 1970 to 1974 (while Condoleezza was an undergraduate), was an organist and choir director while a student at Oxford, and after he retired from politics, he spent much of his time conducting orchestras throughout Europe. Alan Greenspan, chairman of the Federal Reserve, started out as a woodwind player at Juilliard. He studied clarinet and saxophone and played in jazz bands before transferring to New York University to pursue a degree in economics. "I don't regret giving up the music career," said Condi in 2001. "The great thing about music is that you can love it all of your life," Condi said, "you can pick it up at different phases."

Condoleezza has often remarked that Josef Korbel is the reason she entered international politics. Few matched his stature in the field, and his experiences in Europe before, during, and after World War II made him a fascinating mentor to young people eager to understand international relations. He was an Old World figure who had always attracted artistic types to his inner circle. "Korbel had a way of encouraging talented people," said one long-time friend of the family, "He was not an artist, but he attracted artists to him." A student like Condi—multi-lingual, classically trained musician, and extremely bright, poised, and self-reliant—was precisely the type to gravitate to him and to gain his admiration. Korbel immediately took Condi under his wing.

Josef Korbel was born in Czechoslovakia in 1909 and studied in Paris before receiving his law degree from Charles University in Prague. His first position in the Czech government was with the Ministry of Foreign Affairs, and in 1937 he became the press attaché at the Czech Embassy in Belgrade, Yugoslavia. He learned to speak Serbian, and made close friends with Yugoslav journalists, contacts who would become very important to him and his family when Hitler entered Czechoslovakia. Nazi troops enter Prague in March 1939, and Korbel, a Jew, was on a list of those to be arrested. Like several other Jewish families in Czechoslovakia, the Korbels had abandoned their ancestral ties. Whenever Josef had to fill out documents that asked for his religious affiliation, he wrote, "None." "Korbel was one of the very, very few Jews who succeeded in getting into the Foreign Ministry before the war," said one of his Czech colleagues in Michael Dobbs' biography of Madeleine Albright. "He did so by not giving any signs of his Jewishness." For weeks, Josef had been working on an escape plan to get his family to Yugoslavia, and thanks to official letters from two Belgrade newspapers who hired him as a foreign press correspondent, he obtained exit visas for himself, his wife, and their two-year-old daughter, Madeleine. They spent a few weeks in Belgrade, then moved to London where the leaders of the Czech government were living in exile.

Korbel worked as a personal secretary to the Czech foreign minister, Jan Masaryk, then became the chief of the Czech broadcasting service. During the family's

stay in London, Hitler's blitzkrieg pounded their
neighborhood, and back at home, more than twenty
members of their family were killed in the Holocaust.
Three of Madeleine's grandparents, two aunts, one
uncle, a first cousin, and nineteen others died at
Auschwitz or Terezín, the concentration camp in Czechoslovakia.

After the war the Korbels returned to Prague, and
Josef remained a top official in the Czech government.
Madeleine was eight years old, and the family lived in a
luxurious apartment near the presidential palace. Korbel
was part of the Czech delegation to the Paris Peace Conference in 1946 where the new world order was
established. Following the conference, at age thirty-six,
he was appointed Czech ambassador to Yugoslavia. He
traveled back and forth between Prague and Belgrade,
where Madeleine lived a pampered existence in the ambassador's residence. The Korbels hired private tutors for
Madeleine so that she would not be exposed to communist propaganda at the local schools, and when she was
ten, they sent her to a private boarding school in Switzer-
land. The growing tension between the communists and
democrats in Czechoslovakia hung over the family like a
dark cloud, and when the communists seized control of
the Czech government in 1948, the family fled to the
United States. Before leaving Prague, Korbel had been
appointed to a United Nations Commission on India and
Pakistan and began serving in that post at UN headquarters in New York City. Pressure from the new regime in
Prague forced him to leave the job in 1949.

After World War II, several intensive programs in international politics were launched on U.S. campuses. As a
new player on the world stage, America was in need of
expert instruction on the centuries of history leading up

to the formation of the Soviet Union and the Soviet bloc. These new college programs sought out European experts who had immigrated to the United States, and the University of Denver found their expert in Josef Korbel. After leaving the UN, Korbel was hired by the university as professor in international relations. In 1959, he became dean of the Graduate School of International Studies and director of the Social Science Foundation. Throughout his career he was considered an extraordinary teacher; attentive, warm, and generous with his time. He was in demand throughout the world and acted as a visiting professor at Oxford, Harvard, Columbia, MIT and other colleges. He published six books and countless articles that focused on Eastern Europe and the Cold War.

Korbel became the second most important man in Condi's life, next to her father. John Rice had sparked Condi's interest in world affairs and politics when she was very young, spending time with her to discuss the news of the day. She would pattern her life after him in many ways. She has described Josef Korbel as the "intellectual father" she shared with Madeleine Albright who, like Condi, was very much her father's daughter. "There is no doubt that Madeleine was the object of her parents' hopes and dreams from an early age," wrote Dobbs. "She was the oldest, the brightest, the most driven." Madeleine described her father as strict but "very loving" and supportive.

An integral part of Condi's new major in political science was learning Russian. Sometimes called a "ten-year language" because of the difficulty of learning its Cyrillic alphabet and grasping its complexity, this is a formidable challenge for many students. But Condi's early lessons in French, Spanish, and German had given her an affinity for language study that helped her proceed quickly. Previous language experience gave her a solid grounding in the grammatical terms that many English students quickly forget, but are the keys to learning a new language. "It helps to have another foreign language under your belt," said Jason Galie, a Russian instructor and Ph.D. student at Columbia, "because you use a lot of grammatical terms in the beginning, which, if you don't remember from English grammar, makes it more difficult." He explained that the Russian alphabet is a challenge, but not the most demanding part. "Russian is much more difficult than the Romance languages," he said, "in part because of the alphabet. You start writing English letters instead of Russian at first. But even more difficult is understanding the role that the words are playing, which, unlike English, isn't determined by the placement of the words in the sentence but by the endings of the words themselves. For some students that's very difficult to grasp."

Month by month, Condi's increasing grasp of the language gave her a more intimate connection to the land that would become central to her life and work. With only two years to go before graduation, she did not have time to take a large group of courses in her major, but she satisfied all the requirements and did an extensive amount of reading on her own.

When the Rices moved to Denver, John became an associate pastor of Montview Presbyterian Church, and Condi spent every Thursday evening at choir practice with the church's eighty-voice, semi-professional choir. Montview played an important role in helping Denver's Park Hill neighborhood integrate during the 1960s. Park Hill embraced integration during the Civil Rights era and formed successful action committees similar to those that helped integrate Hyde Park in Chicago. Montview Presbyterian teamed up with Blessed Sacrament Catholic Church and Park Hill Methodist to found the Parkview Action Committee. This organization successfully curbed white flight from the neighborhood when black families began moving in. "The membership of these churches got together and said, 'We're not going to have that happen in our community,'" said Russ Wehner, a long-time member of Montview Presbyterian who knew the Rices, "and together we created an economically, socially, and racially integrated community." According to the church's biography, *The Spirit of Montview: 1902–2002*, "church members were asked to sign a nondiscriminatory two-way pledge when buying or selling real estate. Montview joined other churches . . . in working to make Park Hill Denver's first racially integrated community, indeed one of the first in the United States."

In the 1960s, Montview's senior pastor Arthur Miller invited black leaders to speak at the church before most everyone else. "He got Martin Luther King, Jr., to come to Denver and preach at Montview during the height of the Civil Rights movement," said Wehner, "and it took an enormous amount of courage on his part because this was before it was an acceptable thing to do." In 1969, Montview invited Duke Ellington to perform his "Second Sacred Service" at the church. The production included the Montview choir and members of the Denver Symphony Orchestra, and it was a widely attended, sensational event in the history of the church and the community.

As one of four associate pastors, John Rice preached about once every month, worked as a counselor, and directed an adult education program called the 49ers. The study group derived its name from the Colorado Gold

Rush and was also scheduled to last forty-nine minutes. "Under Rice's direction, the popular 49ers Contemporary Forum flourished," states the church's biography. Most of John's work at the church involved pastoral duties such as visiting shut-ins and sick parishioners in the hospitals. His position as a dean and instructor at the university prevented him from being a full-time clergyman. Wehner recalled that Reverend Rice was a prominent figure in the community and a highly respected member of the clergy. "He brought an enormous amount of prestige to the church because of his affiliation with the university and because he was an African-American person who was very well respected," he said.

Just as he did with his students at the university, John helped his fellow parishioners at Montview look at things from a new perspective. "When John came on the staff he worked with a group we had organized called The Integration of Montview," said former pastor Richard Hutchison. "He was very helpful and gave us all a real revelation at one meeting. We were talking about how we could attract more black members, and he said, 'Well, do all of you agree with integration?' We answered that of course we did, and he then asked us where the nearest black Presbyterian church was located. We told him there was one just a couple of miles away. Then he asked, 'Why don't some of you join it?' We realized that we believed in integration, but we put the burden of doing it onto blacks.

"John was always forthright, honest, and challenging," Richard continued, "a very interesting man. He was so honest and secure in his selfhood that he didn't get defensive or angry. Condi inherited some of that from him."

The classical music tradition at Montview was very appealing to Condi. They sang masterworks from all periods of the sacred repertoire, and were known as one of the best choirs in the city. "She had a beautiful voice," said fellow choir member Margaret Wehner. "She also gave a piano recital at the church, and that's why I felt at that time she was going on in music. I remember her very outgoing, bubbly personality—she was a talented and lovely young lady." Some of the pieces performed by the choir made a deep and lasting impression on Condi. "We performed . . . the Beethoven *Christ on the Mount of Olives*," she recalled in an interview on public radio, "and I fell in love with the piece; it isn't a very oft-performed oratorio. And for me, one of the great moments was when I was in Israel for the first time in August of 2000 standing on the Mount of Olives. And as often happens in memory, this great oratorio just comes flooding back and puts it all together for me."

In addition to his work as a university dean, an educator, and a pastor, John Rice also served in Denver city government and made trips to Washington, D.C., to serve as a counselor on the Foreign Service Generalist Selection Board. In 1978, he was appointed by Mayor W.H. McNichols, Jr., to the Denver Urban Renewal Authority. He was a member of various organizations, such as the Kiwanis Club and Optimist Club, that put him in touch with city businessmen and leaders, and at the university he was a member of the Phi Delta Kappa and Alpha Phi Alpha fraternities.

Condi was no less ambitious or busy. Skating had become very important to her, and she looks back at her training on the rink as a vital part of shaping her into the person she is today. "I believe that sports has a place," she said in 1999. "I myself was an athlete, and I believe I may have learned more from my failed figure-skating career than I did from anything else. Athletics gives you a kind of toughness and discipline that nothing else really does." This was another life lesson inherited from her father.

Condi was very pleased that she choose to stay at the university for her entire undergraduate program. "The University of Denver is a gem of a school," she said several years later, "and I have tremendous affection for the place." She graduated with a B.A. in political science at age nineteen in 1974, and was one of the most honored *cum laude* graduates of the year. She graduated with honors, having completed a special sequence of courses in addition to getting excellent grades in the regularly assigned coursework. She was one of ten to win the Political Science Honors Award for "outstanding accomplishment and promise in the field of political science." In the commencement bulletin she was also listed as a member of the Mortar Board, a women's senior honorary organization. Her excellent grades and breadth of coursework earned her entry into Phi Beta Kappa, the honorary scholastic society. The Greek letters of this organization make a fitting motto for the entire Rice-Ray family line: "Love of wisdom, the guide of life."

Each of these honors distinguished Condi as a top student, but another even more prominent award announced at graduation drew wide attention to her outstanding achievements: Outstanding Senior Woman. The university describes this as "the highest honor granted to the female member of the senior class whose personal scholarship, responsibilities, achievements and contributions to the University throughout her University career deserve recognition." Condoleezza Rice, once described as "not college material," was the most highly honored undergraduate woman of the 1974 class.

The commencement speech that year was given by

Watergate prosecutor Archibald Cox, who stressed that each of the students were personally responsible for helping the nation recover from the constitutional chaos that the Watergate scandal revealed. Condi was overwhelmed by the weight of that calling. "Since he didn't tell me precisely how I was going to do that," she recalled, "I wasn't sure that the one course I'd had in American politics had prepared me for that, and I started to think maybe I should just stay in college or get a nine-to-five job and forget all of those challenges that everyone's giving me because I don't have a chance." That speech helped her refine her approach to problem-solving, and when she became a professor, she would advise her students to tackle the big problems of the world with whatever contributions they were prepared to offer, however small.

Leaving the university with such distinction gave her smooth entrée into graduate-level work, a highly anticipated labor of love in which she could pursue Russian and Soviet studies in-depth. She chose to begin at one of the best international politics departments in the country, and packed her bags for Notre Dame, Indiana.

FIVE

The Scholar

"Culture is something you can adopt,
and I have a great affinity for Russia. . . .
There is something about certain cultures that you just take to . . . . It's like
love—you can't explain why you fall in
love."

—*Condoleezza Rice*

ONCE *upon a time in Old Russia, a beautiful young
Princess was turned into a frog by her father, a wizard,
who was jealous of her powers. One day Tsarevna Lyagushka
(the Frog Princess) sees an arrow falling from the sky and
catches it in her mouth. A prince steps out from the woods looking for his arrow. Prince Ivan has been instructed that it will
lead him to his bride, so he marries the frog.*

*When the couple return to the kingdom, the king announces a
contest in which he hopes to find the most talented, capable, and
creative woman in the land, a woman everyone can admire. The
first task in his competition is to sew a shirt. Prince Ivan walks
home very unhappy, but his frog bride tells him not to worry.
That night she hops outside and turns into a beautiful princess,
Vasilia the Wise. She summons her mystical sisters to help her
make a fine shirt of gold and silver threads. In the morning, the
prince brings the shirt to the king, who proclaims that it far sur-
passes any shirt he has ever seen. The frog continues to astound
the king with each new task, while others scoff and grow angry at*

*her cleverness. No one, not even her dear Prince Ivan, knows
that she is a royal being in disguise.*

*When the king invites everyone to a grand ball, Prince Ivan
is once again sad because he knows that everyone will laugh at
him and his frog bride. The Frog Princess tells him not to worry
and to wait for her at the palace table. That night she arrives as
Vasilia the Wise in all her glory. After the prince successfully
overcomes a difficult set of tasks himself, the spell is broken and
Vasilia the Wise upholds her true form forever.*

In both undergraduate and graduate school, Condoleezza Rice's academic accomplishments in her chosen field gave her a kinship with Tsarevna Lyagushka. In newly desegregated America, it was still considered exceptional for a black woman to attend graduate school, excel in foreign languages, and become a leading scholar in any field. At times Condi has winced over the assumption that because she is black these accomplishments are somehow more exceptional. She has used a fairy tale-like term to describe this reaction—the "Condi in Wonderland" phenomenon. She feels that those who consider it a rare and extraordinary feat for a black woman to excel in the way she has cast her as a larger-than-life, wondrous figure. But, as she explains—and as the Russian story says—amazing things can come in all kinds of packages. "I'm five-foot-eight, black and female," she said. "I can't go back and repackage myself. I can't do an experiment to figure out whether any of this would have happened to me had I been white and male, or white and female, or black and male. So I spend no time worrying about it."

Condi's attraction to Russia, the Russian language, and the Soviet Union had blossomed into an obsession by the time she entered graduate school. She couldn't explain why she felt such a strong attraction to that part of the world; she simply followed her bliss. Years later, she would meet others in foreign policy who, like her, had devoted themselves to Soviet history and the Russian language without having an ancestral background that could explain their interest.

Choosing a graduate school wasn't difficult as John and Angelena Rice were virtual encyclopedias of information about post-secondary education. Since Condi's birth, her parents had discussed which colleges could provide her with the best opportunities, and the family tours of college campuses during their summer road trips had also filled them with facts that they had filed away for future use. John Rice's dual careers in the church and academia allowed him to become acquainted with prominent people in both areas who could make recommendations about college choices. One such figure was Reverend Theodore Hesburgh, president of the University of Notre Dame. The Rices knew that Notre Dame was one of America's most competitive private universities, but John's conversations with Father Hesburgh gave him a closer view of the school's conservative, value-oriented philosophy.

From the date of its formation by a Roman Catholic priest in 1842, Notre Dame's mission has been to provide an education "that addresses questions of value and meaning." Although a large percentage of Notre Dame's students are not Catholic, part of the university's mission is to encourage students to partake in community service and approach life as a way to "experience the invisible God" who works through "persons, events and material things." Another tenet of the school's Roman Catholic framework is that "God's grace prompts human activity to assist the world in creating justice grounded in love."

This view—spiritual development on a par with

scholarly work—was very attractive to Reverend Rice, a man who had devoted himself to guiding young people to develop their faith as well as their minds. He thought it would be the ideal place for Condi to pursue her graduate studies.

Condi's new mentor at Notre Dame, George Brinkley, recalled that she shared her father's conservative outlook and his attraction to the school's ideals. "Condoleezza came to Notre Dame in part, I think, because of its conservative reputation," he said. "She's a very complicated person and it's hard to say that this is the reason she came—she's very much her own person. But I think she also liked it because it was a relatively small university with a commitment to values and philosophy and fundamental ideas as well as practical programs and training. I liked it for that reason, although I'm not Catholic, and neither is Condi . . . The faculty is about one-half non-Catholic. The graduate programs in particular have always been much broader and tend to draw students of all backgrounds."

In addition to her father's endorsement and the small class sizes, Condi had another excellent reason to apply to Notre Dame's political science program. The Department of Government and International Studies contained one of the country's top Soviet studies centers, launched by another European émigré who, like Korbel at Denver, was recruited to help the American effort in catching up on Russian and Soviet history. Stephen D. Kertesz, a Hungarian diplomat who fled his country when the communists took power in 1947, was invited to help set up the program on the recommendation of Philip Mosely, head of Columbia University's Russian Institute (now the Harriman Institute). Notre Dame had been consulting with Mosely about forming its own program, as his directorship of the Russian Institute at Columbia gave him access to many of the political émigrés from Europe.

Philip Mosely's Russian Institute—the nation's first Soviet/Russian studies program—spawned a host of programs like the international studies department Condi entered at Notre Dame. As the nuclear superpower rivalry between the United States and the USSR continued through the 1950s, 1960s, and 1970s, these programs attracted students who sought government and academic careers. "The government gathered all those it could collect to inform and guide our wartime relations and our planning for the postwar period," wrote Mark L. von Hagen, director of the Harriman Institute. "Most graduates of these institutes found jobs waiting for them, with government almost a guaranteed employer."

Stephen Kertesz, slated to head up Notre Dame's program, had been an official in Hungary's foreign ministry, including one post as first secretary of the Hungarian legation in Bucharest where he was responsible for the Hungarian minority population in southern Transylvania. He wrote extensively on Eastern European politics after he joined the faculty at Notre Dame.

Among the new scholars at the Russian Institute was George Brinkley, who completed the institute's certificate program and also earned a Ph.D. in political science from Columbia. As part of the second generation of Soviet scholars from that institute, he chose the academic route and joined Kertesz and the rest of the Notre Dame faculty in 1958. Brinkley became one of the distinguished draws to the Notre Dame program and launched a distinguished publishing career with early papers such as "Leninism: What It Was and What It Was Not," "The 'Withering' of the State under Khrushchev," and "The

Soviet Union and the United Nations: The Changing Role of the Developing Countries." One of his first books, *The Volunteer Army and the Revolution in South Russia*, was awarded the American History Association's George Louis Beer Prize.

Notre Dame's government and international studies department became an important center for study of Russia and the Soviet Union in the late 1940s. Scholarship in these areas was very focused, and academics had the luxury of studying one nation, unlike the demands on scholars in other departments to cover an entire region. Soviet studies captivated those who wanted to get inside the Cold War and do some of the most cutting-edge research in history and politics. Those who came to Notre Dame's department could look forward to careers in foreign policy or international relations or use it as groundwork for further graduate work in law or academia. Condi had not decided which route to take when she entered Notre Dame, but she felt that her job options were better than they had been when she was a music major. When asked what she was going to do with degrees in her new area, she responded, "Well, the job market's a lot better in Russian history than it is in concert piano."

Condi was accepted into the graduate school at Notre Dame and began a specialized master's program under George Brinkley. He was flexible about Condi's program, and helped the department carefully construct a degree plan that drew upon her strengths and interests. He recalled that Condi, like many students in the department, arrived without extensive previous work in Soviet studies. "Most students had little background," he said, "so we had to teach them basics [like] history and background so they would understand the Soviet Union and communism."

Condi stood out, however, due to the extra reading she had done while immersing herself in the topic during her junior and senior years at Denver. She had read extensively about World War II and about military conflicts in general, and also delved into Russia's novelists including Dostoevsky and Solzhenitsyn. "He understood the dark side of Russia better than anyone else," she said of Solzhenitsyn. "Like most Russian [novelists], it was tragedy without redemption." In addition to the history books and novels, Condi's Russian language lessons provided insight into Russian literature and culture. Ever since her first course with Korbel, she had devoured the topic and considered her expanding reading list an adventure, an ardent labor of love.

Brinkley immediately recognized that she was a quick study and very gifted. "Our graduate program in Soviet and East European studies has a base of required courses," he said. "But she was extremely bright, so she came better prepared than most students." As he got to know her over the course of the year, he came to understand her parents' role in developing her remarkable confidence and academic abilities. "She was one of those self-driven students," he said. "Since she was a small child she has had a sense of self worth that comes out of a certain kind of experience. Her father motivated her with the idea that regardless of what life held during her childhood, there were very important things like education that enabled her to do what she wanted and be a success in whatever she wanted to go into."

Brinkley also remarked on Condi's knack for the Russian language. "She had some Russian before she came to Notre Dame," he said, "but my impression was that she learned very quickly and just had a talent. Where it was extremely difficult for me, she picked it up quite readily."

The department set out to create a specialized program for Condi, one that would give her the challenge she desired. "It was clear from the beginning that we couldn't put her in a fixed set of requirements," said Brinkley. "I could see that she was someone who was so highly motivated, and who had also read a tremendous amount, that she would benefit from a lot of opportunities to work on her own. And she wanted to do that." Brinkley organized her graduate work to include some regular courses plus a great deal of independent work through a course of study called directed readings. Condi did far more independent study work than any of the other students in the program. In that arrangement, she worked directly with Professor Brinkley, first settling on a topic, then creating a reading list and conducting research. Through the year she had frequent tutoring sessions with Brinkley, which created an enormously focused, highly individualized experience. She had been attracted to Notre Dame for its small graduate class sizes, but what she actually received was much more: a virtual one-on-one, expert guide to the Soviet Union with one of the leading scholars in the field.

At Denver, Condi had become interested in the balance-of-power aspects of international relations and had launched her foray into political studies by reading the work of Hans Morgenthau. She found an affinity for Morgenthau's political realism. "I read early on and was influenced by Hans Morgenthau," she said, adding that Zbigniew Brzezinski and John Erickson were also major influences." Realism, or realpolitik/power politics, was a dominant theme in the study of international relations being conducted in Soviet studies programs at Columbia, Notre Dame, the University of Denver, and elsewhere during the Cold War. The view described in the pages of Morgenthau's *Politics Among Nations* would come to shape Condi's foreign policy outlook throughout her career.

She was drawn to the pragmatic approach of realism, which asserts that the actions of nation-states are based on basic human nature—like a person, a nation will fight to protect its own self-interest. "Power is the control of man over man," wrote Morgenthau, who explained that each nation must act in its national interest. Power struggles, including wars, ensue when other nations threaten this interest. Idealism, or liberal politics, on the other hand, contends that war marks a failure in international relations and that the best chances for peace lie in cooperation and the formation of a higher organization such as the UN or the European Union. Idealists are motivated by morality issues and ideologies whereas realists concern themselves with what Morgenthau calls the "rational, objective and unemotional" outlook the nation must assume to ensure its survival. Condi agreed with the notion that the nation's best interest was not served by trying to enforce ideological causes throughout the world.

To the realist, military force is the nation's most significant power resource and shifts in relative power among nations often result in war. Realism is not devoid of ethics, however—any post-war social scientist had to address the moral issues of nations facing potential nuclear devastation. "Realists insisted that the national interest could and should be an expression of American values," wrote Joel H. Rosenthal. Among those values he listed prudence, humility, the preservation of freedom and a "good-faith effort to balance ideals and self-interests."

Condi describes herself as a realpolitiker and explains that from the beginning she was "attracted to the Byzantine nature of Soviet politics and by power: how it operates, how it's used." She also upholds the moral component that Americans traditionally bring to the table. "I am a realist," she said. "Power matters. But there can be no absence of moral content in American foreign policy and, furthermore, the American people wouldn't accept such an absence." As summarized by Ann Reilly Dowd in a Rice profile for *George* magazine, "Condi came to see the cold war not as a war of ideas between communism and democracy but as something more primordial—a raw contest between two great competing powers with conflicting national interests."

Condi's interest in military strategy became the focus of her graduate work. "While she was at Notre Dame, Condi developed a very strong interest in the Soviet military and in the problems of arms control and Soviet-American relations," said Professor Brinkley. "She did her master's work with some focus on the study of the Soviet military."

Condi's year of study at Notre Dame culminated in a research paper on that topic, which she continued to work on with Brinkley as she developed it into a doctoral dissertation at the University of Denver. "She and I worked to develop her proposal for her doctoral dissertation, and even after she went to Denver, we corresponded and talked on the telephone to get started on the doctoral research program," he said.

Looking back on Condi's career in academia and politics, Brinkley sees a logical progression that begins with her research at Notre Dame. Her research paper led to her doctoral dissertation, her first professorship, her work at the Pentagon, and her National Security Council posts at the White House. Her attraction for Soviet studies, ignited at Denver, became focused and cohesive for the first time at Notre Dame. She honed her research skills and gained detailed insights from a new mentor who continued to play a vital role in her graduate studies after she returned to the University of Denver.

The autumn of 1974 to the spring of 1975 was a challenging and productive time, but it wasn't *all* work. Condi socialized with her new friends in South Bend and, being the type of student who can get more done in a few hours than many do in a week, she could afford to stay out late from time to time. A night out didn't compromise her next day at school because she rarely had to attend morning classes. And she was living away from her parents for the first time, so her leisure time felt more freeing than it had in Denver. Disco had just hit the dance floors in 1974 and college towns everywhere were pounding out tunes like "The Hustle," "Get Down Tonight," and the new sounds of ABBA and Elton John. Condi may have been bred on Brahms and Mozart, but she also loved pop music like any other twenty-year-old. "She partied quite a bit there," said one of her long-time friends, Deborah Carson. "She and her friends used to hang out all the time and sometimes stay out on the town until five o'clock in the morning."

During her year at Notre Dame, Condi thought seriously about entering law school after finishing her M.A. degree. Her second cousin Connie Rice was just starting her undergraduate degree at Harvard and was interested in the profession; a few years later, she would enter the New York University School of Law. Condi applied to and was accepted into several law schools throughout the country, including the one at the University of Denver. But when Condi discussed her plans with her former professor Josef Korbel, he convinced her otherwise. "You are very talented," he told her, "you have to become a professor." Before that conversation, the idea of a life in academia had never entered her mind. "When I think back on that moment," Condi said, "I don't know if it was a subliminal message, but I had such respect and admiration for him that I took the idea seriously for the first time."

Condi put off law school and spent the next year taking courses at the University of Denver's Graduate School of International Studies (GSIS) in the hope that she would discover exactly what she wanted to do. Her parents had instilled in her an interest in world affairs, and as she matured, she felt it was important to become involved in the larger issues, not only as a black person, but as a well-informed, concerned American. "Thinking broadly about the whole world out there has been one of the most important things in my life," she said. "It has been crucial to me to learn about issues which seem far removed, yet are important in all our lives."

The courses she took that year made her realize how much she enjoyed analyzing the big issues and seeing how this analysis is put into practice to literally change the world. In her modest way, she explained that this year of search and study led her into the Graduate School of International Studies at Denver. "I realized that I liked political science more than law," she said, "and I sort of stumbled into a Ph.D. program." With Korbel's encouragement, she decided to continue graduate work in political science and enrolled in his program. "He was nothing but supportive and insistent, even pushy, about me going into this field," she said.

Condi received her master of arts degree in government from Notre Dame on August 8, 1975, and moved back to Denver. She would return to Notre Dame several years later as one of the university's leaders—a member of the board of trustees.

When Condi returned to Denver, she moved back into her parents' house and slipped comfortably into her old activities—singing in the Montview Presbyterian choir, practicing and giving piano lessons to keep up her technique, and watching as much football as humanly possible. Many weekends she would have a few friends over to watch games at her house, and her colleagues soon learned that she was much more than an ordinary fan. "She is one of the few people I have ever met who knows as much about the sport as I do," said Robby Laitos, a GSIS student who first met Condi at a football party. Laitos, who now directs an international consulting company out of Denver, describes himself as a football fanatic who takes the sport "very, very seriously." In his first year at the school, he and other new graduate students were invited to a cabin in the mountains outside of Denver one Saturday afternoon for a day of "food, music, and good company," he said.

"That day there was a particularly exciting college football game on, I believe it was Oklahoma-Ohio State, and the game had just ended when I arrived," said Laitos. "I was discussing the game with someone else when Condi walked up and joined the conversation. This was the first time I had met her. It was immediately apparent that she *knew* football, and was not just faking it. That started a two-year 'football relationship' between us. We never talked about Russia or school, we just talked about football." Laitos also recalled going over to the Rices' on Sunday afternoons to watch football and enjoy Angelena's famous gumbo. "I remember her mother made us all gumbo soup," he said, "and we all thoroughly enjoyed the afternoon of football and gumbo and good cheer."

The doctoral program that Condi entered at the University of Denver had a distinguished history in both its faculty and its curriculum. Denver's Graduate School of International Studies differed from the East Coast Soviet programs in that its curriculum has always been broad-based. Columbia's Russian Institute, for example, had a "predominant intellectual orientation on regime studies, rather than social, economic, and cultural processes," said its current director, Mark von Hagen. The East Coast institutes were keenly focused on the Moscow infrastructure and Cold War strategies, and after the Soviet Union dismantled they were compelled to expand dramatically to encompass cultural, economic, and social aspects of the region. Denver, on the other hand, included those themes in its curriculum from the start. "Looking back," said GSIS professor Karen Feste, "the school doesn't seem a lot different today than it was in the beginning because we were never caught up in the Cold War politics that some of the East Coast schools were. Broader coverage was a matter of routine for us. We had always been interested in social development and human justice in addition to the East-West divide. As a result, when the Cold War ended, our curriculum had less dramatic changes than our sister schools."

This program, exploring several aspects of the Soviet/Russian experience, was very attractive to Condi when she enrolled in 1976. Josef Korbel had not always welcomed women to the department—when he founded GSIS, he opposed the idea of bringing in female students and faculty because he doubted the graduates would go out and get high-ranking positions that could contribute to the stature of the department. When Karen Feste joined the department in the early 1970s, for example, Korbel voted against her appointment to the faculty. The majority voted for Feste, however, and she was brought in as a professor of international politics and research methodology. She remained the only woman on the faculty for many years, but she witnessed Korbel's view change over time. His initial reluctance was ironic in that he strongly supported his daughter's academic track in political science. In the 1960s, Madeleine Albright pursued her master's and doctoral degrees in Columbia's Department of Public Law and Government and also completed the university's Russian Institute program. When Condi began taking classes in international studies at Denver in 1975, after returning from Notre Dame, Madeleine was running Senator Edwin Muskie's national fund-raising campaign.

Karen Feste, one of Condi's professors and academic advisors, became a good friend of Korbel within the first two years of her appointment, and she observed a dramatic transformation in his view about women in the program. "He and I were close," she said. "He was the oldest one on the faculty, I was youngest; he was Old World in his approach, I was modern; and we seemed to click." By the time Condi arrived at Denver he had thoroughly changed his outlook. He was interested in attracting the best and the brightest and, as Feste observed, "gender factors were not important."

Karen Feste had earned her Ph.D. at the University of Minnesota before joining the faculty at Denver and, in addition to teaching, has worked as a political consultant throughout the world for organizations such as Egypt's Institute of National Planning and Kuwait University. Another of Condi's professors, Jonathan Adelman, had received his Ph.D. in political science at Columbia (as had

Brinkley, her Notre Dame professor). Since joining the faculty at GSIS, Adelman has been a visiting scholar at universities in Beijing and Moscow and has traveled extensively on speaking tours for the State Department. A prominent member of the American Israel Public Affairs Committee, he was a member of the Allied Jewish Federation's mission to Israel in 2002.

At GSIS, Condi also studied with Catherine Kelleher, a professor who has become one the world's foremost experts on security issues and whose career has encompassed both academia and government. She worked at the Pentagon as deputy assistant secretary of defense for Russia, Ukraine, and Eurasia, and later served as defense advisor and personal representative of the secretary of defense at NATO. She was also the director of the Aspen Institute Berlin, the German office of the organization that conducts policy seminars for American and European leaders. In the spring of 2002, she was awarded the Bundeswehr Golden Cross of Honor, Germany's highest military decoration, for her "contributions to transatlantic relations, especially the promotion of political dialogue between European and American decision-makers." She is currently a professor at the Naval War College in Newport, Rhode Island.

The 1970s and 1980s were an extremely exciting time to be studying international relations and the Soviet Union. Major Cold War events that coincided with Condi's college years included the Strategic Arms Limitation Treaty (SALT I) signed by the United States and the Soviet Union in 1972. By the time Condi started graduate school the talks had reached an impasse and India had developed nuclear weapons. In 1975, the United States and the USSR joined thirty-three other nations at the Conference on Security and Cooperation in

Europe and included their signatures on the Final Act of the conference, the Helsinki Accords. This pledge to protect human rights also established the borders of Europe as they stood at the end of World War II, recognizing the Soviet Union's domination over the Baltic States of Estonia, Latvia, and Lithuania.

Another episode for Condi to follow as she developed her Russian reading skills in the pages of *Pravda* was the sale of U.S. grain to the Soviet Union in 1975. Near-famine conditions in the USSR compelled the nation to sign a long-term contract for U.S. grain. A less dour motivation for U.S.-Soviet relations also occurred that year—the spacelink of the U.S. *Apollo* and the Soviet *Soyuz* spacecraft. In the six years since the *Apollo* moonwalk, NASA administrators had been working to convert the *Apollo* mission into a program of American-Soviet cooperation. "As with so many aspects of American national policy, NASA's programs had always reflected the current environment of foreign affairs," stated a NASA article on the *Apollo-Soyuz* spacelink. "The joint flight could be seen as a part of détente, but the people at NASA saw it as much more."

The *Apollo-Soyuz* Test Project (ASTP) kept NASA in the manned space mission, kept the flight team working, and paved the way for the international space cooperation that was essential for the next phase of space technology. The spacelink was covered on TV, which provided images of U.S.-Soviet cooperation that were painfully absent in the arms race. Statements by the astronauts and cosmonauts described the unity of the world as seen from space, a refreshing change from political stories that stressed the tensions between the superpowers. "Dear American TV people," said cosmonaut Valeriy Kubasov during one televised spot, "It would be wrong to ask which country's more beautiful. It would be right to say there is nothing more beautiful than our blue planet."

In 1976, the year Condi began her Ph.D. program, she registered as a Democrat and voted for Jimmy Carter in the election. Carter's handling of the USSR's invasion of Afghanistan in late December 1979, however, changed her mind about him and the Democratic party. The president called the invasion "a deliberate effort by a powerful atheistic government to subjugate an independent Islamic people" and warned that a "Soviet-occupied Afghanistan threatens both Iran and Pakistan and is a steppingstone to their possible control over much of the world's oil supplies." He also said that he was shocked and saddened by the attack and that his "opinion of the Russians has changed most drastically in the last week [more] than even in the previous two and one-half years before that." In response, he issued an embargo on grain and technology, cut back Soviet fishing privileges in American waters, postponed discussion and ratification of the SALT II treaty that he and Brezhnev had hammered out earlier that year, and called for a U.S. boycott of the 1980 Moscow Summer Olympics. Condi thought that Carter's shock and surprise were naive and his actions too weak. "I remember thinking, What did you think you were dealing with?" she said. "This is a horrible government—of course they invaded some foreign country! I thought it was time to have a tougher policy toward this repressive regime."

Had it not been for Carter's treatment of the Soviets during that crisis, Condi would probably still be a Democrat. "I was a registered Democrat and might never have changed parties were it not for what I thought was our mishandling of the Cold War," she said in 2000. "I thought the Soviets were aggressive and playing us like a violin. I thought Carter didn't understand the true nature of the Soviet Union, which was pretty dark."

Condi was so passionate in her criticism of the U.S. policy toward the Soviet Union that her attitude overpowered her high regard for the Democratic party's support of the Civil Rights movement. During the presidential campaign of 1980, she registered as a Republican and voted for Ronald Reagan. "I admired what Lyndon Johnson did for civil rights in 1964," she said. "But by 1980 I just thought the U.S. was not pursuing an effective foreign policy, and I was attracted to Reagan's strength. Then my political views developed in favor of smaller government."

Condi's Democratic beginnings are still evident in her moderate social views, such as her pro-choice stance. This makes her a self-described "all-over-the-map Republican" who is "'very conservative' in foreign policy, 'ultra-conservative' in other areas, 'almost shockingly libertarian' on some issues, 'moderate' on others, and 'liberal' on probably nothing."

Many Americans who were introduced to Condi for the first time through her speech at the 2000 Republican National Convention got the impression that she became a Republican in the footsteps of her father who had been rejected by the Democrats in Jim Crow Alabama. But Condi had her own reasons. "It was the constitution and foreign policy, not social issues, that drew me to the Republican party," she said. Condi takes a ribbing from her black friends for being a Republican, but she is firm and confident in her position. "I'm in the GOP for the right reasons," she said. "I like our foreign policy stance better. I really am a smaller government person. I don't think every solution is in Washington."

In the final year of Condi's doctoral program, Polish

shipyard worker Lech Walesa was named the official chairman of his non-communist trade union, Solidarity. After years of daring, illegal strikes, Walesa had gained rights for Polish workers and brought international attention to Poland's struggles under communist rule. Not even the closest followers of these events dreamed that they signaled the beginning of the end of communism in Eastern Europe and the Soviet Union.

Following world events like these fueled Condi's passion for Soviet studies. Unlike the other subjects she had explored as an undergraduate, this field had powerful, real-world immediacy that impacted the way nations behaved, the way people lived, and the way history unfolded.

To Josef Korbel, Condi stood out among her fellow students at GSIS because she possessed the complete package—academic brilliance, self-motivation, and a Russian-language background. "Korbel liked Condi because she was smart, she was quick, she was energetic *and she knew Russian*," said Feste. "Those are factors that mattered to him." Foreign language was a crucial part of the program in Korbel's view, and he demanded that students start working on a Slavic language before entering the program. "Korbel told students who wanted to study East or Central Europe or the former Soviet Union that they better have a language before they came to study with him," said Feste. "Condi was a perfect candidate because she did have a background in Russian. Others didn't; they had followed the politics but hadn't studied a language. He told them to come back after they had studied one of the languages such as Czech, Polish, or Russian."

Condi not only continued her Russian lessons but also began studying Czech, as her Russian professor

Libor Brom was Czech and encouraged her to pursue it. Today, her professional resume states that she is fluent in Russian and has "research ability" in Czech and French.

Korbel was known for being extremely gracious with those he liked and severe with those who did not measure up to his standards. "He expected a lot out of people," said Feste. "He gravitated toward people who he thought were very intelligent." Condi got along very well with him, and he pushed her relentlessly to aim high in the field. Korbel's support and enthusiasm for Condi's career echoed the support he gave his daughter, and this attention made him a new father figure. "He was as proud of [Madeleine], and as aggressive about her prospects, as he was about me," Condi said. His faith in her talent proved to be well justified.

One of Korbel's themes that would come to light in Condi's work with George W. Bush was his insistence that students learn to translate policy into clear, concise language. "It was Josef Korbel who taught her that a leader must articulate foreign policy in ways ordinary people can understand," wrote Ann Blackman in her biography of Madeleine Albright, "that in times of crisis, citizens will not rally to the cause if they do not understand the impact it will have on their daily lives." Condi took this lesson to heart and developed a reputation as someone who can bring the most complex policy issues down to earth. That ability made her George W.'s first choice as foreign policy tutor during the presidential campaign, and it is a central part of her job as national security advisor.

Although Korbel was Condi's mentor and favorite teacher, they did not always agree. She said he was "probably more liberal on domestic politics than I was," but added, "he was a wonderful storyteller and very attentive to his students. It was that attentiveness, plus his ability to weave larger conceptual issues around very interesting stories, that made him such a powerful teacher."

The large amount of independent study work that Condi did at Notre Dame prepared her well for the rigorous process at GSIS. "Our program works best for students who work autonomously," said Feste, "and she was one of those people. She was willing to seek out help when she needed it and just do the work; that was Condi's approach." Coursework in the program included topics such as military history, Soviet foreign policy, Soviet and Russian history, communism, international politics, and Soviet and Russian culture. She narrowed her research for her dissertation to comparative military regimes, working closely with Jonathan Adelman who cochaired her dissertation committee and with George Brinkley, her former professor at Notre Dame. Her study analyzed the Czech military and its effects upon the nation's society and politics. It was pioneering research that resulted in a unique contribution to the field. "There wasn't a lot written about the subject," said Adelman. "There wasn't a lot of information out there, [but] that didn't stop her. She rolled up her sleeves." To Adelman, her eagerness to meet this challenge revealed a lot about her character. "People might see her as contained," he said. "But she can be quite daring, flexible, and innovative."

Her study included a seven-week trip to the Soviet Union with a brief stop in Poland. In Moscow, she was forced to be unusually creative in her research methods due to the scarcity of documented information. Her relatively brief visit put a real face on the research topics she pursued in the libraries at the University of Denver.

"The General Staff [of the USSR] was my life for five years," she said. "I would go to Moscow and count the windows in the Ministry of Defense General Staff building to figure out how many people worked there because the data was never published." Later, when she was working in Bush Senior's administration, she discussed the subject with Sergei Akhromoyev, who had been the leader of the Soviet General Staff for many years. She had estimated that there were about 5,000 members of the staff, and when she asked him for the figure, he said, "About 5,000." Her creative research methods had worked.

On her research trip, Condi finally had the opportunity to experience the culture that had enthralled her for years. In Moscow and St. Petersburg, she could visit the concert halls in which Tchaikovsky conducted his symphonies, Rubinstein poured out Chopin, and young Rachmaninov conducted opera. She saw firsthand how the solid authority of the state manifested itself in the imposing walls surrounding the Kremlin, the sprawling memorials to the nation's heroes, and the majestic architecture of the subway system. She was surrounded by the beauty of the Russian language, which swirled through the steamy coffeehouses and which by now she could speak and read with confidence.

Very few black individuals lived in Moscow, and although Condi had grown accustomed to predominantly white classrooms, she was a minority as both a black person and an American in the USSR capital. According to one Russian native, this would have made her a very popular character. Dmitri Gerasamenko, a native of St. Petersburg and graduate of the St. Petersburg State Theatre Arts Academy, noted the extraordinary phase in which foreigners, including black people, first trickled into the Soviet Union. "The majority of Soviets didn't have the opportunity to interact with blacks before 1957, the year of the International Students Festival in Moscow," he said. "The Iron Curtain had been up for forty years and suddenly people from all over the world were coming to Moscow for the first time. The visitors were astounded by the wonderful energy in Moscow, although the people were so poor, they were proud to share whatever they had, to have some room in their communal apartments to entertain.

"Foreigners saw that the people were generous and cheerful in spite of their poverty," he added. "After that, foreigners began to visit the city, and many Moscow people saw blacks for the first time. In the 1960s you could see black people being followed down the street by curious Russians who would touch them to be sure they were real; they couldn't believe their eyes. This was done with a sense of innocent curiosity. We students in the 1970s and 1980s were so hungry for another culture that we went out of our way to talk to foreigners, to try to make them feel comfortable in our culture and to learn about their lives and where they came from. The capitalist countries were of real interest to people. Our people didn't know anything about life in America or other democratic countries."

Reflecting on the five-year period in the late 1970s and early 1980s in which Condi traveled to Moscow for her dissertation research, Gerasamenko said, "A black student from a prestigious American university who could speak Russian would have been treated with much hospitality and respect," he said. "In the first place, the Russians were so grateful to meet people who spoke Russian, even if it was just 'Hi' or 'How are you,' any attempt was met with great delight. I would assume that

Rice's knowledge and unique American experience must have been fascinating to the Russians who met her during those years."

In the summer of 1977, Condi went on a domestic trip as part of her research, which gave her a glimpse into the U.S. military complex for the first time. She went to Washington to work as an intern at the Department of State, spending weeks inside the Pentagon. Later in her program she took on another summer internship at the Rand Corporation, the policy research organization that had been founded by the military airpower supplier, Douglas Aircraft, after World War II. Headquartered in Santa Monica, California, and Arlington, Virginia, Rand was a perfect fit for a student focusing on international security. Its research areas include world political, military, and economic trends; sources of potential regional conflict; and emerging threats to U.S. security.

Back home in Denver, Condi's social life continued to revolve around football—but with an added dimension. During those years she dated a member of the Denver Broncos and their romance turned into a very serious relationship. Condi's boyfriend was a "very major player," according to her friend Deborah Carson, and the couple got engaged. Condi socialized with NFL wives, sat in the good seats at games with them and became a well-loved member of that intimate inner circle of the NFL. She picked out her wedding gown and started to work with her mother on all the arrangements, but the couple broke up before the wedding. "She was seriously going to marry him," said Carson, "and I really don't know what happened. It wasn't anything like a major blowup; I think they just got to the point where they didn't get along."

When Condi finished her doctoral program at Denver, she was twenty-six years old. She would date more football players, as well as men in other lines of work, but she did not get engaged again (up to the time of this writing in 2002).

The final product of Condi's work was a dissertation entitled *The Politics of Client Command: The Case of Czechoslovakia 1948–1975.* This would become the basis for her first book, *Uncertain Alliance: The Soviet Union and the Czechoslovak Army, 1948–1963*, which was published by Princeton University Press in 1984.

On the morning of August 14, 1981, she joined her graduating colleagues in the outdoor commencement ceremony on the University of Denver's Margery Reed Quadrangle. With a Ph.D. in international studies and a post-doctoral position at Stanford in the wings, twenty-six-year-old Condi was set to embark upon a distinguished academic career. Although her parents and other family members stood proudly by, the absence of one person made the day bittersweet. Josef Korbel had died of cancer in 1977. He did not live to see his star pupil or his daughter become prominent world figures. "He died of stomach cancer, and he had a tough time at the end," said Karen Feste, "but he was active to the last minute." On his sickbed, Korbel continued working on a new manuscript about Czech soldiers in World War I.

From the mentoring she received from Korbel to the stimulating challenges of her research topic, Condi's experience at Denver was extremely positive, and she remembers it warmly. "Because of the small, interactive faculty in the GSIS, I received solid training in political philosophy and methodology," she said. "I liked the interdisciplinary curriculum and unrestricted choices." Receiving her diploma that summer morning, Condi completed her college years in a field that she had not even heard of when she first began taking undergraduate music courses at the university. Later, she would recommend her students to make an active search for a field that ignites their passion, as she did. "I tell students, 'If you don't know what you want, start exploring. Find a class you like and a professor with whom you have a rapport.'" The life-altering switch from music to Soviet studies had taught her a lesson in flexibility, in the virtues of not limiting yourself with a rigid plan. "[For years] I structured my life to be a concert musician," she said. "That was all I wanted to do. And it fell apart on me. I'm never going to do that again." This realization appeared to affect her career significantly—from that point on, she committed herself to working diligently on the job at hand while staying open to whatever might come.

The GSIS faculty attending commencement that day knew that they would hear much more from Condoleezza Rice. "I think we all knew that she was going to do something quite superior to the average student," said Arthur Gilbert, another professor who reviewed Condi's dissertation. Karen Feste echoed that prediction. "We always thought Condi would be successful," recalled Karen Feste. "Over the years we have had some excellent students in our program who stand out during their time at Denver, and with each of them we know it's going to happen—we don't know when, but we know it's going to happen." With Condi, it all began to happen in California.

SIX

Professor Rice

"The understanding of arms control, the respective views and needs of all the nations, is fundamental to our very existence. Blacks should be part of this understanding, as they should be in every other field of American thought and progress. It would be a shame to leave such a vital national concern in the hands of white males over forty!"

—*Condoleezza Rice, 1983*

ON the morning of December 1, 1989, a light rain put a sheen on the deck of the USS *Belknap*, a guided-missile cruiser docked with the Sixth Fleet in Valletta Harbor at Malta. The weather outlook for the Mediterranean islands was not good that week, and by nightfall gale force winds created sixteen-foot swells that jerked the massive ship up and down like a toy. President Bush settled into the comfortable admiral's quarters and tried to get some rest before the momentous conference to come. At the Malta Summit the president would meet Soviet President Mikhail Gorbachev and present U.S. positions on several issues as well as express support for Gorbachev's *perestroika* reforms. The Malta summit—dubbed by the press as the "seasick summit"—was the first superpower meeting ever held on a ship, and the opening talks had to be postponed for a day because of the choppy waters.

The U.S. delegation to the summit included Secretary of State James A. Baker III, White House Chief of Staff John H. Sununu and National Security Advisor Brent Scowcroft. Joining Scowcroft was the National Security Council's Soviet expert, thirty-five-year-old Condoleezza Rice. When Bush introduced Rice to Gorbachev, he described her as the woman who "tells me everything I know about the Soviet Union." Others in the room watched as Gorbachev, looking surprised and skeptical, turned to Condi and said, "I hope you know a lot."

One of the reasons Condi had become a Soviet expert was the fact that it was a hands-on, ever-changing field in which history was being rewritten every day. As an undergraduate taking her first courses in international relations, little did she know that one day she would be front-and-center at one of the most historic scenes in modern political history—the end of the Cold War. The first day of talks took place in a book-lined room of the Soviet cruiser *Maxim Gorky*, the only ship in the harbor heavy enough to withstand the rolling waves. In eight hours of talks held over two days, Bush and Gorbachev discussed arms control, trade policies, Soviet emigration laws, military conventional forces in Europe, and other issues. The most profound outcome was the two leaders' agreement that the old rivalry between their nations was history. "[The] characteristics of the Cold War should be abandoned," said Gorbachev at the end of the Malta Summit. "The arms race, mistrust, psychological and ideological struggle, all these things should be of the past." President Bush agreed, stating that the world was on the "threshold of a brand new era of U.S.-Soviet relations." At Malta, Bush and Gorbachev opened up a new age of cooperation between the superpowers. And Condi Rice was there.

Condi's career as both an academic and a policy maker had begun eight years previously at Stanford University. Following graduation at Denver at age twenty-six, she received a post-doctorate fellowship to continue her research at Stanford's Center for International Security and Arms Control, part of the university's Institute for International Studies. Stanford, about thirty-five miles south of San Francisco, boasted a renowned faculty of Nobel laureates and Pulitzer Prize winners and offered one of the most beautiful campuses in the country. The cluster of California Mission-style buildings with their red-tiled roofs, surrounded by thousands of oak, palm, and eucalyptus trees, formed the oldest section of the colossal campus situated on 8,000 acres of land in sight of San Francisco Bay.

The fellowship gave Condi a stipend of about $30,000, an office, and access to all of Stanford's libraries, research facilities, and department faculty. As a Soviet scholar, she joined policymakers, business people, security specialists, and other experts at the Center to study contemporary issues of international security. It was the only department to offer "a fully disciplinary course in arms control in the whole nation," and students who took its courses were training to become arms control and security specialists. Most graduates went on to hold a variety of government arms-control positions. (The department is now called the Center for International Security and Cooperation.)

The fellowship was to last for one academic year, but a few months after she arrived, Condi made such a big impression at a talk she presented to the political science department that she was asked to join the faculty. The department was seeking qualified minorities and Condi fit the bill for affirmative action not only as a black person, but also as a woman in a field dominated by men. Once she got in, however, there would be no guarantees that her position would be renewed unless she proved herself worthy of the job. "They didn't need another Soviet specialist," said Condi, "but they asked themselves, 'How often does a black female who could diversify our ranks come along?'" The department chair explained his position: "We have a three-year period here," he told her, "and then you have to be renewed. And nobody's going to look at race, nobody's going to look at gender; and you don't get any special breaks; and you surely don't get any special breaks when you come up for tenure." Condi thought, "Well, yeah, that seems perfectly fair."

In the fall of 1981 Condi began the semester as an assistant professor of political science. She was also named assistant director of the Center for International Security and Arms Control. At twenty-six, her scholarship, knack for teaching, and personality stood out and earned her respect from faculty and students. "I think what struck people at the time was a combination of all the personal stuff—charm and very gracious personality . . . a kind of intellectual agility mixed with velvet-glove forcefulness," said Coit Blacker, one of her fellow professors. "She's a steel magnolia," he continued, adding that her Southern graciousness is mixed with "a very steely inner core" and extreme self-discipline.

John Ferejohn, who joined Stanford's political science department as a professor in 1983, recalled that Condi was the only black person on the faculty at the time. He recognized her qualities of leadership and persuasiveness—traits that she has carried throughout her career. "She got along well with everybody," he said, "and even when she was just an assistant professor she exhibited a lot of what you see now—a very effective leader, decisive, clear-headed. Even when you disagree with her about something, she has good reasons. She's effective when she's opposing you—she often wins."

Over the next decade she taught several classes, most of which she called "applied" political science that dealt with the military, national security, and foreign policy. Her courses included:

"Soviet Bloc and the Third World": an exploration of the political, military, and economic activities of the Soviet Union and its allies in the Third World.

"The Role of the Military in Politics": a survey of the interaction between military and political leaders in three types of governments: Western-industrial, communist, and that of developing countries. Condi used examples of leaders in the United States, the USSR, China, Brazil, and Nigeria.

"The Politics of Alliances": this class examined NATO, the Warsaw Pact, and other nineteenth and twentieth century military-political alliances in the international system.

"Political Elites": a seminar on the recruitment and behavior of political decision-makers in the legislative, administrative, executive, and military departments of government.

"U.S. and Soviet National Security Policies: The Responsibilities of Empire in the Nuclear Age": a comparison of how the two superpowers balance domestic and international responsibilities with a close look at their national security systems

"The Institutions of Violence": a seminar on revolutionary change, the role of the military and the police.

"The Transformation of Europe": explored through

the eyes of decision-makers in Washington, Bonn, Moscow, Paris, and London, this course discussed the changes in Europe between 1989 and 1990.

One of her favorite teaching methods was to have her students re-create major foreign policy decisions in a series of role-playing sessions. After the students researched and wrote papers about the event, they were each assigned to play a particular figure. She felt that this gave the students a broader understanding of what actually goes on in decision-making situations and provided more insight than simply reading a text. "It is increasingly difficult to generate in students a sense of the complexity involved in foreign policy with the methods available in the literature of political science and history," she said. She felt that role-playing helped students grasp the importance of the key players' personalities and emotional reactions as well as the roles played by members of Congress, the press, bureaucrats, and special interest groups. She explained that the "orderly, post hoc re-creations that we teach" in textbooks leave out many important aspects of the story. While re-enacting an event, students were often shocked at their own behavior. "It's interesting to watch students come to terms with how they behave," said Condi. "They will say, 'I never thought I could behave that way.'"

One student, Troy Eid, recalled the drama of a role-playing session in which he played a Soviet defense minister, complete with a Russian Army officer's coat. The reenactment lasted an entire week, and at one point he fell asleep, exhausted, in Condi's office. She woke him up and gave him coffee so he could keep with the program. "It is still the most intense week I've ever had," he said, which is saying a lot from a man who went on to graduate from the University of Chicago Law School, become chief counsel to Colorado Governor Bill Owens, and subsequently CEO of a large Internet systems development company.

As a Republican, Condi did not fit the traditionally liberal mold of academia. And she did not try to keep her conservative views under wraps. One student recalled that she was known as "Condi the Hawk," and John Ferejohn stated that her Republican Party affiliation "wasn't a surprise, it was commonly known about her. She was active in the community. She doesn't hide her light under a bushel. She's very straightforward."

In her classes on military topics, Condi often opened her first lecture with a football analogy. Anyone who knew her understood that one of her favorite topics was the comparison of football to war. Paul Brest, former dean of Stanford Law School and current president of the Hewlett Foundation, recalled going to a Stanford Cardinal's game with Condi. He had scheduled an event at the law school for the head of the San Francisco 49ers. "Condi heard about it," he said, "and told me, 'I'm not going to let you embarrass the university because I know you don't know anything about football, so I'm going to take you to a Stanford football game." She sat down between Paul and his wife and gave them a crash course in the game. "The first thing she said was, 'Football is like war, it's about taking territory,'" Paul said.

Condi is not the first to make this analogy. Stephen Crane, author of the Civil War novel *The Red Badge of Courage* (1895), was asked how he could write so convincingly about a war that he had not experienced. "I believe that I got my sense of the rage of the conflict on the football field," he answered. Teddy Roosevelt once said, "In life, as in a football game, the principle to follow is: Hit the line hard; don't foul and don't shirk, but hit the line hard." And Walter Camp (1859–1925), the man who created American football, described a "remarkable and interesting likeness between the theories which underlie great battles and the miniature contests of the gridiron."

Many football players and other jocks attended Condi's large survey classes and connected with the analogy. One female student commented that she felt a bit alienated by the approach, however. She took a freshman class from Condi just as war was breaking out in Bosnia in 1992. "It was a large lecture class that focused on military action and intervention," she said, "and it was very interesting because it was going on just as the Yugoslav crisis was happening. Dr. Rice started out the class by giving a football analogy, comparing football strategies to turf battles between nations. It struck me to hear this because she was a woman; it had a kind of stereotypically male bent to it. I think that for impressionistic students it's a tool and it works, but unfortunately it's sort of dangerous when you have a lot of football players in your class who are out there playing the game every day. I think that it brings war down to the football level rather than vice versa. To me it was an unappealing analogy for that reason. But that didn't make her a bad teacher; the class was very interesting and I learned a ton."

One of Condi's colleagues remarked that the passion she brought to teaching was obvious even after she left the classroom. "Anyone who has had the good fortune to have a meeting with Professor Rice immediately after one of her lectures can sense the excitement she brings to the classroom," he said. "Just by the way she talks about the lecture she has just given, it is obvious that she is still completely engaged in her subject and in her students to a truly extraordinary degree." Students who had Condi as an academic advisor knew that she was seriously committed to them. "I will always remember the fifty-five-minute phone conversation in the middle of the day to get back to me on a draft of my dissertation proposal," said one graduate student. Another graduate student described her as "a marvelous facilitator, a teacher in an ancient Socratic sense. Her command for guiding our discussions and ensuring our eventual arrival at major conceptual understandings was outstanding among the teachers I had at Stanford." Condi left a lasting impression as a role model on a group of students who attended one of her seminar courses. "She . . . treated us all like we were her favorite students," she said. "By the end of the seminar, several of the students were wistfully thinking about how much we wanted to be like her. This was not idle hero-worship. She seemed to be the embodiment of everything we admired about academia. She was knowledgeable without being close-minded, prestigious without being pompous, and her lectures were complex without being dry."

When Condi's three-year trial period was over the university gave her a positive appraisal and renewed her assistant professorship. She had, in fact, become one of the university's most highly regarded instructors. In 1984 Stanford awarded her the Walter J. Gores Award for Excellence in Teaching, the school's highest honor for teaching. Presenting the award during the commencement ceremonies on June 17, Provost Albert Hastorf praised her "for bringing enthusiasm and insight to her lectures and sparking the sense of curiosity and fascination in her students that she herself feels." He also remarked that she was renowned for giving "incalculable support, encouragement and inspiration to her undergraduate advisees."

Condi advised both undergraduates and graduate stu-

dents, and one of her Ph.D. students is a rising star in foreign policy. Jendayi Frazier was hired to teach at Condi's
alma mater, Denver's Graduate School of International
Studies, after graduating from Stanford in the early 1990s.
Her training as an Africa policy expert included a research position at the University of Nairobi, Kenya.
Harvard hired her away from Denver, making her an assistant professor of public policy at the Kennedy School
of Government. When Condi became George W.'s national security advisor, she appointed Jendayi to the
National Security Council as its Africa expert. Her official
title is special assistant to the president and senior director for African affairs.

Josef Korbel's assessment that Condi had the mak-
ings of a talented professor was borne out as she
continued to climb the academic ladder at Stanford. In
1987, she was promoted to associate professor and in
1993, at age thirty-eight, became a full professor. That
year she received another distinguished honor: the
School of Humanities and Sciences Dean's Award for
Distinguished Teaching. The award came with a $5,000
cash prize and a $1,000 increase in salary.

By 1984, Condi had become good friends with fellow
professor Coit Blacker, who in the early 1980s worked as
an aide to Democrat Senator Gary Hart. They discussed
Hart's presidential campaign and his military reform
ideas, which Condi found interesting. Coit introduced
Condi to Senator Hart, who was taken by "her intellect
and charm—charm in the profound sense, not the silly
sense. And I'd add a third dimension: inner strength."
Condi helped him briefly on the campaign as a foreign
policy advisor.

Working with Hart gave Condi a glimpse into policy
at work, but her first hands-on experience in government

took place in 1986 when she was sent to the Pentagon for a year by the Council on Foreign Relations. The mission of this nonpartisan research and membership organization, which publishes the journal *Foreign Policy*, is to increase "America's understanding of the world and [contribute] ideas to U.S. foreign policy." Each year the Council awards highly competitive International Affairs Fellowships that allow academic professionals to swap places with government officers. This gives the scholars exposure to government and allows the government personnel to pursue academic interests in their fields. Condi's Notre Dame professor George Brinkley suggested she apply for the opportunity and helped her obtain one of the twenty fellowships that were given to academics that year. "I was affiliated with the Council on Foreign Relations and was one of several who recommended her for that fellowship," he said.

It was a fascinating time to be in the corridors of military power. Condi's position as special assistant to the director-Joint Chiefs of Staff brought her to the Pentagon during Reagan's massive buildup of the military. In his first term, defense spending increased by 7 percent each year. When Condi arrived in the administration, Reagan was gearing up for an arms limitations summit with Gorbachev. The Iceland summit in October 1986 began on a high note with a tentative agreement by both leaders to ban all nuclear ballistic missiles within ten years. They even made progress on a handful of human rights issues. But Gorbachev demanded that Reagan scale down his space-based missile defense program, commonly known as "Star Wars," and the talks were deadlocked. They met again the following year to sign the Intermediate-Range Nuclear Forces (INF) Treaty, which eliminated all ground-launched missiles (approximately 2,700) with ranges between 300 and 3,500 miles.

Condi studied nuclear planning and reveled in the military culture at the Pentagon. She considered her stint there a "reality check" into the complex workings of the military and gained a deeper respect and admiration for military personnel. She was captivated by the nuclear arms issues that were on the front burner at the time, by the focus of her work, and by her surroundings. She later remarked that the defense and military are "ill understood by the academic community and the civilian community at large," and she was grateful to get an inside look. "I found them welcoming, happy to have the contact with academics," she said. In an interview held one year after her return to Stanford from her fellowship, she said that her Pentagon post stood out "as one of the greatest experiences in my life."

When she moved to California for the Stanford job, Condi had left her parents for the second time. Unlike her Notre Dame year, Stanford was a more long-term move, and she had truly left the nest. Church had always been a family activity, so in that first year on her own, she didn't attend regularly. One Sunday she found herself chatting with a man at the grocery store who said he needed a piano player for his small church. She said she'd be happy to do it and spent the next six months playing for his congregation. "I realized then the long arm of the Lord reaches all the way to Lucky's Super Market," she told a prayer group in Denver in 2000.

Condi became reacquainted with her childhood friend Deborah Carson in Palo Alto, and the two often got together to talk about their dates, have dinner, or go shopping. Shoes are Condi's biggest shopping obsession, and she quickly came to love an exclusive shop on San

Francisco's Union Square that carried all the top-of-the-line brands. Deborah remembered one trip in which Condi loaded up her arms with eight pair of Ferragamos. A few months later, she and Deborah showed up at the store again, and the salespeople literally fell all over themselves. "We walked in the door," said Deborah, "and a salesman from the back of the store started jumping over the benches to get at Condi! We were laughing so hard, and I said, 'Condi, you're going to kill them!' They must have told each other the previous time that when this person comes back, that's a *good* day."

Condi kept to a vigorous workout routine which included strength training with personal trainers in Stanford's athletic department. Her friends fixed her up on blind dates from time to time, but she had better luck finding interesting men on her own. She dated a university coach, a visiting professional from a Fortune 500 company in the East who was taking a Stanford seminar, and others. Football continued to be her favorite theme for romance, however, and one of her more long-term boyfriends at Stanford was San Francisco 49ers wide receiver Gene Washington. A graduate of Stanford, he played with the San Francisco team from 1969 to 1977. Washington, the superstar, appeared in cameo roles as himself in movies and television shows such as a 1972 episode of "Banacek." He and Condi had two major connections: they both loved football and they both came from Birmingham. "They were a real couple for a while," said Deborah Carson, "and even after they stopped dating they remained friends. They still attend social events together from time to time." Gene is now one of the top officials of the NFL as its director of football operations.

Football took up a healthy percentage of Condi's time, and she once remarked that if it weren't for all the coverage on TV she would be much more published. In truth, she hit the ground running as soon she got to Stanford with articles appearing in major journals and compilations. She wrote three books during her Stanford years, beginning with *Uncertain Alliance: The Soviet Union and the Czechoslovak Army*, which, as mentioned in the previous chapter, was an extension of her doctoral dissertation. Next came *The Gorbachev Era*, a collection of articles on Russian and Soviet history, which she co-edited with Alexander Dallin. A leading scholar in Soviet and East European studies, Dallin was a professor in international history at Stanford. Their book was published by the Stanford Alumni Press Service in 1986.

She co-authored her third book, *Germany Unified and Europe Transformed: A Study in Statecraft*, with Philip Zelikow, with whom she served in Bush Senior's administration during the period of German reunification. The book, published by Harvard University Press in 1995, won critical acclaim and is considered the definitive insiders' look into Germany's reunification process. Both authors drew upon their own experiences during that landmark time in history as well as upon thousands of classified government documents. Following is an excerpt from the book's compelling narrative about the day the Berlin Wall crumbled:

> The opening of the Berlin Wall was as electrifying and emotional an event as the world had seen in many years. Although the wall's collapse immediately called into question the postwar order and Germany's future, those were hardly the concerns that dominated the moment. Rather, there were, first and foremost, the scenes of Germany overcoming its division in the most human of terms as families were reunited after years of separation.

There were the expressions of giddy East German citizens encountering the casual prosperity most West Germans took for granted, the bewildering array of material goods that had been nothing more than an image on West German television. And there were the feelings of nationhood that welled up in Germans on both sides of the divide. . . . About 9 million East Germans visited the West during that first week.

This book was one of three awarded the Akira Iriye International History Book Award for 1994–1995, an honor given by the Foundation for Pacific Quest to recognize excellence in scholarship in international history. *Germany Unified* was also named a co-winner of the 1996 Book of Distinction on American Diplomacy by the American Academy of Diplomacy, and awarded a Citation for Excellence for nonfiction foreign affairs by the Overseas Press Club of America.

Condi found her passions in Soviet studies and teaching, and her life at Stanford was rich on many levels. She juggled classes, advising, research, writing, playing the piano, weight training, exercising, dating, and gluing herself to the television for twelve-hour football-watching marathons. Her academic career would take two dramatic turns in the 1990s, however. First, she answered the call to Washington for a post at the White House. Second, she made a quantum leap up the academic ladder.

SEVEN

Bush I

"Condi was brilliant. . . . She has a manner and presence that disarms the
biggest of the big shots. Why? Because
they know she knows what she is talking about."

—*Former President
George H. W. Bush*

IN her fourth year at Stanford, Condi was invited to address the graduates on Senior Class Day. At thirty, the
assistant professor looked as young as the twenty-two-
year-old students, but her words of advice revealed a
good deal of worldly experience. She talked to them
about tackling the problems of the Cold War world without becoming overwhelmed, suggesting that any
contribution to a solution, however small, was valuable.
"All you have to do with the large, huge, and very frightening problems that we face is to make a contribution,"
she said. "If you focus too much on solving that problem,
rather than just making a contribution to its solution, I'm
afraid that you will become paralyzed at the enormity of
the task and unable to do anything at all. People say that
time is running out for us. Well, maybe. . . . All that we
can do is hope that we have the time and to work consistently to make sure that we make good use of that time."

For Condi, making good use of her time included public service. Growing up in Birmingham, she had watched her parents devote their lives to children, outside the classroom as much as in. Their strategy for combating civil injustice was to arm the youth with confidence, education, and opportunity, constantly and patiently preparing them to thrive in an unfair world. This sense of responsibility and commitment was ingrained in Condi, and she hoped to channel her knowledge into making a contribution to the decision-making processes that shaped national security.

Her year-long job at the Pentagon gave her a hint of how policy was transformed into action, and she was eager to have a hand in the process. Even though she was not interested in partisan politics, she had devoted her academic career to the study of conflict resolution and military strategy and she hoped to one day have the opportunity to put her expertise to use in Washington. In the meantime, she became involved in problem-solving in her own community of Stanford, California.

In 1986, Condi joined the Board of Directors of the Stanford Mid-Peninsula Urban Coalition, an organization that helped minorities with health, housing, education, business start-up, and other issues. One of the primary functions of the Coalition was helping run the Peninsula Academies, which provided vocational and academic training to minority students at high risk of dropping out of high school. The academies were founded in 1981 with the goals of improving students' grades, developing positive attitudes about education, learning about work and responsibility, improving attendance, and preparing for work and/or college. Back in Birmingham, John Rice had done exactly the same in his youth fellowship program at Westminster Presbyterian Church. Condi served on the board for three years.

In 1988, she was elected to the leadership of another education-oriented organization, KQED, San Francisco's public broadcasting network. The mission of this television and radio network was (and remains) to promote "lifelong learning, the power of ideas and the importance of community service and civic participation." In her candidate's letter to KQED, Condi described the assets she felt she could bring to the station's Board of Directors:

> Television and radio play a major, perhaps the major, role in informing Americans about the problems and opportunities that we face as a polity. . . . Directors should be thought of as committed representatives of the viewing public; able from different perspectives to identify those areas in which public broadcasting, through information and exploration of ideas, can make a difference. The Bay Area is an international community with a major stake in America's international economic and political future and KQED must provide programming commensurate with that stake. As a professor of international politics and Soviet affairs, I am particularly concerned that this challenge be met. I can bring concern and expertise on these important issues to the Board.

Just one month after being elected to the Board, however, Condi accepted the position with the National Security Council in Washington. She submitted her resignation before having the opportunity to attend any Board meetings.

Condi reached a large audience in the Bay Area community when she was asked to give a speech at the Commonwealth Club, the public affairs forum that hosts hundreds of events each year to explore politics, society, culture, and other contemporary issues. The Club began its public speech series in 1911 with Teddy Roosevelt, and those who have followed include celebrity politicians and national figures such as Martin Luther King, Jr., Ronald Reagan, Erin Brockovich, and Bill Gates. On May 9, 1988, Condi delivered a speech entitled "U.S.-Soviet Relations: The Gorbachev Era" for the Club's Friday Luncheon Program at the Sheraton Palace Hotel in San Francisco. The speech was heard throughout the country via live radio broadcast.

Two other speaking engagements highlighted thirty-three-year-old Professor Rice's calendar in that period. In November 1987, she was invited to be a visiting scholar for a few days at the University of Michigan in Ann Arbor. She lectured and led a seminar for students in the university's Center for Russian and East European Studies, and also gave a public speech about Gorbachev. The following spring, in April 1988, she made a trip to the USSR to give a speech at the U.S. ambassador's residence in Moscow.

Condi's community activities were motivated by a genuine desire to do public service, a characteristic that did not go unnoticed by her colleagues. "I think of people as being one of two types," said John Raisian, Director of the Hoover Institution at Stanford. "One group looks at the politics of an organization and thinks strategically as they climb the career ladder. Others look for opportunities to make a difference, independent of where that puts them on the ladder. Condi is very much the latter." He added that she is the sort of person who thrives on taking on many things at once. In addition to her teaching, writing, and research, "she has always had advisory interests and capacities," he said. "She's always been a very busy and full-plate–type person."

Her plate began to fill up during her first year at Stanford when she started serving on several university committees and other administrative organizations. Her committee involvement included the Public Service Center Steering Committee, which she chaired (1987 and 1991–1999); the Committee on Undergraduate Admissions and Financial Aid, which she also chaired for one year (1982–1985 and 1988–1989); the Executive Committee of the Institute for International Studies (1988–1989 and 1991–1993); and the Graduate Admissions Committee, which she chaired for one year (1991–1992). She was also the Director of Graduate Studies and a member of the Faculty Senate in 1988 and 1989. The Senate handles the internal administration of the university, from setting policy to drafting new rules and statutes regarding degree programs. The Senate's proposals are forwarded to the Board of Trustees for approval.

In 1985, Condi was awarded a National Fellowship from the Hoover Institution on War, Revolution and Peace, which allowed her to take a break from her classroom work and devote an entire year to research. Founded by Herbert Hoover in 1919, the Institution was one of the first think tanks in the United States and has amassed one of the world's largest archives and libraries on twentieth century politics, economics, and social issues. In its mission statement, Hoover defines itself as a research organization committed to "generating ideas that define a free society. . . . [and] contributing to the pursuits of securing and safeguarding peace, improving the human condition and limiting government intrusion into the lives of individuals."

Among the research opportunities for scholars at Hoover is the National Fellows Program, which supports

Condi atop her uncle's car, age five, in 1959.

Courtesy of Condoleezza Rice

A school picture in Birmingham, age seven.

Courtesy of Condoleezza Rice

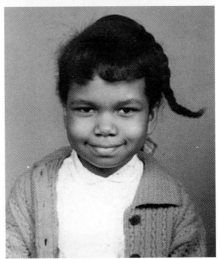

The Rice home in Birmingham, just a few blocks from Westminster Presbyterian Church where Condi's father was the pastor. The home was built by the church to serve as the parish house shortly after Condi was born. Photo by Antonia Felix

Westminster Presbyterian Church on South Sixth Avenue (Titusville) in Birmingham.
Photo by Antonia Felix

Inside Westminster Presbyterian Church. During Sunday services, Condi played the piano (front left) while her mother played the organ (front right) and her father preached from the center pulpit.
Photo by Antonia Felix

A portrait of Condi's grandfather, John Wesley Rice, whom she discussed in her speech at the Republican National Convention in 2000. Reverend Rice left sharecropping to attend college and become a Presbyterian minister, and he founded Westminster Presbyterian Church in Birmingham. His son, Condi's father, took over as minister of the church in 1951.

Courtesy of Westminster Presbyterian Church

Condi skating at age thirteen in Denver, Colorado, 1967. Condi's parents spent several summers taking graduate school courses at the University of Denver, and while they were in class during the day, Condi practiced figure skating. She once referred to her lessons on the rink as "high-priced child care." The Rices moved to Denver permanently in 1969. Courtesy of Condoleezza Rice

*Condi, age seventeen, with her mother, Angelena, and father,
John Wesley Rice III, on the day Condi was named Outstanding
Junior Woman at the University of Denver, 1972.*

Courtesy of Condoleezza Rice

Two undergraduate portraits taken at the University of Denver.

Courtesy of the
University of Denver

Condi's father in a public speaking engagement at the University of Denver. John Rice was a lecturer as well as an administrator during his career at the university, teaching courses in black studies and serving as an associate dean, vice chancellor, and in other posts.

Courtesy of the University of Denver

Josef Korbel, University of Denver professor, father of Madeleine Albright, and Condi's mentor in Russian and Soviet studies. Condi remembers him as one of the most important people in her life.

Courtesy of the University of Denver

At Denver's Graduate School of International Studies with Dean Edward Thomas Rowe (left), and university Chancellor Dan Ritchie (right).

Courtesy of the University of Denver

Guest commencement speaker at the University of Notre Dame, where she received her master's degree in government in 1975.

Courtesy of the University of Notre Dame

*Assistant professor of
political science at
Stanford University,
age twenty-six.*
Courtesy of Stanford
University News Service

Professor Rice teaching at Stanford, May 1993, at thirty-nine.
Courtesy of Stanford University News Service

Provost of Stanford, 1995, enjoying a return to the classroom to discuss the fall of communism.

Courtesy of Stanford University News Service

Working out in the strength training room at Stanford. Exercise is a high priority in Condi's life, and she keeps a rigorous daily workout schedule. "I put her through the same regimes I did with any athlete at Stanford," said Stanford trainer Mark Mateska.

Photo by Frederic Neema/Corbis Sygma

*On George W. Bush's campaign trail in October 2000 with
Laura Bush (left) and Barbara Bush (center) to support the
"W is for Women" push.*

Photo by Rebecca Cook/© Reuters 2000

*The White House senior staff swearing-in ceremony on January 22,
2001. Condi is the first woman and the second black person to
become a national security advisor.*

Photo by Larry Downing/© Reuters 2001

National Security Advisor Rice in the Oval Office with President Bush, April 11, 2001. She is one of the president's closest confidants as well as a long-time Bush family friend who previously served as one of Bush Senior's top Soviet advisors. Photo by Ho/© Reuters 2001

A pat on the cheek for Secretary of State Colin Powell in the Oval Office. As national security advisor, Condi's job is to referee the often very differing views of the secretary of state, secretary of defense, and other members of the National Security Council and bring their opinions to the president.

Photo by Kevin Lamarque/© Reuters 2002

Shaking hands with Russian President Vladimir Putin at the Kremlin on May 24, 2002. Condi speaks fluent Russian, and devoted her academic career to the study of Russia and the former Soviet Union.

Photo by Kevin Lamarque/© Reuters 2002

An impassioned moment with the Moscow press in July 2001, after meetings about arms control talks between the United States and Russia.

Photo by Sergei Karpukhin/
© Reuters 2001

Accepting the NAACP President's Award at the Image Awards ceremony on February 23, 2002.

Photo by Jim Ruymen/© Reuters 2002

Fielding a question at a White House briefing on November 1, 2001. After the attacks of September 11, 2001, Condi came to the forefront as one of the White House's lead spokespeople on the war on terrorism.

Photo by Kevin Lamarque/© Reuters 2001

Condi the collectible— the TOPPS "Enduring Freedom" trading card featuring National Security Advisor Rice.

Courtesy of TOPPS 2001

Accompanying cellist Yo-Yo Ma in a Brahms piece performed at the
National Medal of Arts Ceremony in Washington on April 22, 2002.
Condi, who started lessons at age three, is an accomplished pianist who
trained for a professional career until her junior year in college, when
she changed her major to international relations.

Photo by Larry Downing/ © Reuters 2002

The official White House
portrait of National Security
Advisor Condoleezza Rice.

White House photo by Tina Hager

Condoleezza Rice is sworn in to testify before the 9/11 Commission, April 8, 2004. © Larry Downing/Reuters/Corbis

President George W. Bush nominates Condoleezza Rice as Secretary of State, November 16, 2004. © Kevin Lamarque/Reuters/Corbis

junior scholars who are completing research projects. That year, Condi was among fourteen people selected from throughout the country for the fellowship. It was the first of three Hoover fellowships she would receive during her years at Stanford. As a National Fellow from September 1985 to the August 1986, she completed *The Gorbachev Era* with Alexander Dallin, one of her three published books. Dallin was an emeritus professor of political science and history at Stanford when he died in July 2000, and his colleagues at the university's Center for Russian and East European Studies described him as "a distinguished scholar and a kind and wise human being." Working on a book with Dallin was an honor in itself, as he was one of the country's foremost experts on the Soviet Union and one of the first generation of graduates from Columbia University's Russian Institute.

The Gorbachev Era is a collection of essays by leading figures in the field of Soviet studies, many from Stanford, which had been presented at a summer program at Stanford in 1985. In addition to editing the book, Condi contributed two essays entitled "The Development of Soviet Military Power" and "The Soviet Alliance System." Dallin's entries were "The Legacy of the Past" and "A Soviet Master Plan? The Non-Existent 'Grand Design' in World Affairs."

Dallin's wife, a Soviet specialist at the University of California at Berkeley, also contributed two essays to the book, and she recalled how the project got started. "The Stanford Alumni Association had asked Alex to develop a series of lectures for its summer program while Chernenko was still the Party's General Secretary," she said. "By the time of the lectures Gorbachev was the country's new leader and a major transition was under way in the USSR. The chapters examine the nature of the various crises confronting the Soviet system—economic, political, social, military, foreign policy—and also represent one of the early efforts to speculate about what possible direction Soviet policy might take under Gorbachev." Dr. Lapidus contributed two chapters to the book, "Soviet Society in Transition" and "The Soviet Nationality Question," and she recalled that her husband and Condi worked well together in spite of their differing political views. "Clearly they approached international affairs and the USSR from rather different political perspectives," she said, "but these differences didn't stand in the way of a warm personal relationship, and Condi paid a touching tribute to Alex at a memorial service in our garden when he died."

The most difficult part of Condi's life in 1985 was being far away from her parents. Back in Denver, her mother was battling breast cancer and that year, at age sixty-one, she died. Condi flew home to attend the funeral and to grieve with her father and the many relatives who flew to Denver to be with them. Friends recall that music—which was so central to Angelena's life—encircled them as they thought about her quietly back at the Rice home. "I never shall forget the day we returned from her mother's funeral," said Evelyn Glover, a family friend from Birmingham. "When we came in, Condoleezza prayed with everyone and said, 'Let's play some of mother's favorite hymns.' And she went to the piano."

During the year of her first Hoover fellowship, Condi also began work on a book about the history and development of military staffs in the United States and the Soviet Union. She continued working on the book after she returned to her teaching, but it was slow going with all of the other responsibilities on her schedule. A couple of years later that book was put on hold indefinitely. In February of 1989 she got a call from an old acquaintance, Brent Scowcroft, who convinced her to take a leave of absence from teaching and put her Soviet expertise into practice.

Scowcroft had just been named national security advisor to newly elected President George Bush, and he wanted Condi to be part of his team on the National Security Council. A moderate Republican and long-time career military man and academic, he would have an enormous influence on Condi's development as a foreign policy specialist. They shared a passion for Soviet history, they both had academic careers teaching Soviet history, they both spoke Russian and they both held a power politics outlook on international relations.

Stepping in as national security advisor was a smooth transition for Brent because he had served in that post under President Gerald Ford. In that administration, Henry Kissinger was both national security advisor and secretary of state, and Brent was his deputy, his right-hand man in national security. When Kissinger stepped down as national security advisor to devote all of his time and energy to his role as secretary of state, Brent replaced him as national security advisor.

Brent, who describes himself as someone who likes to stay out of the limelight, never gave press interviews as national security advisor. He kept eighteen-hour days in the White House, and was widely respected as a consensus builder and expert organizer. In the Ford administration, everyone understood that Kissinger made the foreign policy, and Scowcroft managed, organized, and coordinated it between various agencies and the Oval Office. In terms of recognition, Kissinger's term as national security advisor was the most high-profile in history and Scowcroft's the most low-key.

Despite his quiet and unassuming demeanor, Brent is a foreign policy luminary with a long career in the military and the departments of state and defense. Born in Ogden, Utah, he is a Mormon who neither smokes nor drinks. He and his wife, Marian, who have been married since 1951, have one daughter. After graduating from West Point Brent planned on a career as a pilot in the Air Force, but an accident in a defective plane ruined his chances for flying. He went on to get a master's degree in international relations from Columbia University and returned to West Point as a professor of Russian history. He learned to speak Russian fluently and pursued more Slavic language study at Georgetown University in Washington, D.C., after which he used his skills in a foreign service post at the United States embassy in Belgrade, Yugoslavia.

In the early 1960s he was an associate professor of political science at the United States Air Force Academy in Colorado, where he eventually became full professor and chair of the department. His academic career progressed after he finished his Ph.D. in international relations at Columbia University, and was hired to teach military strategy and security to senior military at the National War College. His career continued to span both academia and government, with a post on the long-range planning staff at Air Force headquarters in Washington and several national security jobs at the Pentagon.

By the time he reached the rank of colonel in 1971, he was appointed one of President Nixon's military aides and helped construct the realpolitik diplomatic stance with China that culminated in Nixon's historic trip to China in 1972. After returning from the trip, Brent was promoted to brigadier general. He then went to Moscow as the leader of the advance team to organize Nixon's trip to the Soviet Union in 1972.

During the Nixon years, Brent was at the center of nuclear arms policy, helping craft the SALT II treaty. He was also given the job of organizing the withdrawal of Americans from Saigon during the evacuation in April 1975.

In contrast to the Nixon/Kissinger strategy of détente, President Reagan took a more aggressive approach to the Soviet Union and Brent was not appointed to a defense or state department post. But the administration needed his military expertise, particularly on analyzing the newly developed multiple-warhead weaponry that was part of Reagan's fast-growing arsenal. He led the Commission on Strategic Forces to analyze how this weapon could be used. His national security background was also put to use in that administration. Reagan appointed him head of the Tower Commission to investigate the National Security Council's role in the Iran-Contra affair. In his report, Brent placed the greatest blame on Reagan's chief of staff but also criticized the president for not keeping track of the Council members and their activities. He concluded that the structure of the National Security Council was not the problem, but the people who were serving in it.

After Brent met Condi at a dinner hosted by the Stanford political science department in 1987, he followed up with her and sat in on one of her classes. Her lecture on the MX missile convinced him that she would be a great asset to his national security team in the new Bush administration. He talked to her at length at a foreign policy strategy meeting in Aspen, Colorado, then invited her on board at the National Security Council.

As national security advisor, Brent's job was to gather foreign policy opinions and strategies from cabinet members such as Secretary of Defense Dick Cheney,

Secretary of State James Baker, and chairman of the Joint Chiefs of Staff General Colin Powell. All three were members of the National Security Council (NSC), the advisory group that discussed foreign policy issues and drafted strategies for implementing that policy.

Scowcroft presented various NSC members' ideas to the president and made it a priority to keep conflicts and rivalries in check to ensure a smooth-running operation. "Scowcroft and Baker placed a premium on cooperation," wrote Condoleezza and Philip Zelikow in their book about German unification. "Bitter rivalries between the State Department and the National Security Council staff had been a standard feature of Washington politics since the 1960s," they added, and although disagreements were part of the territory in any administration, a hallmark of Scowcroft's style was to prevent upheaval and concentrate on cooperation. "Disputes arose but were always quickly contained," wrote Condi and Philip.

In January 1989, Condi became director of Soviet and East European affairs at the National Security Council. "I had chosen Condi," said Brent, "because she had extensive knowledge of Soviet history and politics, great objective balance in evaluating what was going on, and a penetrating mind with an affinity for strategy and conceptualization. She [was] . . . conversant and up to date with military affairs." He also felt that she could hold her own when the job got rough. "She was charming and affable, but could be tough as nails when the situation required," he said. Four months later she was upgraded to senior director for Soviet affairs and also named special assistant to the president for national security affairs. Condi's closest associates were Philip Zelikow, manager of European policy and Dennis Ross, another Soviet specialist and director of policy planning. Condi knew

Dennis from California, where he had been a professor at Berkeley. All three were accountable to Robert Blackwill, the senior director for European and Soviet affairs.

Besides the president and cabinet members mentioned above, other members of the president's National Security Council included Brent's deputy, Robert Gates, and Robert Hutchings, head of the Council's Southeastern Europe and Germany departments. Others with whom Condi worked closely included Robert Zoellick in the state department and Paul Wolfowitz in the department of defense.

Condi held three major job responsibilities as part of the National Security Council staff. First, she helped coordinate the policy-making process by gathering information from those at the assistant secretary or undersecretary level. Second, she served as an aid to Brent Scowcroft, helping him decide which foreign officials to see and preparing for those visits. "We went to the meetings," she said, "and I would write a paper for him suggesting issues he might want to raise. If an issue couldn't be settled at my level and it had to go to the Scowcroft, Baker, Cheney, Powell level, then it was my responsibility to make sure Brent was prepared." Her third area of responsibility was acting as the president's "personal foreign policy staff." In this function, she wrote briefing papers about issues to be raised at foreign policy meetings with other heads of state.

The first job she faced as one of the president's top political minds was cracking the case of the 500-pound cake.

On the administration's first day at work in January, the White House received a huge box with a Soviet postmark but no other identifying information. The Secret Service's bomb squad carefully transported it to a secure

area and, decked out in full bomb-proof regalia, opened
it. Inside was a slightly crushed but magnificently deco-
rated, gigantic cake. Condi was enlisted to track down
who sent it. With only a postmark to go on, she launched
a personal investigation and discovered that a bakers' collective from a small Soviet town had made the cake for
President Bush to congratulate him on his inauguration.

The president found this very touching, and he asked
that a photo be taken of him and his family by the cake
and sent to the bakers' group. He then wanted the cake
sent to a charity that could distribute and enjoy it. The
photo session took several days to organize and by the
time the cake was to be sent away the rats in the Secret
Service warehouse had polished most of it off.

In March, Condi was given her first critical assignment—one that put her at the center of the
policy-making process. The president had just received a
lengthy National Security Review outlining the United
States' policy history with the Soviet Union. He had requested this report in an effort to begin formulating his
own approach to Gorbachev. Brent Scowcroft thought the
report was sorely lacking in both detail and ideas, and he
instructed Condi to lead a National Security Council
team in writing up a "think piece" that focused on Gorbachev—the policies he had already formed and the
ideas he had for the future.

Up until then, Condi had written about Gorbachev,
publishing articles about him in journals and book compilations and adding substance to the study of the Soviet
Union. With this assignment, she had an opportunity to
put her knowledge of Gorbachev and the Soviet system
to work as a shaper of U.S. policy for the first time. The
document that came out of her group formed the basis of
the Bush administration's policy with the Soviet Union.

"Condi's memo laid out the premises that I believed should guide the development of an overall strategy for U.S.-Soviet relations," wrote Scowcroft, "and it evolved into a four-part approach for coping with Gorbachev."

He described these four steps as strengthening America's foreign policy image with a clear, confident policy agenda; ensuring that America's allies understand the U.S. commitment to them and to arms control; taking action—including economic aid—in Eastern Europe to promote the independence launched by Gorbachev's reforms; and working "aggressively to promote regional stability" in the world through U.S.-Soviet cooperation.

Condi's input to this blueprint for American foreign policy included a supporting memo that discussed the turmoil within the Soviet Union. She pointed out that as Moscow's old political structures crumbled, it was forced to look for guidance in the outside world. This opened up the possibility of an ambitious and dramatic new approach to the Soviet Union, one that involved "setting our sights literally on transforming the behavior of the Soviet Union at home and abroad," according to Brent Scowcroft.

Condi's next assignment, like the cake incident, involved more sleuthing. The new administration was being criticized for not defining its foreign policy position or announcing goals or strategies that would signal where the government's policy was headed. The decision was made to schedule the president's policy speeches during the coming spring commencement season. But an event in Eastern Europe prompted the administration to bump up that schedule. In early April, Solidarity was made legal in Poland, and the nation broke away from forty-five years of Communist rule. With Poland's new rush toward democracy, the administration had a cause around which to form its Eastern European policy. They scheduled the president's Poland/Eastern European policy speech to take place in Hamtramck, Michigan, on April 17. Brent described Hamtramck as a "natural" choice because "it had a high concentration of families with ties to Eastern Europe, particularly Poland. . . . It was the right place to talk about change inside the Soviet Union and our aspirations for Poland's freedom."

With the speech only two weeks away, Bush's aides had to work fast. In this case, he immediately put Condi to work searching for money within government programs that could be pulled to use as economic aid to Poland. This was a difficult task in an environment of tight budgets and a huge deficit. The president also had to decide about whether or not to make economic aid a big part of his policy. The National Security Council meeting devoted to that topic brought up two views: sending money to Poland was risky because the country may not be able to make good use of it yet. One member argued that the United States had sent economic aid to Poland in the 1970s to support some political changes, but it had made no difference because the infrastructure wasn't ready for it yet. The same thing could happen this time. On the other side, President Bush and Secretary of State James Baker argued that Poland was making great economic strides this time and it was a completely different situation. The president had to make his own decision, and he ultimately decided to try to find as much financial aid as possible to include in his policy toward Poland.

The question of who would write the speech sparked a controversy between the national security staff and the president's speechwriters. Brent felt that the National Security Council was the logical choice because they were closest to the substance of the issue. The speech-writers argued that they were perfectly capable of nailing down the content as well, and they resented the fact that anyone would call that into question. Brent compromised and assigned the first draft to Condoleezza and chief speechwriter Mark Davis. President Bush then put his own mark on the speech, adding his own nuance and tone until he felt it perfectly reflected his view as well as his voice.

In July 1989, Condi joined President Bush, Brent Scowcroft, and their official delegation to Poland and Hungary, where the president addressed the crowds with promises of economic support for Eastern European democracy movements. In Warsaw and Gdansk, Poland, they met with Solidarity leaders Lech Walesa and General Wojciech Jaruzelski, and Bush made an address at the National Assembly. In Budapest, they met with Communist leaders including Prime Minister Miklòs Nèmeth, who presented the president with a memento that hinted at the monumental changes to come. "Nèmeth presented President Bush with a plaque containing a piece of the barbed wire from the border fence between Hungary and Austria—a literal piece of the Iron Curtain," wrote Scowcroft. Hungary had opened its border with Austria, and although this created a problem with East Germans trying to flee to the West via Hungary, it portrayed Hungary as a "beacon of light" in Eastern Europe.

In the fall of 1989, Condi faced a situation in which she proved Brent correct about her ability to handle herself when the going got tough. She was to greet Boris Yeltsin—the garrulous, heavy-drinking Soviet official—at the White House entrance and direct him to a meeting. Yeltsin, then a member of the Soviet parliament, was

Gorbachev's most vocal critic, frequently lashing out about how slowly his economic reforms were moving. During his U.S. tour that September he became a press magnet for his unpredictable, red-faced outbursts and colorful personality.

President Bush and Scowcroft had to decide whether or not Yeltsin would get a White House visit. Their carefully planned structure for meeting foreign political guests had three levels. The most prestigious visit was a scheduled meeting with the president. One step down was a meeting with Brent, with a "drop by" visit from the president that could last as long as the president desired. The third type was a meeting with Brent alone. Entrance to the White House was another factor—if Brent wanted the press to have access to the guest, the official would be brought in through the West Lobby. Those whom he wished to keep away from the press were brought through the West Basement doors.

President Bush wanted to meet Yeltsin and he asked Brent to schedule a drop-by meeting in Brent's office. On September 12, Yeltsin was instructed to arrive at the basement entrance, where Condi was waiting for him. True to form, Yeltsin refused to budge from his car unless Condi promised to take him to the Oval Office. "This isn't the door you go in to see the president," he yelled at Condi, who reminded him that his meeting was with the national security advisor, not President Bush. "I've never heard of General Scowcroft," he barked at her. "He's not important enough to meet with me." Fuming, with arms crossed defiantly over his chest, he sat in the car and glared at Condi, who glared back without saying a word. The stare-down lasted five minutes. Then Condi began to turn away and said, in an impassive tone, that he might as well return to his hotel as she would inform the general that he was not coming. Yeltsin relented, agreed to see Scowcroft, and stomped out of the car. Condi grabbed him by the elbow and brusquely led him up the stairs.

Those who witnessed this exchange were amazed at Condi's complete lack of intimidation. They knew she was confident and self-assured, but until that day they had not seen the depth of her fortitude.

Yeltsin was delighted when the president dropped by the meeting for a few minutes. When he left and his car began leaving the White House grounds, he spotted a cluster of reporters taping their stand-up reports. He jumped from the car, attracted the crowd, and proceeded to speak to several journalists. Although it was not the quiet exit Brent had orchestrated, "no harm was done," and Yeltsin soon returned to Moscow.

Two months later, the fall of the Berlin Wall revealed the groundbreaking changes taking place in Eastern Europe. A few weeks after that jubilant event, Condi accompanied President Bush and his national security delegation to the Malta Summit, where they presented their position to Gorbachev. As described in Chapter Six, this was Condi's first meeting with Gorbachev and other top-ranking Soviet officials. The Soviet president's attitude upon meeting her was just one of many surprised reactions she would receive. "I think the Russians would sometimes feel, 'What's a girl like you doing here amidst bombs and bullets?'" she said. Other than that, she was not certain exactly how the white male Soviet power structure actually felt about her. "It was initially hard for the Russians to accept me," she said. "I never figured out if it was because I was female, or black, or young. But by and large, they've managed to deal with it." Her schedule didn't give her time to worry about it and her attitude has never been one of intimidation. "I never have felt lonely or stressed in these environments," she said. "You just get caught up in the fourteen-to-fifteen-hour days."

From time to time, Condi ran into problems as a black/female minority within the foreign policy ranks. When Gorbachev made his first visit across the United States in June 1990, for example, Condi was chosen to lead the American delegation that escorted him to various cities. At the airport in San Francisco, a secret service agent—who for some odd reason had no idea who Condi was—tried to prevent her from stepping out onto the tarmac with the rest of the group. "He was right in my face in a confrontational way," she recalled. "And that provokes a confrontational attitude from me." The incident was reported in the press and proved highly embarrassing for the secret service. The image of a white agent brusquely keeping the only black person in the group away from the leader of the Soviet Union did not paint a good portrait of American race relations. Condi remarked that she is no "shrinking violet" in situations like this.

Another episode that illustrates the sexism any woman is likely to face in the field of international relations came years later when Condi was working in the second Bush administration and on an official visit to Israel. Ariel Sharon, then a candidate for prime minister, told journalists, "I have to confess, it was hard for me to concentrate in the conversation with Condoleezza Rice because she has very nice legs." Another journalist explained that such remarks are generally overlooked in Israel because of the prevalence of the macho military attitude. "You know these people who serve too many years in the army," she said, "it's the way they see things."

A priority of the Malta Summit of December 1989 was discussion of the reunification of Germany, a prospect that the Soviets feared "would rip the heart out of the Soviet security system." Gorbachev, whose proposals for more economic freedom in the Soviet satellite countries led to bold demonstrations and border openings, had not anticipated the swift rush toward independence that these nations would take. Condi was among the small group that developed the policy that Bush brought to Malta as well as to other European summits that year. The policy-making group consisted of Condi, Philip Zelikow (with whom she would write a book about German reunification), Robert Blackwill, Peter Zoellick, and Dennis Ross. They were Scowcroft's top aides regarding German reunification.

Condi's group crafted an American policy toward Germany and the "new Europe" that involved Germany's self-determination and commitment to NATO. It also stressed that all transformation be "peaceful, gradual, and part of a step-by-step process." Another goal was to have reunification take place quickly, before the Soviets and others could hamper the process with formal counterproposals. Condi played a major role in shaping this part of the policy. In an early 1990 memo to Scowcroft she stated that the five-year plan announced by German Chancellor Helmut Kohl was too slow, allowing too much time for the USSR to intervene and play a strong hand. She persuaded Scowcroft and his staff that time was of the essence. "It was a risky move," said Philip Zelikow. "But it turned out to be accurate."

The sweeping transformation of Germany did occur quickly. In March 1990, the first free East German election was held, and pro-unification parties won the majority. In September, European leaders met in Moscow to sign the Treaty on the Final Settlement with Respect to Germany, which recognized East Germany's union with West Germany. "Today's agreement settles the external aspects of the establishment of German unity and makes the achievement of a unified, free, and democratic Germany just a short step away," said White House Press Secretary Marlin Fitzwater. A photo included in Condi's book *Germany Unified and Europe Transformed* shows her standing in the crowd behind the signer's table at this historic event. Of the approximately thirty-five people shown, she appears to be one of only two women in the room. On October 3, 1990, the two Germanys signed the official unification treaty.

With the loss of East Germany, the Soviet Union was firmly set on a course of destruction that the world had not anticipated. Condi was at the center of American policy during this process until she left her post in March 1991. In January of that year, Lithuania and Latvia's struggle for independence erupted in violence—one of the few bloody episodes in the entire transformation. More Baltic states broke away in a domino effect, and in June 1991, Russia was allowed to vote for its own president for the first time, and Yeltsin became the Russian leader while Gorbachev remained the head of the Soviet Union. In December, leaders of Ukraine, Russia, and Belarus secretly met to form the Commonwealth of Independent States (CIS), and the Soviet Union was permanently disbanded. On Christmas Day, Gorbachev announced that he was stepping down. At the Kremlin, the red and yellow-sickle Soviet flag was replaced by the white, blue, and red flag of the new Russian Federation.

During Condi's two-year term with the National Security Council, she had not only become close friends of President George Bush and his wife Barbara, but had made an indelible impression upon him and the rest of his staff. Bush was enormously impressed in her performance and it came as no surprise that he wanted George W. to meet her when he won his first political campaign and became governor of Texas. Bush Senior appreciated Condi's diplomatic style as much as her intellectual resources, as expressed in a note he wrote to a journalist in 2000:

> Condi was brilliant, but she never tried to flaunt it while in meetings with foreign leaders. . . . Her temperament was such that she had an amazing way of getting along with people, of making a strong point without being disagreeable to those who differed. . . . She has a manner and presence that disarms the biggest of the big shots. Why? Because they know she knows what she is talking about.

Others who have worked with Condi agree that her dynamic personality, combined with her intellect, make up a formidable package that contributes to her success. George Brinkley, her Notre Dame professor, summed it up when he said, "She's not only a person with extraordinary ambition and intellectual abilities, she has quite a remarkable personality that has played a role in her advancement."

For Condi, those two years in the Bush administration were a life experience that she knew she could never repeat. "It was an exciting time," she said. "You could go to bed one night and wake up with some country having changed its social system overnight, with a new democracy to deal with." She felt gratified to be part of an administration that helped make Germany's transition a smooth and positive one for the United States and its allies. "Was it inevitable that Germany unified on completely Western terms, within NATO," she said, "that Soviet troops went home, with dignity and without incident; that American troops stayed; that all of Eastern Europe was liberated and joined the Western bloc? No, it was not inevitable—and that leaves a lot of room for statecraft."

She was also grateful for the people with whom she practiced that statecraft. "My colleagues were the smartest people I had ever met, and we all hit the ground together with resolution of the issues that I had been taught were the most important in the international policy field on the table," she said in 1995. "I ask myself if I would ever have that constellation of forces, events and personalities again . . . [including] a president I adored . . . George Bush, for whom the great issues at the end of the Cold War were priority number one."

Overall, working with her immediate boss stood out as the personal highlight of the job. "The most personally satisfying was working with Brent Scowcroft," she said.

Condi knew she had been spoiled by working in Washington during one of the most eventful periods in political history—and having such a vital role in the process—and she didn't expect to return to the White House any time soon. In a speech given several years later, President Bush reiterated his admiration for his staff during that turbulent and exciting time, a staff that included his good friend Condoleezza Rice:

> Excellence describes the people that I had at my side, and it was a joy, a blessing to work with each of them.
>
> Make no mistake, they were good and decent people, but they were tough, too, with strong views, and they were mature men and women who understood that power had a purpose. And moreover, seeing them work together it was clear that they respected one another.

As we debated one issue or another, they would often argue views very forcefully. But once the decision, once the President made the decision, we closed up the ranks. That's the way it ought to be.

EIGHT

Room at the Top

"I tell my students, 'If you find yourself
in the company of people who agree with
you, you're in the wrong company.'"
—*Condoleezza Rice, 1993*

BY the spring of 1991, when German unification was
complete, Condi had proven herself to Scowcroft
and he asked her to continue in her post. The Gulf War
ended on March 1, closing another chapter in the Bush
administration, and Condi decided it was time to leave
Washington and return to academic life. She didn't want
to reach burnout in what she called an "all-consuming"
job, and according to Scowcroft, she was listening to her
biological clock. At thirty-six, she wanted to settle down
and have a family. Condi did not confirm this explana-
tion, but said rather that her teaching career took
precedence over everything. "It wasn't an easy decision,"
she said. "I felt that it's hard to keep an academic career
intact if you don't come back in about two years." She
recognized the importance of her senior-level job with
the National Security Council, but she felt she needed to
put academics and public service in balance. "We're fortunate in the U.S. that we can go in and out," she said.

"But I think of myself as an academic first. That means that you want to keep some coherence and integrity in your career." The fact that she had not been available to her upper-level students for two years ground away at her conscience. "I tried to keep up with my graduate students but it was hard," she said. "You can't be away from that for too long."

The prospect of staying on at the NSC for another two years conjured up images of seemingly endless fourteen-hour days and no time for the small, normal things that make up a balanced lifestyle. "I wanted a life," she said. She felt she had been extremely fortunate in being in the NSC during one of the most amazing, transforming periods in European political history, and it was time to return to the pleasures and routines of teaching, doing research, playing the piano, and going to the grocery store. She had worked hard to achieve her academic status and didn't think it was necessary to risk it all for one job, no matter how prestigious. "When the time came and I was asked to stay," she said, "I thought if I stayed, I should stay to the end of the term and I didn't think I was prepared to do that. I was getting tired—it is a very demanding job. The real stress of White House jobs is that it's a really small staff—forty people in the whole NSC staff. It's a burn-out job."

Condi moved out of Watergate and returned to the West Coast, eager to leap into academia and share her experiences with her students. Her recent experience gave her much more to offer, especially regarding the "story behind the story" element of world events. In her classes she had always stressed the importance of the personal element in international relations—the attitudes and emotions and relationships that underlie the bigger story—and now she could bring some of that information to her classes through first-hand experience. "I've always tried to teach some of the decision-making aspects of politics," she said upon her return to Stanford. "I think I have a better sense for that now. It's important to understand what people were really thinking . . . I think I can bring some perspective on what it was like to go through those events from that vantage point."

When she left Washington in March 1991, Condi had no idea that the events in the Soviet Union would proceed so quickly. In her first weeks back at Stanford she said, "The events in the Soviet Union will unfold over a period of time. It was not likely that by being in Washington I would have been able to see the Soviet Union's problems through this period." Like everyone else, she was surprised when the entire system fell apart before the end of the year. In a public speech in December, she expressed the magnitude of change that had swept the world since she was a political science neophyte at the University of Denver. "All the assumptions that I started out with as a student of international studies have simply been blown away," she said. "The old assumption—that Europe was permanently divided, that the East-West conflict was a permanent fixture of the international system, that Soviet forces would remain deep in Eastern Europe . . . no longer hold. A great power—the USSR— has collapsed."

Once she got resettled, Condi delved back into publishing and wrote an article that appeared in *Time* magazine in September 1991. Four weeks earlier a group of Communist hard-liners had staged a coup in Moscow, trying to oust Gorbachev who was about to sign an agreement giving the republics more freedom. But enormous public opposition coupled with the reluctance of the armed forces to support the coup caused the hard-liners to back down. Condi's article, "A New Army for a New State," discussed the military's role in the coup and Gorbachev's arsenal as the leader of a new, non-Communist nation. "The Soviet Army still has as chance to find a place in a stable and democratic successor the communist Soviet Union," she wrote. "If that is to happen, personnel changes are not enough. A stable democracy needs sturdy institutions, not just charismatic personalities."

She reached another national audience three months later with her second appearance at the Commonwealth Club, where she gave a speech entitled "End of the Cold War: Challenge for U.S. Policy." Like her previous speech for the Club, this one was broadcast live over the radio and was part of the Friday Luncheon Program. In this speech, given at the St. Francis Hotel in San Francisco on December 13, 1991, Condi discussed the formidable challenges facing the former Soviet Union, from its struggle to initiate a market economy to its political instability. She shared insider perceptions gleaned from her two years in the Bush administration, including a vivid portrayal of Gorbachev's reputation among his people. One question from the floor after her speech asked her to explain the difference between the world's view of Gorbachev as the great redeemer who brought down Communism and that of the Soviet people, who blamed him for making things worse. She responded:

> People in the Soviet Union associate Gorbachev with the domestic disintegration of the country. If they're now standing in lines three or four times longer than they used to, then it's because of Gorbachev. What is missing in that analysis is that it was the years of stagnation under Brezhnev that led to these problems. Gorbachev didn't understand the economic problems very well when he came to

power. He sort of messed around at the edges, trying to squeeze productivity, and then one day just
realized that the whole system was rotten. He tried
to break it up, but didn't have the courage to leap
into a market system and therefore probably wors-
ened the transition. His lack of popularity comes
from the association of *perestroika* with the disinte-
gration of the Soviet economy. Yet if you probe,
Russians will say that they understand that he was
the father of something important. They blame him
simply in the manner of: what's he done for us
lately?

In her first eight years at Stanford, Condi wrote fifteen articles that appeared either in journals or in foreign
policy/Soviet history book compilations. In the six years
following her return from Washington, she published five
more articles and co-wrote her third book, *Germany Unified and Europe Transformed: A Study in Statecraft.*

She also resumed public service work, including a
stint on the governor's advisory panel of redistricting California in 1991. She was well acquainted with newly
elected Republican Governor Pete Wilson who, after his
election in 1990, had put Condi on his short list of ap-
pointees for the U.S. Senate seat that he would be
vacating that year. Deep into her Washington job at the
time, Condi told him she wasn't interested and later told
the press that she didn't think she would have received
the appointment anyway. Wilson appointed California
State Senator John Seymour to the Senate seat. As part of
Wilson's advisory panel in 1991, Condi contributed ideas
for redrawing the state's assembly, state senate, and Congressional district boundaries.

Another government service appointment took Condi
away on short trips over a period of several weeks but

kept her involved in military policy. In 1997, she was appointed to the Federal Advisory Committee on Gender Integrated Training in the Military, a committee set up by Secretary of Defense William S. Cohen. The 11-member civilian group, which included one retired admiral and three retired generals, met with hundreds of military personnel in an effort to "assess the current training programs of the Army, Navy, Air Force and Marine Corps and to determine how best to train our gender-integrated, all-volunteer force to ensure that they are disciplined, effective and ready." The committee delivered a long list of recommendations included improving the training of drill sergeants, revamping recruiting policies, toughening basic training, expanding sexual harassment instruction, providing separate barracks for men and women, and hiring more women trainers.

Utilizing her background in military systems was gratifying, but Condi's pet project was the Center for a New Generation, an after-school enrichment program she cofounded for children of the impoverished Ravenswood School District in East Palo Alto. The idea came out of a dinner table conversation Condi had with her father, who had moved to California after Angelena's death and his retirement from the University of Denver in 1982, and his new wife, Clara Bailey Rice. "I was a principal at Menlo Oaks Middle School," said Clara, "and Condi had come to speak for my middle school's 'graduation' ceremony. They were about to enter high school and they organized a little program. I asked Condi to speak for their graduation services, and she was impressed with how they carried the whole service by themselves and did such a beautiful job with so few resources. She asked me what sort of support the district had for these kids to be successful."

John was doing some consulting at Stanford and volunteering in Clara's school district. Like Condi, he was concerned about the students at Menlo Oaks school. He was working at improving the quality of East Palo Alto education as well as its environment. "He really didn't like the way the grounds looked or the areas where the kids played," said Clara, "so he got people to go over and redo the lawns and playing fields." Clara, seventeen years his junior, met John through his volunteer work in the schools and they soon learned they had many common friends back in Birmingham. Before becoming a principal, Clara had been a middle school science and math teacher. They were married in July 1989.

Although John was retired, he did not slow down very much in California. His public service work included an appointment to the Board of Governors of California Community Colleges, made by Governor Pete Wilson. His long academic career had been honored in 1995 when he received the National Alliance of Black School Educators' Living Legend Award. That year he also received an honorary doctorate from Daniel Hale University in Chicago, which prompted some friends and family to begin calling him Dr. Rice.

Condi learned that the Ravenswood School District had a well-funded program for below-average readers, but nothing beyond that to help students qualify for college. No students from the school district had ever gone to Stanford, which was only five minutes away. That seemed to clinch it. "The three of us—John, Condi and I—came up with the idea for an after-school center at the dinner table one night," said Clara.

The Center for a New Generation, held at Clara's school, was open to children in the third through eighth grades with good potential who had at least a C+ average and were recommended by their teachers. At the Center, they received first-time exposure to foreign languages, computer training, and tutoring in math and science— given by Stanford students whom John Rice enlisted for the job. "He was retired," said Clara, "and he put all kinds of energy into the Center, so it would have the resources it needed." John organized a band as part of the musical arts program and found funding for instruments and uniforms. He also arranged a bus schedule with the school district for transportation to and from the Center and found vendors to donate food and snacks.

Condi officially cofounded the Center with Susan Ford, a well-known philanthropist active in the business and medical community and director of the Sand Hill Foundation. The program enrolled from 100 to 120 students during the school year and about 150 during the summer. They established a formal relationship with Stanford, which contributed student volunteers as well as education professionals who helped form the curriculum. John organized a group of school counselors to follow up with the students once they entered high school and make sure they had the support and encouragement they needed to graduate.

John had taught Condi how effective this type of program could be through his own youth fellowship back in Birmingham. The Center for a New Generation was enormously successful, and within a few years, two of its graduates were accepted at Stanford, and more went to other colleges and universities. In 1996, when Condi's duties at Stanford prevented her from spending as much time at the Center as she felt it deserved, she met with the Boys & Girls Club of the Peninsula to talk about a merger. The administration agreed to adopt the Center and took control of its operation. To keep a hand in the program, Condi became a vice president of the Boys & Girls Club. In 1998, Condi and Susan Ford were honored by the organization for their "extraordinary support of children and youth" at a Leading Citizens Dinner. Condi's father gave the invocation that evening, and the band from the Center for a New Generation played for the guests.

The kids at the Center became Condi's extended family and her work there was extremely important to her. She once told her father, "Those are sort of my kids, all 125 of them." Giving children in disadvantaged circumstances a few breaks became Condi's cause. "Ever since I've been out of school," she said, "most of my efforts outside work have dealt with trying to give kids an opportunity." Her aunt Connie Ray said that Condi's devotion stems from her philosophy of life. "Condoleezza has always felt that to be a complete person you had to be devoted to a cause," she said.

Condi's work with children in East Palo Alto has led some to call her a role model for minority children, and although she doesn't mind that recognition, she hopes that kids will disregard race and gender and simply look at the work their models do. "I have never accepted this notion that you have to see somebody who looks like you doing it to make it possible," she said. At the 2000 Republican National Convention, the "Profiles in Compassion" video series included a film about the Center for a New Generation.

Another California group that identified Condi as a role model was that state's Women Legislator's Caucus. In 1992, they named Condi "Woman of the Year," recognizing her work in the Bush administration and the national status she had achieved. "Dr. Rice has participated in the making of history," said State Senator Becky

Morgan, who named her that year's recipient of the award. "Condoleezza exemplifies everything that a woman can be: intelligent, articulate, capable and highly respected. She is an excellent role model for younger women."

Condi's clout as a Washington veteran gave her more visibility in the media, new stature in the Republican Party, and entrée into some of the nation's top foreign policy organizations. In 1991, for example, her television appearances as a consultant on Soviet affairs for ABC News offered a hint of the media star she would become. In 1992, she gave an address at the Republican National Convention in Houston, where President George Bush was nominated for re-election, and shared the stage with Pat Buchanan and leaders who introduced the new Party agenda as the "Contract for America."

Her foreign policy affiliations expanded to membership in the Lincoln Club of North California, the American Political Science Association, and the Aspen Institute, where she participated in the Aspen Strategy Group from 1991 to 1995. Aspen conducts nonpartisan policy programs for public- and private-sector leaders, and the Aspen Strategy Group focuses specifically on "the role of the U.S. in the post-cold war world, the U.S.-Russian relationship, and the Strategic Defense Initiative." Her former boss at the White House, Brent Scowcroft, has been co-chairman of the Aspen Strategy Group since 1984.

At Stanford, she jumped back into administrative duties by serving on search committees for the Stanford football coach, dean of admissions, and president of the university, all in 1991. The following year, she joined the Provost's Committee on the Status of Women in the University and the University Policy and Planning Board.

A major development in Condi's life—the result of her White House service and new Republican contacts— was her launch onto several corporate boards. Directors are chosen on the basis of their expertise and also because they are identified as professionals who will have a positive reflection on the company and will act harmoniously with the rest of the board.

Those who leave posts in government are attracted to corporate boards as a way of staying connected to the national scene and utilizing their Washington connections. Like the majority of women on corporate boards, Condi came to Chevron, TransAmerica, Hewlett Packard, and other companies with a background very different from that of the white males who served as directors. Albert A. Cannella, Jr., Associate Professor of Management at Texas A&M University's College of Business, has analyzed the difference between the routes women and minorities take to become members of corporate boards and the routes taken by white men. The white-male path has traditionally been a series of advancements from within the company, while the glass ceiling prevents the same for women executives. "White men prove themselves in the industry and get promoted," he explained, "but women and minorities don't tend to get promoted. Rather, the prominent routes for them are law, government service, and academics—having a Ph.D." With a background in both the White House and academia, Condi had the perfect resume for obtaining directorships and maintaining the high-profile contacts she made in Washington. "She's very well connected," said Dr. Cannella. "She knows a lot of people in government, and that's something a corporation is always looking for. In particular, those with a background in government service are in demand on boards of industries where there is a lot of government regulation and oversight."

In his published study about the differing routes men and women take to become corporate directors, Dr. Cannella explained that corporations seek out board members from outside the company who are "business experts, support specialists, and community influentials." Condi fits into the third category, people who provide the board with "non-business perspectives on issues, problems, and ideas, as well as expertise about and influence with powerful groups in the community." These members are often politicians, academics, clergy, or other social leaders. While the first category, business experts, is made up primarily of white males who have worked their way up the business ladder, the other two categories include more women and minorities who came via the academic or political-experience route. Of those, a large number hold doctoral degrees—56 percent of the black women in the study held Ph.D.s as opposed to only 19 percent of white male directors. (Chevron's current CEO, David J. O'Reilly, holds a bachelor's degree in chemical engineering, for example.)

Another pattern observed in Cannella's study is the fact that women and racial minorities tend to sit on several boards at once, unlike the white male majority who serve on fewer at one time. This is true of both Condoleezza and her fellow Chevron board member, Carla Hills. Like Condi, Carla came to the board with a background in government service, having served in the senior Bush administration as U.S. trade representative (while Condi was serving on the National Security Council). During the Ford administration, she was secretary of housing and urban development, and prior to that, she was an assistant district attorney in Los Angeles.

Condi joined the Board of Directors of Chevron Corporation, a multinational with oil operations in twenty-five countries, immediately upon returning to Stanford in 1991. Her expertise on the states that made up the former Soviet Union made her a valuable asset for Chevron's oil interests in Kazakhstan. She worked extensively on those deals, including their plan to help build a pipeline from the Tengiz oil field across southern Russia to a Russian port on the Black Sea.

Like her Hoover Institution colleague, George Shultz, who served as a director of Chevron before she arrived at the company, Condi supplemented her Stanford income with fees from Chevron that included a $35,000-per-year retainer and $1,500 for each board and committee meeting attended. By her tenth year with the company, she held over 3,000 shares of Chevron stock worth $241,000. Also like Shultz, she had a supertanker named after her—the 136,000-deadweight-ton SS *Condoleezza Rice*.

Condi's work on Chevron's oil projects in Kazakhstan formed part of one of the United State's largest overseas energy investments. Construction on the 935-mile Kazakhstan pipeline, a group effort by the Caspian Pipeline Consortium (CPC), began in 1999 and the first barrels of oil from the Tengiz oil field flowed into a waiting tanker at the Russian port of Novorossiysk in November 2001. According to a White House press release that month, the CPC "is the largest, single United States investment in Russia," and American oil companies, primarily Chevron and Exxon, paid for approximately half of the pipeline's $2.6 billion price tag.

Condi's decade-long affiliation with Chevron would raise flags when she joined the George W. Bush administration. Not only did the oil company's holdings in the Middle East, Southeast Asia, and Africa pose conflict-of-interest issues, Chevron was the subject of a lawsuit involving human rights abuses in Nigeria. The corporation was charged with aiding Nigeria's military police in crushing public demonstrations against the exploitation of the nation's delta region, where most of the oil reserves are found.

Condi served on and chaired Chevron's public policy committee, which was responsible for identifying social, political, and environmental issues that concerned the corporation at home and abroad. When Condi's affiliation with Chevron came up during the presidential campaign of 2000, one television news show asked her about George W.'s relationship with "big oil" and how that would affect his administration. "American oil companies are important to our security," she answered, "in that they give us the ability to explore abroad. They give us the ability to explore here in the United States and to protect the energy security of the United States."

The issue of Chevron quelling protests by environmental activists in Africa did not come up in the broadcast, but Condi praised Chevron's environmental policies in the United States. "Oil companies have come a long way in their environmental policies," she said, "actually going so far as to fund environmental projects around the country. They are good citizens. We can't live without oil. And we have to have American oil companies doing it. I'm proud of my association with Chevron . . . and I think we should be very proud of the job that American oil companies are doing in exploration abroad, in exploration at home, and in making certain that we have a safe energy supply."

Condi resigned from the Chevron board on January

15, 2001, after being named Bush's national security advisor. Three months later, in the midst of California's energy crisis, Chevron renamed the tanker that bore her name. As reported in the *San Francisco Chronicle*, the ship was "one of the most visible reminders of the Bush administration's ties to big oil" and "the White House had faced questions over the appropriateness of the tanker's name." Chevron did not comment on whether or not the White House requested the name change, but a company spokesman, Fred Gorell, said, "We made the change to eliminate the unnecessary attention caused by the vessel's original name." The ship is now called *Altair Voyager*.

Condi's background at Chevron put her in the company of many government officials—women as well as men—criticized for having alliances with corporations that may create conflicts of interest or harbor controversial business practices. When Hillary Clinton was running for Senate, for example, stories emerged about her history with Wal-Mart, Arkansas's largest corporation. As first lady of Arkansas, she served on the company's board of directors, and the press pointed out that Wal-Mart's non-union employment policy contrasted with Hillary's support of the Teamsters and other unions during her campaign and that their "Buy American" slogan smacked of irony, as Wal-Mart imports more foreign goods than any other company in the United States.

Chevron was the first of several corporate boards Condi joined in the 1990s. In 1991, she became a director at TransAmerica, the insurance giant based in San Francisco housed in the famous pyramid-shaped skyscraper that bears its name. (In May 2002, as national security advisor, Condi would list the TransAmerica Building as a possible terrorist target along with the Statue of Liberty and the Empire State Building.) Concurrent with her work at Chevron, she served on TransAmerica's board of directors for ten years. TransAmerica was the sixth largest life insurance company in the United States and also offered financial and real estate services. In 1999, when Condi left the board, TransAmerica was bought by the Dutch company Aegon N.V. She stayed in the financial services world, however, by joining the Charles Schwab Corporation's board of directors that same year. Once again, she came to the business on the heels of George Shultz, who had joined the brokerage house two years previously. She and Shultz both served on the compensation and customer quality assurance committees at Schwab.

In 1995, Condi joined another financial company, J. P. Morgan, the 140-year-old investment banking institution whose clients included 30 million individuals as well as corporations, institutions, and governments. She became a member of the International Advisory Council, a group of business and government leaders—chaired by Shultz— that met every eight months to advise the corporation. This post introduced her to many international figures, from a senior Singapore government official to a former Saudi finance minister and chief executives of corporations from South Africa, Brazil, Japan, and Mexico.

The Hewlett-Packard Corporation, headquartered next door to Stanford in Palo Alto and founded by two Stanford engineering graduates, was part of the Silicon Valley explosion of new technology. Condi joined the Board of Directors in 1991 and served for two years, becoming an insider in this very Stanford-friendly corporation.

In addition to corporate boards, Condi obtained director positions in large foundations and research policy research groups. From 1994 to 1997, she was a trustee at the

Carnegie Corporation, one of the country's oldest philanthropic organizations that focuses on education and international security among other areas. During her term at Carnegie, she served on an advisory council for its Commission on Preventing Deadly Conflict, joining a list of world leaders including Jimmy Carter, Robert S. McNamara, Desmond Tutu, and Mikhail Gorbachev. The Commission itself consisted of sixteen members whose tasks included studying methods for obtaining full disclosure of nuclear weapons. Their report, "Comprehensive Disclosure of Fissionable Materials: A Suggested Initiative," was released in 1995. As a member of the advisory council, Condi offered her expertise on the nuclear arsenals of the United States and the former Soviet Union.

This was not her first experience with the Carnegie organization. In 1988 and 1989, she had served on the board of trustees at the Carnegie Endowment for International Peace, the research organization that describes itself as "the oldest international affairs think tank in the country." The Endowment studies "relations among governments, business, international organizations and civil society," and, through its Carnegie Moscow Center, focuses on relations between Russia and the United States.

From 1992 to 1997, Condi served on the Board of Directors of the RAND Corporation, the research association where she had served as a summer intern as a college student. The first organization in the country to be called a "think tank," RAND has expanded its original focus on military technology to include education, health care, international economics, and other issues. Brent Scowcroft was also on the board at RAND during Condi's term.

In 1997, she joined the board of directors of the Hewlett Foundation, a separate entity from the Hewlett-

Packard Corporation she had worked for previously. The foundation gives $120 million in grants to organizations that, according to its mission, "make positive contributions to society." As a member of the board, Condi helped set the budget, made investment decisions, and reviewed the work of many of the institutions receiving financial support from the foundation. Another task of the board during her term was selecting a president, and Paul Brest was the candidate chosen by the selection committee. As both the dean of the Stanford Law School and the president of the Hewlett Foundation, Paul Brest became one of Condi's close friends and colleagues. "Condi's greatest expertise was on the international side of the foundation," said Paul. "She was particularly interested and helpful to the foundation in those areas, but like other directors she had to deal with all the issues. The board meets four times a year."

At the National Endowment for the Humanities, the federal agency that provides grants to cultural institutions and scholars, Condi served on the Board of Trustees from 1991 to 1993. She also became part of San Francisco's cultural leadership as a member of the San Francisco Symphony's Board of Governors.

Starting in 1994, Condi returned to Notre Dame three times a year to serve on the Board of Trustees, the primary administrative arm of the university. She was elected to the fifty-three-person board after having served on the advisory council for the university's College of Arts and Letters. A survey by the *Journal of Blacks in Higher Education* published in 2000 found that Notre Dame had more black trustees than any major university in its study, with seven black members, including Condi, on the board. In 1995, the university recognized her prominence as an educator by giving her an honorary doctorate and inviting her to give the commencement address to that year's graduating class. Two years later, she was honored by Notre Dame once again, named a National Exemplar of service to education in America. This recognition was given during a major fund-raising campaign in which the university produced a film, *Generations: A Celebration of Notre Dame*, that was broadcast to alumni groups throughout the country. The film highlighted four Notre Dame graduates who had contributed to education, the church, and society.

In addition to the honorary doctorate from Notre Dame, Condi was named an honorary doctor of laws at Morehouse College in 1991 and a doctor of humane letters at the University of Alabama in 1994. Morehouse, founded in Atlanta two years after the Civil War, is the nation's oldest black, all-male college with alumni including Martin Luther King, Jr., Olympic track champion Edwin Moses, film director Spike Lee, and actor Samuel L. Jackson. Recognition from the University of Alabama must have served as a personal measure of how far the nation had come, for the university was segregated when John and Angelena Rice wanted to pursue graduate work in the early 1960s.

Condi's prominence in academia was further recognized in the spring of 1997 when she was elected to the American Academy of Arts and Sciences. This honor is given to those who have made "distinguished contributions to science, scholarship, public affairs and the arts," and she was among eleven professors named to the Academy that year. The following year she was named one of forty Young Leaders of American Academia by *Change* magazine, the journal of the American Association for Higher Education. At Stanford, she re-entered the Hoover Institution with a three-year research fellowship that supported new research projects while she continued teaching classes in political science.

From the boardrooms of multinational corporations and policy centers to the academic lecture circuit, Condi grew in stature in the business, academic, and cultural worlds upon her return from the Bush Senior White House. She was promoted to full professor at Stanford in May 1993 at age thirty-eight. Unknown to her, a committee was meeting at the same time to discuss an important new opening at the university, one of the top jobs that traditionally led to the presidency at any number of major universities.

One month after her upgrade to full professor she received a call from Gerhard Casper, president of Stanford. Over the years they had talked frequently about the development of the university and shared a common interest in the political science department, as Gerhard's career included two years as an assistant professor of political science before becoming dean of the University of Chicago Law School. They had met the previous year when Condi traveled to Chicago with the presidential search committee to meet him as a candidate for the position. At that time he was provost of the University of Chicago, the second most powerful position at the institution. As provost, he was the principal budget and academic officer, reporting directly to the president. At that first meeting, Gerhard found Condi to be one of the most exceptional academics he had ever met. "I was greatly impressed by her academic values, her intellectual range, her eloquence," he recalled.

That June day in 1993, just over a year after they first met, Condi had no reason to think Gerhard's invitation to meet him in his office was anything more than another chance to talk about a committee decision or some other administrative matter. The meeting turned out to be anything but routine, however.

"I did not beat around the bush," said Gerhard. "I said to her, 'Condi, I want you to be the next provost.' And there was really silence. You know, Condi is not someone who's easily stunned by anything, but there was absolute silence on the other side of the table."

It was a lot to take in. As provost, she would be the first black person, first woman, and youngest individual ever to hold the job. At thirty-eight, she was more than twenty years younger than all of her predecessors had been when they took the office, and she would go into the number-two power spot, leapfrogging the usual positions of chair and subsequently dean of a department. Without previous experience in managing a department's finances she would be responsible for the university's entire $1.5 billion annual budget. She would also be the chief academic officer, making policy decisions that affected the 1,400-person faculty. But Gerhard was convinced she would perform well in the job. "I knew it would be somewhat controversial because universities have a strong civil service expectation," he said. "If you are to be provost, you should have been dean, you should at least have been a department chair . . . but I was absolutely convinced that she was competent."

Casper also remarked that most of the controversy that followed the announcement revolved not around Condi's race, gender, or lack of experience, but over the fact "that Condi was a Republican and most American universities are primarily made up of Democrats." Some members of the faculty and student body were concerned that Condi's conservative political views would sway the decision-making levels of the university toward the right, but Condi responded to those concerns by stating that her politics would not come into play in her job.

Condi entered the job at a difficult time as Stanford, like other universities, was facing budget cuts in the slowing economy. In addition to the recession, they also had enormous repair costs from the earthquake that rocked the Bay area in October 1989 and caused damage to 200 buildings. The repair bill reached $200 million. When Condi became provost, the university's deficit stood at $20 million. "Stanford—like all universities—is in a maelstrom of change," she said after accepting the position as provost. "Just as I was fortunate to be given a chance to help shape America's response to the extraordinary events that ended the Cold War, I am honored that President Casper has placed faith in my judgment and ability to meet Stanford's challenges." She also described the source of her commitment—a deep admiration for the university that had grown stronger over the years. "When I decided to return to the university two years ago, I did so with even greater commitment to, and appreciation of, the freedom of thought, exploration and expression that the academy allows," she said. "There is no other environment that can match the energy of a place like this."

With her new appointment, Condi changed her plans for the summer. She had scheduled a four-week trip to the oil fields in Kazhakstan, where she would do research for a book, as she told *The New York Times*. As a Chevron director working on a deal in that country, however, her academic and corporate schedules were clearly going to overlap. She cancelled the trip and crammed on the university budgeting process instead. She had never faced a billion-dollar budget, and reducing the deficit would surely entail firings and cutbacks that would make her unpopular on many levels of the university. But winning a popularity contest had never been on her itinerary, and she knew that conflict would be an unpleasant yet necessary part of getting the university's finances on track. She wasn't afraid of the problems that would undoubtedly arise should she have to trim departments and initiate staff layoffs. "I tell my students, 'If you find yourself in the company of people who agree with you, you're in the wrong company,'" she said.

To some people at the university, erasing the budget deficit was a pipe dream that could not be accomplished. But Condi spent the next few months constructing a strategy that she outlined in a memo to deans and administrators in November 1993. The plan called for reductions in department budgets and student services, possible layoffs and the consolidation of support staffs. In an interview with the campus paper, she assured students that the university was not reeling from a crisis but working productively toward solutions like the rest of the nation. "I actually don't think of this as a budgetary crisis," she said. "This is just managing in the '90s. Every American institution out there is going through the same questions."

"There was a sort of conventional wisdom that said it couldn't be done . . . that [the deficit] was structural, that we just had to live with it," said Condi's fellow professor, Coit Blacker. "She said, 'No, we're going to balance the budget in two years.' It involved painful decisions but it worked, and communicated to funders that Stanford could balance its own books and had the effect of generating additional sources of income for the university." Many of those painful decisions involved firing people, a process that Condi dreaded but that she considered absolutely necessary to turn the budget around. "I always feel bad for the dislocation it causes in people's lives," she said. "When I had to lay people off, I eased the transition for them in any way I could. But sometimes you have to make difficult decisions, and you have to make them stick."

Her job was not easy, and often not pleasant. "In the first couple of years, there was very little to which I could say yes," she said. "Also, we had to restructure the administrative units of a lot of departments. That was hard, laying off people. That's not fun." But she felt that making clear decisions and staying on course was more productive than letting issues simmer for months or years. She prided herself on being able to make tough decisions. "I think that you have to have a certain decisiveness about things," she said. "People would rather have an answer of 'no' than have no answer."

In addition to the shadow of the deficit, another dark cloud hung over Stanford's finances when Condi became provost. The university was embroiled in an investigation over alleged overbilling for indirect costs, part of the monies used to perform the thousands of federally supported research projects at the university. Federal research projects are funded with grants that cover two types of expenses, direct and indirect costs. The first are easily identifiable, such as laboratory equipment, supplies, and professors' salaries for a specific project. Indirect costs, however, cover the utilities, library materials, building maintenance, use of support staff, and other items that are not easily attributed to specific projects. The university and the government agree on an overall percentage of those goods and services to be billed as indirect costs. In Stanford's case, the percentage billed for indirect costs were the highest of any university in the nation at 74 percent. This meant that a professor who budgeted $100,000 for a research project would receive an additional $74,000 to cover indirect costs for a total grant of $174,000.

In 1990, the federal office that oversees the research budget claimed that Stanford had overcharged millions for indirect costs. The wide-scale audits that followed made big news in the press and Stanford's reputation was put on the line. The complex auditing process, with dozens of accountants reviewing Stanford's books at any given time, gave Condi additional supervisory duties in an already demanding job. But when the investigations were completed in 1994, no wrongdoing was found. The federal government "concluded that it has no claim against Stanford for fraud or any wrongdoing or misrepresentation regarding indirect cost submissions," wrote Gerhard Casper in a public statement.

In addition to unhappy reactions to the job cuts that came with her budget-slashing plan, Condi made some controversial decisions as provost that put her on the firing line. For years, reports had been submitted about the need to hire more women faculty, pointing out that several departments had never hired a woman professor and that, except for the provost, no woman served in the university cabinet. In 1997, Condi admitted that progress was very slow on the issue. She reported that in 1993 the percentage of women on the faculty was 15.8 percent and by 1996 had risen to 17.8 percent—an improvement, but not an earth-shattering one. "Obviously this is slow, steady progress in the right direction," she said, "but I'd emphasize that the numbers are not flying up."

Studying the problem, Condi came to the conclusion that the most fundamental roadblock was the slow turnover in senior positions. "You see 1 to 2 percent turnover rates in the tenured faculty," she explained. "So you simply know that if you're not enlarging the size of the faculty, percentages are going to move slowly. That's an arithmetic fact. People may not like that arithmetic fact, but it is an arithmetic fact."

One incentive to bring more women into faculty positions involved creating a fund for new positions, tailor-made to outstanding women candidates who did not meet specific criteria for other openings. Other than that, the provost's critics felt that she did not do enough to enforce affirmative action, even though she admitted in meetings that she was a product of affirmative action hiring back in 1981. Condi did not want to send the message to women that Stanford was recruiting them to fill a quota rather than hiring them on their merits. She felt that the positive aspect of showing a commitment to women by setting quotas "is more than outweighed by the downside, which I believe makes people feel as if they are being targeted for the wrong reasons."

Condi did believe in affirmative action as a starting point in some cases, such as her own, where she was given an opportunity to prove herself but only during a probationary period, after which she was judged strictly on her performance in the political science department. "Done in the right way, affirmative action can be very helpful," she said. But this did not compel her to institute quotas or make any other sweeping affirmative action policies at the university.

The provost's affirmative action stance became headline news at Stanford again when she upheld a dean's decision to not grant tenure to Karen Sawislak, assistant professor of history. Outraged students formed demonstrations on campus, but Condi explained that the dean is held responsible for the quality of the faculty and his decision stands. The provost and advisory board review tenure decisions to make certain that proper procedures were followed in making the determination whether or not to grant tenure. In the Sawislak case, Condi explained, all the procedures were in order. "Tenure is granted to those who have achieved true national distinction in research and excellence in teaching," she said. "It is a very tough standard, and the dean must decide whether it has been met and make certain that the standard is applied evenly throughout the school. A departmental vote, even a unanimous one, does not usurp the dean's role in this regard." She added that affirmative action was not a consideration at this stage, citing a Stanford policy written in 1985. The policy states that affirmative action pertains to the time of search and appointment and the assistant professorship years, but not to the period of tenure review. As she had explained in the Senate meetings about the need to hire more women faculty, Condi drove home the university's established policy of using affirmative action as a starting point only.

Another controversial issue during Condi's tenure as provost involved a new core curriculum, "Introduction to the Humanities," which overhauled both the method and the content of the undergraduate humanities experience. This program, launched in 1997, replaced the previous humanities curriculum entitled "Cultures, Ideas and Values" while expanding upon that program's multicultural approach. The new humanities course included updated study plans, such as interactive Internet projects and group projects that took the place of final exams. Both the provost and the president of the university fully supported and helped create the new curriculum in the hope that more freshmen would be attracted to humanities courses. Only 12 percent of freshmen showed an interest in studying the social sciences, philosophy, languages, literature, or the arts, a fact that many faculty and administrators were anxious to reverse. "Introduction to the Humanities" included readings on non-Western cultures as well as courses that covered issues of race, ethnicity, and gender.

Condi supported the multicultural aspect of the new curriculum, stating that the story of Western civilization is incomplete without the story of the cultures that it confronted. "The argument that I have never bought . . . is that the study of Western civilization—devoid of the study of all the other civilizations that helped to shape it—was the smart thing to do," she said. "Human history has been the story of clashes of civilizations and that is the interesting part about it. . . . I never understood the critique that you should teach only Western civilization."

The changes in curriculum and teaching style were a group effort, spearheaded by a faculty committee and strongly encouraged by Provost Rice and President Casper. "I think the experience that an undergraduate has here in the first two years is just 180 degrees from where it was," said Condi after the course was launched. "Much more in touch with faculty members, much more small group oriented, much more research oriented."

Another hot issue that arose during Condi's term as provost was a housing shortage for graduate students. In May 1998, a group of 1,000 students rallied on campus and 100 camped out for a night on the Quadrangle to protest the shortage of affordable housing. Nearly 900 graduate students who applied for on-campus housing were turned away for lack of room. Condi announced that the university would build new facilities but that the project would take approximately two years after being approved. In the meantime, housing remained a major problem, one which she passed on to her successor.

In spite of controversy over affirmative action, new

multicultural programs, and other issues, Condi was widely respected for her achievements with the university budget. At a meeting with the Faculty Senate in May 1996, she announced that the university was not only out of the red, but holding a $14.5 million reserve. "This is something the entire university should be proud of," she said, attributing the success to spending cuts, a large increase in the value of Stanford's endowment, and record-breaking fund-raising successes. "I'm very proud we're fiscally sound now," she said, but cautioned against going back to old habits. "Universities tend in times of relative flush to keep growing and add functions, and to stop thinking of the necessity for consolidation," she said. Positions that had been eliminated would eventually be reinstated, for example, moving the ledgers toward another budget crunch. "It seems almost as if there's a pendulum," she said, "and you have to be very tough to not have the pendulum swing."

During her role as provost, Condi continued to teach as a professor of political science. She also renewed her commitment to the piano, joining a faculty chamber group and studying seriously in private lessons. The man who suggested she begin performing again was a colleague at Stanford. "Condi was the provost when I was dean of the law school," said Paul Brest, who is currently the president of the Hewlett Foundation. A violist, Paul took up the instrument when his children began taking music lessons. "The provost meets with the deans once a month or so," he said, "and I had heard that she had once been a really serious pianist. I came to one of my monthly meetings with the piano part to the Schumann piano quartet and asked her, 'How about we play this?' When she agreed, we started up a piano quartet that played pretty regularly for five years." The group's cellist was

Walter Hewlitt and the violinists varied, but were primarily Stanford Law School graduate Andrea Chavez and staff member Karen Lindblaum.

Paul said that Condi loved playing piano quartets and quintets and was an excellent chamber music musician. "There's always a lot of give and take in a quartet," he said, "with comments like 'please don't rush that' or 'please play a little bit softer.' Condi goes so easily with that. She has a very good ear, and she's a wonderful pianist. String players are always complaining that the piano is playing too loud, it becomes kind of a joke; but she's able to take criticism, give criticism, and just work with the group. She's a real team player. You have to do that if you're playing chamber music."

This group gave informal recitals in each other's homes, and enjoyed exploring piano trios, quartets, and quintets by Schumann, Brahms, and others. It offered a challenging musical outlet without the pressure of public performances. But eventually Condi became more serious and set her sights on performing with the Muir String Quartet, a world-class group that often came to Stanford to perform as a scheduled stop on its North American concert tours. Formed in 1980, the Muir Quartet is the resident quartet at the Boston University School for the Arts and winner of the 1981 Naumburg Chamber Music Award. The group is named for the legendary naturalist and Sierra Club founder John Muir, and donates the profits of its recordings to environmental organizations.

Condi had become friends with the Muir Quartet by reading through pieces with them during their Stanford visits. The quartet always played an informal concert in someone's home before their Stanford performance, and Condi wanted to work up a piece that she could play with them at one of these pre-concerts. The quartet agreed, and Condi began rehearsing the Brahms Piano Quintet in F minor. This work, considered the pinnacle of Brahms' chamber music, demands virtuosic technique, especially in the third movement, a scherzo marked *Allegro*. Condi was already taking piano lessons with associate professor George Barth when she decided to tackle this piece.

"When we began working I didn't know what to expect," said George. "She's a busy woman, and I thought that maybe she would just have a dilettante approach to things. We started working on a Chopin nocturne and the Beethoven Sonata No. 7 in D Major. She soon said she wanted to 'put more time into this,' so I decided to turn up the heat and see how far we could go. I discovered that there was no upper limit to what she could do. I pushed and she responded, every week she came ready to go, intensively working on everything. She worked with great intensity and concentration and remembered everything I said—all the nuts and bolts. She made great progress, and I was really impressed."

Condi worked with George about ten hours a week while she was preparing to do the Brahms with the Muir Quartet. Whether she was rehearsing for a performance or simply working on new repertoire, she considered her lessons a "sacred" time and would not allow any interruptions. This wasn't an easy feat for the person with the number-two job at the university. "If she got a call from the office she'd say, 'I'm doing Brahms now,' and she told them to wait. She wanted them to know that this was her time to do music."

George recalled that the Brahms Piano Quintet performance, although in an informal setting, was an exhilarating event. "She played it very well," he said. "I was amazed at her tempo in the scherzo; it was very exciting." From the beginning of that November evening, her friendship with the Muir Quartet came through. "They began to play," said George, "and Condi noticed a funny look on the string players' faces. The opening lines turned into 'Happy Birthday' because it was her birthday. They played it through while everyone in the house sang along. Then they started over for real."

George prefers to work with people like Condi, non-music majors who have a unique commitment to their art. "Most of my students are neurobiologists and geologists who go on to incredible careers in other fields and happen to be great players," he said. "I'm interested in how far amateurs can go, and I've taught some amazing pianists. When I find, for example, someone in physics who has very difficult work to do but has time for piano, I know he's going to put in the work. A student like this will tell his lab, 'I'm playing in a chamber competition this week, I won't be in.' These are not amateurs in the sense of just messing around, they're really serious. As a political scientist and provost, Condi was definitely in that group."

Regularly scheduled faculty talent shows at Stanford revealed just how skilled many of the engineers and math professors really were. Condi appeared on one of these programs with George after mastering another Brahms piece, the two-piano version of his *Variations on a Theme by Haydn*. "We worked on that and performed it at a faculty talent show," said George. "It was really fun performing with her. At faculty performances you find all these amazing people crawling out of the woodwork, people who are renowned in other fields and who are also great musicians." George recalled that Condi later performed the Brahms *Liebeslieder Waltzes*, a collection of joyful, short pieces scored for two pianos and chorus.

Condi's connection with the Muir String Quartet

prompted her and her Stanford string player friends to attend Muir's summer music workshops. They have traveled to Utah to study at the Advanced Quartet Program at the Institute at Deer Valley, making music against the glorious backdrop of the Wasatch Mountains. George Barth came along for two summers to coach them on some of the piano quartet repertoire. Condi has also followed the Muir Quartet to Montana for summer retreats, where she reads through music with them and practices some of her favorite chamber music repertoire. "I now play almost exclusively chamber music," she said in 2001, "and I have to be selective. I don't have that much time to practice. And I do like the social aspects of playing chamber music." Before she began playing with Paul Brest and the other members of the quartet at Stanford, she had only worked on solo piano music. Chamber music opened a new world to her, one that she continues to explore and enjoy. Given the choice, she would prefer playing with a string quartet or giving a solo recital rather than performing a concerto with an orchestra. "I played with orchestras a couple of times," she said, "and always found it overwhelming."

George Barth noted that Condi's skills as a chamber musician—being a good listener and collaborator—were just an extension of her personality. In departmental meetings, Condi the provost was equally attentive. "She would pay attention to everyone and find ways of incorporating everyone," he said. "That is something one would expect to see reflected in her chamber playing, and I think that is why she's always taken to this kind of playing. I think she enjoys both things. I also know that her friendships at Stanford are important to her and doing chamber music is one of the best ways to pursue friendships." George saw first-hand how much dedication

Condi put into her music; in spite of her heavy schedule of teaching, researching, and administering the university, she made music a priority and therefore kept a balance of work, art, and soul in her life. "Condi is very self-disciplined," he said. "She finds time to do things that matter. This is one way that she tries to not let go of things that matter to her."

Another high priority in Condi's lifestyle was her commitment to exercise. Stanford had an excellent strength-training department, and she is proud to claim that she worked with Karen Branick, who was Tiger Woods' strength coach when he was a student at Stanford. After Branick left, Condi trained regularly with Mark Wateska, who developed a rigorous program for her.

Twice a week she put on her sweats, went to the varsity weight room, and began a one-hour workout with ten minutes on the treadmill and fifteen minutes of stretching. She then proceeded to the weights and performed bicep curls, shoulder and leg presses, isolateral pull-downs, abdominal crunches, and many other routines, capped off by a cooldown on the treadmill and more stretching. "I put her through the same regimes I did with any athlete at Stanford," said Mark. "She felt that her workouts kept her sharp physically as well as mentally."

Condi, who is five-foot-eight and weighs 140 pounds, trained in order to develop more quickness and agility in her tennis game, to control the stress of her job, and to just see how far she could push herself. She also liked the fact that her regime allowed her to eat whatever she wanted without gaining weight. Photos of Condi in sleeveless gowns, such as the one she wore to the televised NAACP Image Awards in February 2002, reveal her well-toned arms. Condi described her workouts as a crucial break from her work, one of the few activities that get her away from her desk and her meetings. She explained that, unlike people who have children, she has to find another outlet that takes her away from work. "If you don't have children who are a break on working all the time, you can work all the time," she said. She also uses her stints on the treadmill to focus on pressing issues, plugging in either rock or classical music, depending on her mood. "I do some of my best thinking on the treadmill," she said. This is the only time she uses music as an accompaniment to whatever she's doing. "I get very caught up in what's going on with the music," she said, "so only when I'm exercising can I have music as background music." She often times her treadmill workout to familiar music rather than the clock. "I have to do something to get my mind off that fact that I'm droning on a treadmill for 30 minutes and I usually play on the CD pieces that I know, usually pieces that I've played, because I can kind of time my workout to the start of a Scherzo, to know that I ought to run to the end of the Scherzo, or something like that."

"She's very goal-oriented, very driven, very competitive," said Mark. "I would not want to come up against her in any situation." Each year on her birthday, Mark's "present" was to coach her through one repetition for each year of her life on the 100-pound leg press. "I don't think she liked receiving gifts from me," said Mark, "but that was the challenge—you're one year better. That's the approach we took. Age was not something that held you back."

Mark was impressed with Condi's self-discipline as well as her unassuming personality. "As a strength coach, I guess I was the low man on the totem poll in the scheme of things, but she never acted like the provost; she didn't want special treatment, she wanted me to kick her butt. So I never felt intimidated by her position; I felt comfortable being myself and doing my job. That made for a good relationship." Mark attended one of Condi's informal performances at Stanford and was astounded by the physicality that her playing required. "He said, 'You know, that's every bit as physical playing that piece as anything that I watch with the Stanford football team,'" said Condi. "Pianists don't often get enough credit for the physical side of playing something like Brahms, which can be quite physically demanding."

In her first years as provost and professor, Condi had no desire to go back into government service. She was fulfilled in teaching, advising freshman, and guiding the academic course of her graduate students, and she did not miss the pace of Washington. She spent quality time trying to convince her undergraduate students to go for a career in academia, outlining the many perks that had enriched her life—including travel. "I . . . tell them that I've been to Europe thirty times or so now, and I've never paid my own way," she said in 1993. Such arguments may also have served to convince herself that she was better off as a professor than as a foreign policy official in Washington.

"I don't suffer from Potomac fever in the way it afflicts many people who have worked in Washington and spend the rest of their lives wanting to go back," she said in 1995. "I can say in all honesty that I don't spend a waking moment thinking about whether to go. I had a chance to finish so much in those two years that I have no thirst to try to do it again." But by the end of 1998, she had changed her tune.

Five years had passed since she left the Bush administration, and she sorely missed the hands-on foreign policy world. The former president's son, George W., was seeking her advice on foreign affairs, and these meetings pulled her further toward the practicalities of her field. It appeared to be time for a change, and Condi decided to leave Stanford. "The most important thing became to get back to what I do, which is international politics," she said in March 1999. "I haven't been to Russia in two and a half years. For me, going to Russia is like breathing."

She planned on entering the business world to apply her international relations background in that area. "I'm going to take a leave from the university to pursue opportunities in the private sector that will give me practical experience in economic and political reform," she said. She hoped to get the most experience in witnessing "the impact of globalization on international financial and political institutions." She added that she planned to return to Stanford one day, but that "it's time to get back to my passion: international relations and politics."

In his remarks at Condi's farewell celebration, Gerhard Casper joked that no one really believed she was leaving to pursue international politics. "We all know her *real* passion," he said, "and the fact that NFL training camps open in only a few weeks." He also thanked her "for investing as much talent and energy into consolidating the Stanford budget as into unifying Germany. The former may have been a tougher task than the latter and ended up taking more time."

The ceremony turned poignant when Brenda Sepolen sang two of Condi's favorite gospel songs, "His Eye Is on the Sparrow" and "I Need Thee Every Hour." Most of the more than 100 people in the room, including Condi, were moved to tears. Later, Gerhard presented Condi with a pricey gift he had acquired with the help of an entire group of Condi well-wishers. She opened the package to find, much to her amazement, a rare, six-volume first edition of Tolstoy's *War and Peace*. Inside, the dedication read:

To Condoleezza Rice
May War be the fiction,
And Peace the reality
With the greatest appreciation and deep gratitude
for her service as Stanford's 9th Provost.

At the final meeting of the Faculty Senate for that academic year, Condi's colleague Brad Efron talked about the "warm grace and tough-love honesty" Condi displayed as provost and professor. He also reminded her, during the champagne toast, that her job as a tenured professor at Stanford would not be going anywhere. "It's like the Mafia," he told her. "It's not just something you quit."

When Condi officially stepped down as provost on July 1, 1999, she declared a one-year leave of absence from the university and re-entered the Hoover Institution as a senior fellow. As an expert in the states of the former Soviet Union and Eastern Europe, she brought years of both academic and government service experience to the Stanford-based research organization, which is dedicated to studying a wide range of contemporary policy issues.

John Raisian, director of the Hoover Institution, remarked that her connections are as impressive as her background. "She has this incredible reputation even though her experiences are somewhat limited by the mere fact of her age," he said. John described her ability to maintain a power network of Washington contacts by drawing a comparison to another Hoover member,

George Shultz, who has been a distinguished fellow at the institution since 1989. "George has this star quality appeal," he said. "He left the Reagan Administration in 1989 and over the last more than a decade he continues to be very popular and very in touch with significant people around the world. At a junior level, Condi has the same kind of appeal. When she established friendships and associations some ten years ago with people like Colin Powell and Dick Cheney and Paul Wolfowitz, she's maintained them. She's always had her finger in lots of foreign policy issues even while she was out here on the West Coast."

John also pointed out Condi's publishing history and background in various public service organizations. "She has had other sort of advisory interests and capacities, and these are things that matter a lot to a place like Hoover," she said. "What we're trying to do is generate ideas that will make the world a little better place, a safer place. We comment on ideas that are in the world of policy and educate people about the facts underlying policies in the United States. This is right up her alley and what she does." In the Hoover newsletter, John added that "Condi is one of the brightest people I have ever met. She has a wealth of experience, and her enthusiasm is highly contagious. She will become an integral part of Hoover's foreign policy outlook."

Two weeks after her entry into the Hoover Institution, Condi was named the recipient of a new endowment donated by philanthropists Thomas and Barbara Stephenson. They created the fund to support a Hoover fellow who has "achieved stature as one of the most outstanding scholars in his or her field with a demonstrated commitment to research of public policy." The benefactors added, "We are thrilled by this opportunity to support both an institution and an individual who can have a significant, positive impact on an emerging new world."

❦

One year after Condi became provost of Stanford, she was listed among *Time* magazine's "50 Young Leaders to Watch." They based their selections on people age forty and under who had made "civic and social impact" and whom they thought would "make a difference." The article predicted that for some of the honorees "solving one problem will inevitably lead to another and another: until, eventually, the new leaders will be ministering not to a neighborhood but to a nation, perhaps to the world. Assuming that we will let them."

In the article's brief biographical sketch of Condi, Michael Mandelbaum of Johns Hopkins University predicted that "she has the ability to have a Cabinet-level job—she could be Secretary of State." This was five years before Condi joined George W.'s presidential campaign as his foreign policy advisor, six years before she was named his national security advisor. At forty, she had already become a major figure in her field and those who followed her career anticipated that she would one day appear on the national political stage. She would not disappoint.

When her friend George W. Bush began pulling together his presidential campaign, she was invited to put her expertise to work for him. She became head tutor among the candidate's foreign policy experts, head writer of the nuclear strategy speech, and front-and-center figure in the "W is for Women" campaign. By the time it was all over, George W. went a step further. He asked her to stay at his side as his national security advisor. He pulled her all the way into the West Wing, just around the corner and down the hall from the Oval Office.

NINE

Portals of Power: Bush II

> "If there is any lesson from history, it is that small powers with everything to lose are often more stubborn than big powers. . . . The lesson, too, is that if it is worth fighting for, you had better be prepared to win."
>
> —*Condoleezza Rice, 2000*

THE morning of September 11, 2001, Condi arrived at her office, as usual, at 6:30. She anticipated another typical, long day, in which she would not go home until 9:00 that night. Her job involved a certain amount of repetitiveness, such as scheduled daily briefings, but working in national security is never routine. About two hours into her day, an unusual message signaled that this day would be no exception.

Her secretary appeared at the door at 8:45 A.M. to say that a plane had hit the World Trade Center. What a strange accident, Condi thought. She called President Bush, who was in Florida speaking about his education agenda, and gave him the news. "What a weird accident," he said. A short time later, Condi was in a staff meeting when her secretary walked in and handed her a note. A second plane had struck the other tower. In a flash, she realized it was a terrorist attack.

Her second thought was to call a meeting of the top

members of the National Security Council. She went downstairs to the Situation Room, the military command center located in the basement of the West Wing, and got on the phone. Besides the president, the principal members of the NSC have historically been the vice president (Dick Cheney), secretary of state (Colin Powell), and secretary of defense (Donald Rumsfeld). Another cabinet member in the council is the secretary of the treasury (Paul O'Neill), and the top military and intelligence advisors are the chairman of the Joint Chiefs of Staff (Henry Shelton) and CIA director (George Tenet).

The president was not the only one unavailable for an emergency sit-down meeting. Donald Rumsfeld was in his office in the Pentagon, but just after American Airlines Flight 77 crashed into the building at 9:43 A.M., he was rushing through the corridors to get to the wreckage and help the injured. He would later move to a basement command center and take part in NSC meetings by phone. General Powell was having breakfast with the new president of Peru in Lima, but by 10:45 A.M., he was on his way back to Washington. Shelton was in a plane over the Atlantic on his way to Europe.

Two minutes after the plane hit the Pentagon, the White House was ordered to evacuate, and Condi was instructed to leave the Sit Room and go to an underground bunker. Cheney was already there, but before Condi left, she called the president once more to urge him not to return to the White House. She told him that his cabinet and staff feared there could be another hit on Washington. The president heeded their advice and was flown to various locations throughout the day. He didn't return to the White House until 6:30 that evening.

The first thing Condi did when she arrived at the bunker was telephone her aunt and uncle, Connie and

Alto Ray, in Birmingham. She asked them to tell everyone she was OK. Her next calls were to heads of state throughout the world, notifying them that the United States government was intact and "up and running." Throughout the day she set up conference-call NSC meetings with the president. At 3:55 in the afternoon, for example, Dick Cheney and Condi were on the phone from the bunker while the president was hooked in from Offutt Air Force Base in Nebraska.

That Friday, still numb like the rest of the country, Condi rode in the presidential motorcade to the National Cathedral to attend the memorial service, a moving ceremony in which speakers from many faiths gave messages of solace and unity. That first week, Condi's faith kept her going, as it always has. "Since I was a girl I have relied on faith—a belief that I'm never alone, that the bottom will never fall out too far. That has always been a part of me, and I'm drawing on that now," she said in early 2002.

Less than a year earlier, Condi had gone through another heartbreak with the death of her father. John had suffered a heart attack in the spring of 2000, and his health had never returned. He held on through the Bush campaign and the post-election crisis, and Condi spent as much time as possible by his side. He lived to hear the president-elect appoint his Little Star the next national security advisor. Six days later, on Christmas Eve, 2000, he died. He was seventy-seven years old.

After the attacks of September 11, Condi became much more visible on the national scene. She delivered many of the media updates on the war on terrorism, withdrawing from the style she learned from her NSA mentor, Brent Scowcroft. In his term as NSA for Bush, Sr., Brent never spoke to the press and kept a low profile outside the White House. He exerted most of his energy coordinating foreign policy for the president and did not get involved in public communication. A few months after Condi's appointment, Brent said, "If she's doing her job well, the president is getting the attention." In visibility, however, Condi now more closely resembles former national security advisors like Henry Kissinger (Nixon administration) and Samuel Berger (Clinton administration), who worked more as policy makers than policy coordinators and managers and thus received a higher profile than their predecessors.

In the first several weeks following 9/11, Condi was on the phone every morning at 7:15 with Secretary of State Powell and Secretary of Defense Rumsfeld. They discussed newly gathered information and ideas, which Condi sifted and later shared with the president. The role of assistant to the president for national security affairs, commonly called the national security advisor (NSA), is to gather foreign policy information and present the various views to the president. The NSA is a managerial role rather than a policy-making position, although past NSAs have assumed powerful decision-making roles. Technically, the NSA is an inside manager who keeps a low-profile outside the White House. But each president has had his own unique relationship with the NSA and has drawn different expectations of the advisor. Unlike most NSAs, Condoleezza Rice has become a media star, especially after the attacks of September 11 when she began holding press conferences about the war on terrorism.

"I try very hard to remember that I have to be very disciplined about making sure I'm giving the president the whole story," said Condi, "that I'm making sure he knows everything." She stressed that she makes it very clear to the president when she is talking about her own view and that it is offered only as one part of several other views. "I am responsible for making sure that I've checked things out before I tell them to the president—and for not abusing the privilege of sitting down the hallway from him."

The personal foreign policy views that Condi shares with the president are the product of her conservative, political realism outlook. This includes a call for less American military cooperation in conflicts in other countries. This non-interventionist approach is a classic tenet of "power politics" and views the military as a tool to be used with great discrimination. This view was voiced loudly and clearly in one of Condi's speeches in the final weeks of the campaign. In October 2000, she stated that if elected, Bush would withdraw U.S. troops from the Balkans and leave the Europeans in charge of the peace-keeping forces. She explained that the U.S. presence there detracted from its readiness in other areas of the world like Asia and the Persian Gulf. Her speech created an uproar in Europe. Later, George W. would admit that "we had gotten off on the wrong foot in Europe."

During the campaign Condi had also outlined her foreign policy approach—which she had shared with George W.—in a lengthy essay in *Foreign Affairs*. Included were clear statements about military restraint. "Using the American armed forces as the world's '911' will degrade capabilities, bog soldiers down in peacekeeping roles, and fuel concern among other great powers that the United States has decided to enforce notions of 'limited sovereignty' worldwide in the name of humanitarianism. . . . The president must remember that the military is a special instrument. It is lethal, and it is meant to be. It is not a civilian police force. It is not a political referee. And it is most certainly not designed to build a civilian society.

Military force is best used to support clear political goals."

This view would be made clear in the first months of the Bush administration, most notably in its hands-off approach to the Middle East.

Condi is calm and steady under pressure, a major factor in her selection as a White House spokesperson after 9/11. She never appears flustered, can think on her feet, and explains complex subjects clearly and simply. These are characteristics that have made her stand out among many of her colleagues and that prompted George W. to ask her to coach him on foreign policy during the campaign. Her Stanford friend Coit Blacker calls her "lightning brained," and her director at the Hoover Institution, John Raisian, said she has a "rare ability" at extemporaneous speaking. "When you see her giving talks," he said, "she does so most of the time with virtually no notes. She maps out in her head what she wants to say and is so articulate that she doesn't have to write it out first." While Condi would probably argue that this ability is not rare among professors who spend most of their time talking and fielding questions in front of a classroom, she appears to have developed this skill to a high degree.

Speaking on the Sunday morning Washington talk shows and fielding questions about foreign policy are perhaps the simplest jobs in Condi's schedule. At this time in history, her job requires analyzing the National Security Council's varying views on the war on terrorism, war in the Middle East, potential war in India, relations with North Korea and China, and other monumental concerns. "On a scale of one to ten in degree of difficulty, this is a fifteen," said Samuel Berger two months after the terrorist attacks. "I have enormous respect for her and for what she's doing right now."

The National Security Council was created during the Truman administration, when the complex policy decisions of postwar America called for better communication between the president's diplomatic and military staffs. Truman faced a host of thorny policy issues at the beginning of his administration. He learned about the United States' newly created atomic bomb soon after taking office and faced the agonizing decision of whether to use it on the Japanese. The Soviet Union had installed military regimes in several Eastern European countries, and in Western Europe nations were suffering financial collapse and starvation in the wake of the war. These and other conditions in the fast-changing world drove Truman to write the National Security Act of 1947, which included a new advisory board of "chiefs of staff and service commanders" called the National Security Council.

Truman was explicit about the council's role as advisory only, stating that he would have "complete freedom to accept, reject and amend the Council's advice and to consult with other members of his official family." The president would have the last word as well as the authority to "determine such policy and enforce it."

The first NSC policy papers provided the president with facts and opinion consolidated into one document, streamlining Truman's policy-making process. One of the first NSC papers, for example, helped define the content and logistics of the Marshall Plan, the gigantic financial aid package that America sent to Western Europe. Overseeing the policy paper assignments and other activities of the Council was the manager, then called the executive secretary. Truman's executive secretary of the NSC was Rear Admiral Sidney William

Souers, a close associate who had helped him reorganize the intelligence agencies after the war. Souers had a background in both the military and business, and he served for a time as the first CIA director. Like many national security advisors to come, Souers was a trusted confidant of the president. "A poker-playing crony of the president's, Admiral Souers was on easy terms with Harry Truman," wrote John Prados in his history of the NSC.

What was George W. looking for in a national security advisor when he began selecting his senior staff? The essential qualities of this position were spelled out clearly by the first man to hold the job. When Souers told Truman he was leaving the White House to return to the business sector, Truman asked him to describe the traits he should seek in his replacement. In his book, Prados includes excerpts from the memo that Souers gave to Truman in reply and explains that these criteria still hold true today:

- He should be a non-political confidant of the president.
- He must be objective and willing to subordinate his personal views on policy to his task of coordinating the views of all responsible officials.
- He must be willing to forego publicity and personal aggrandizement.

Prados writes that in the decades since the NSC's creation, its staff has acquired "power rivaling that of Cabinet officers, diplomats, and generals." As manager of that powerful staff, and as one of the closest presidential advisors, the national security advisor has become a central figure in the White House.

The nation's twentieth national security advisor,

Condi is the first woman to hold the post. She is the second black person, following General Colin Powell who was appointed national security advisor in the Reagan administration.

Condi's appointment made her the most prominent woman in foreign policy, the new poster-child for the slow but steadily increasing ranks of women in the field. Madeleine Albright's appointment as secretary of state in President Clinton's second term threw open the gates for more women in foreign policy. Throughout her career, Madeleine has been committed to the advancement of women in the field, and she considered her Cabinet appointment a victory for all women.

During George W.'s presidential campaign, one of Condi's Stanford colleagues made a remark about her shakeup of the status quo. "Foreign policy is dominated by bald, graying white men," said Michael McFaul, "and they're not used to someone like Condi Rice." According to a recent study by the Women's Foreign Policy Group, men still dominate in terms of numbers, but increasing numbers of women are making their mark in the field. "The foreign policy establishment, comprised primarily by males, is in the midst of a transformation," states the WFPG study. "In record numbers, women in the U.S. are entering the field of international affairs, assuming leadership roles and breaking with centuries of tradition. . . . Their faces are seen and their voices are heard in the corridors and staterooms of power as never before."

The summary of this study states that the post-Cold War era offers more opportunities for women in diplomacy and defense in areas such as human rights, law, humanitarian relief, trade, the environment, and the media. The study also reiterates the importance of Madeleine Albright in this trend. "The appointment of Madeleine

Albright to serve as sixty-fourth Secretary of State dramatically symbolized the changes underway in the profession.
. . . As recently as 1970, women constituted only 4.8 percent of U.S. Foreign Service officers. . . . By 1997, women
comprised 18 percent of the career senior foreign service,
24 percent of career senior executive service, 22 percent
of ambassadors . . . 40 percent of under secretaries . . . 28
percent of assistant secretaries . . . and 31 percent of
deputy assistant secretaries.

With input from nearly 600 women, the WFPG study
reveals the characteristics that these women claim have
helped them succeed in the field. The findings could be
a summary of Condoleezza Rice's own experience:

> High self-esteem and confidence went hand-
> in-hand with a third characteristic the women
> mentioned as important to their professional
> success: consistently exceeding performance ex-
> pectations (95 percent). There was a definite sense
> that women must work harder than male colleagues
> to earn the same levels of respect, trust and salary.
> Eighty percent of women agreed that gaining inter-
> national experience was important to advancing
> one's career. Seventy-four percent of women agreed
> that "developing a style with which male colleagues
> are comfortable" was important.

Although Condi and Madeleine Albright have had
very different careers in international relations, their lives
do share a few common themes; for one, they both admired and emulated their fathers. Madeleine ascended in
the field of international relations in the hopes of mirror-
ing the career of her father, Josef Korbel. "I tried to
pattern myself after him," she said. "A good deal of what
I did, I did because I wanted to be like my father." Condi
followed in her father's footsteps as well. Like him, her

career in academia spanned both teaching and administration. She also relives John Rice's commitment to underprivileged youth, as in her cofounding of the Center for a New Generation in California. Also like her father, she places her faith at the center of her life.

Additional similarities in Condi and Madeleine's youth were their parents' protectiveness and zealous commitment to their education. Madeleine described her parents as overly protective, and her father went to great lengths to oversee her education. "He corrected her essays . . . fretted about whether she would get into the best schools, plotted her future," wrote Dobbs. Condi's parents went to great extremes to shield her from the horrors of segregation and devoted themselves to her education, providing nearly as much instruction at home as she ever got in a classroom.

Another comparison can be drawn in terms of Condi and Madeleine's "outsider" status in their early years. Madeleine came to the United States at age eleven, a Czech who spoke English with a British accent and "spent a lot of time worrying, trying to make sure that I would fit in." Condi's situation was more dramatic, of course—a black child growing up in the most segregated city in the nation—but her upbringing was carefully guided to ensure that she would not only fit in, but succeed exceptionally in the culture at large.

As scholars, Condi and Madeleine both concentrated on Eastern Europe and the Soviet Union, and although they are both major figures in foreign affairs, they resemble each other least in the political arena. Madeleine, who knew of Condi for many years as her father's protégée at the University of Denver, discovered this in 1988 when she called Condi to ask if she would like to help her with Democrat Michael Dukakis's presidential campaign.

After an awkward silence on the phone, Condi said, "Madeleine, I don't know how to tell you this. I'm a Republican."

Condi states that in spite of their differences, she and Madeleine share important common ground. "I know and like Madeleine very much," she said. "You can have the same intellectual father and different outcomes. . . . On issues of how you use power we probably don't agree . . . but there are some powerful core values that we share."

Other women stars of foreign policy include Jeane Kirkpatrick, America's first woman ambassador to the United Nations, appointed by President Reagan. A political scientist with a career in both academia and government service, Kirkpatrick worked in the defense department for many years and, like Condi, served as a foreign policy advisor to a presidential candidate (Reagan). Another prominent women in the field is Swanee Hunt, who served as ambassador to Austria during four years of the Clinton administration. She is widely praised for the peacekeeping work she did in Bosnia during the war, and she currently teaches at Harvard's John F. Kennedy School of Government.

When Condi moved to Washington to start her term as NSA, she bought an apartment at the Watergate, the luxury residence on the Potomac that is home to Supreme Court justices and other Washington luminaries. The grand piano that her parents bought her when she was thirteen came along, as well as her treadmill and piles of Ferragamo shoes. She doesn't have as much time to practice as she did at Stanford, but on occasion she works up a few pieces for informal gatherings. In April 2002, she was surprised to get a call to do a "command performance" at a ceremony that would present a number of performers with the National Medal of the Arts.

Cellist Yo-Yo Ma, one of the award recipients, requested that Condi accompany him on a piece at the ceremony. One of the world's most famous classical musicians, Yo-Yo Ma enjoys collaborating with serious amateurs, partly to expose them to the large audiences he feels they deserve. He had heard that the national security advisor was a pianist, and he asked her if she had time to work something up for the ceremony at Constitution Hall on April 24. She was able to squeeze him in—the afternoon of the performance. He chose a piece by Brahms—Condi's favorite composer—the Adagio movement from his Violin Sonata No. 3 in D Minor (arranged for cello).

When President Bush presented Yo-Yo with his medal that night, he described him as a "world-renowned cellist who represents the very best in classical music." He hinted at his advisor's upcoming appearance when he said, "Later on this great American figure will be performing with another world-renowned figure." When the time came, First Lady Laura Bush introduced the pair. She revealed her West Texas roots when she told the audience that Condoleezza Rice would be performing on the "pi-AN-ah," and one critic was notably touched by the First Lady's "down-home and unabashed" appreciation of the artists. Laura loves classical music and Condi appreciates having another classical music fan in the White House.

The lush, solemn duet went beautifully and they were given a rousing standing ovation. "It's my great pleasure to say that she's very good," reported Greg Sandow in *The Wall Street Journal* a few days later. "Ms. Rice . . . was all music." He continued:

Her touch was authoritative, her rhythm firm, her phrasing thoughtful. Or at least this was true in places where she just accompanied Mr. Ma. When she had to step out a little more, she didn't find the focus a professional would have, and seemed reticent, or even shy. But my heart went out to her. Afterward, I thought, she looked as if this had been a peak moment in her life, and who could blame her? She seemed thrilled, and had every right to be. She did herself, the arts and her country proud.

Yo-Yo Ma understands how gratifying it is for serious amateur musicians to show their stuff to their colleagues and peers and prove to them that their music is more than a hobby. Condi did this during an interview with a visiting journalist one day at Stanford, popping a cassette into the player when they hopped into her Mercedes. The speakers blasted out her recording of the lightning-quick scherzo movement of the Brahms Piano Quintet she had prepared so diligently with the Muir Quartet. "I thought you'd like to hear me play," she told Ann Reilly Dowd of *George* magazine.

Before September 11, the National Security Council met twice a month. After the attacks, it began to meet three times per week. The hunt for Osama bin Laden, bombing strikes in Afghanistan, anthrax assaults, airport security concerns, and threats of more terrorist attacks put the Council in high gear. Before the attacks, Condi said her job was "to help make sure the government is speaking with one voice." She reiterated that after September 11, stating, "I probe to see if there is a consensus. I don't see any reason to continually take split decisions to the president if that's not necessary," adding that it was sometimes necessary to present a range of split opinions.

But the goals of the administration came into sharper focus, to a degree, after the attacks. Condi said that the administration's aim was "to leave the world not just safer . . . but better."

The president's primary advisors on foreign policy are Vice President Dick Cheney, Defense Secretary Donald Rumsfeld, and Secretary of State Colin Powell. As referee between these three—as well as between other members of National Security Council—Condi is sandwiched between the widely differing views of a team of powerful Washington veterans. On one side, Cheney, Rumsfeld, and his deputy, Paul Wolfowitz, are hard-line, conservative hawks who promote military strength and intervention. Cheney and Rumsfeld have been linked since the Ford administration, in which Rumsfeld was secretary of defense and Cheney, his protégée, served as White House chief of staff. Rumsfeld has been described as "a bureaucratic infighter without equal," and is famous for foiling Kissinger's SALT II plans during the Ford years. In his memoirs, Kissinger describes him as "a special Washington phenomenon: the skilled full-time politician-bureaucrat in whom ambition, ability and substance fuse seamlessly."

On the other side stands General Powell, a centrist who advises against military intervention and, like Condi, does not believe the nation's role is that of global policeman. During the first Bush administration, Cheney, then secretary of defense, was at constant odds with Powell, chairman of the Joint Chiefs of Staff. "Now the jockeying has picked up where it left off a decade ago," wrote Lawrence Kaplan in the *New Republic* after George W.'s election. The president anticipated these clashes of philosophy when he made his Cabinet appointments. Colliding egos and ideologies go with the territory and they're worth it, as the end result is a broad perspective from which he can make his own decisions. "There's going to be disagreements," the newly elected president said. "I hope there is disagreement."

Although Condi's views coincide more closely to Powell's than to Cheney's and Rumsfeld's, this did not guarantee an instant cozy alliance. "According to several Bush advisers," wrote Kaplan, "Powell has demanded, and been assured, that Rice's duties won't impede his ability to guide U.S. foreign policy. Rather, members of the Bush team predict, Rice will manage the day-to-day interagency paper flow and keep the trains running on time." Former Secretary of State George Shultz, one of the conservatives who has promoted Condi's career and worked with her at the Hoover Institution, sees Rice and Powell as two strong-willed people who work well together. "They have a very nice, easy, friendly style [together] and a lot of mutual respect," he said. "But they are both strong people. Neither one is a pushover."

Eighteen months into her term, Condi has managed more than "keeping the trains running on time." She has run a tight ship, keeping the egos at bay as the administration works through one crisis to the next. That's her job. And whatever she lacks in experience, compared to Cheney, Rumsfeld, and Powell, she makes up for with her own power-alliance—her bond with the president. "She not only spends the most time with the President, but in the pantheon of foreign policy advisors, his comfort level is highest with her," said a *Business Week* source.

In the aftermath of the Chinese fighter jet/U.S. spy plane collision in early April 2001—the administration's first crisis—Condi took on the customary NSA role of coordinating information for the president. The State Department was primarily responsible for negotiating with the Chinese and getting the crew home. During this period she fulfilled other, more policy-oriented duties, however, such as meeting with Indian Foreign Minister Jaswant Singh. And four months later, it was clear that she would be a foreign policy operator as well as manager with her trip to Moscow to meet with Russian President Vladimir Putin.

Condi's trip preceded President Bush's European visit, paving the way for his talks with Putin about missile defense. One of the president's top priorities is a missile defense shield in the tradition of the Star Wars program, a plan that Russia vehemently opposes. Bush chose Condi to make the trip because of her expertise in arms as well as in Russia. She was the first senior foreign policy person in the administration to visit Moscow, a significant event in the history of national security advisors. "Her mission to Moscow was unprecedented," said Brookings Institution fellow Ivo Daalder, author of several books about foreign policy. Not since Kissinger had a national security advisor made a "routine diplomatic mission to Moscow," he said.

Condi knew that much of her message would not be popular with Russian officials, especially the plan to withdraw from the 1972 Anti-Ballistic Missile Treaty, which Bush and Rice consider an outdated relic of the Cold War. "We've always said that we believe that the ABM Treaty is not only a problem for the limitations it places on testing and evaluation, but it's the wrong treaty for the wrong era," Condi said in a press briefing before leaving for Moscow. "And it inculcates and hardens a hostile relationship that no longer exists. But we'll talk to the Russians as to form. I think that's part of the consultation that needs to go on."

The primary purpose of the trip was to clarify which

topics Bush and Putin would discuss and set up a rough timetable. Condi's talks with Putin, Defense Minister Sergie Ivanov, and other officials helped set the tone for the arms talks to come, including the president's meetings with Putin at the G-8 Summit in Italy that summer. At that meeting, the two presidents agreed to talk in the future about reducing their stockpiles.

The Russian press relished Condi's appearance in Moscow, praising her "beautiful Russian" and gushing over her fondness for St. Petersburg (formerly Leningrad), where she spent a few weeks as a graduate student. Her meetings were covered extensively on television news and in the newspapers. When she returned to Washington, she remarked that Putin's style was refreshingly different than that of his predecessors. "I've been in lots of meetings with Russian leaders and they tend to turn into an exchange of monologues," she said. "[Putin] is much more conversational. He has a good sense of humor and loves to tell little jokes and stories."

Working on the U.S.–Russian dialogue on missile defense is one of Condi's primary assignments. In a summit held at Bush's Texas ranch, both Bush and Putin agreed to major cuts in their nuclear arsenals, but they did not come to an agreement about revoking the ABM Treaty. They were upbeat throughout the three-day summit and expressed a warm regard for each other, but the treaty remained a thorny issue.

After September 11, the vital alliance between the two countries in fighting terrorism had an effect on the ongoing arms talks. The Bush administration went ahead with its plan to withdraw from the ABM Treaty, but this did not have a harmful effect on the historic arms reduction treaty Bush and Putin signed in the spring of 2002. Bush traveled to Moscow and St. Petersburg for a summit with Putin in May, and the talks resulted in an agreement to "remove from deployment" two-thirds of each nation's long-range nuclear missiles over a period of ten years. The United States officially withdrew from the ABM Treaty in June 2002. Deputy Secretary of Defense Paul Wolfowitz discussed the relevance of that step in *The Wall Street Journal*:

> As a result of hard work and determination on both sides, relations with Russia—and between Russia and our NATO allies—are entering a new and promising era. Future U.S.-Russian summits will not be dominated by the question: What treaty are you planning to sign to regulate the nuclear balance of terror? Instead, we will focus on cooperating to meet the security challenges facing both our nations, the war on terrorism, and what we can do to enrich the lives of our peoples through closer economic, cultural, and political ties.

With her contributions to Bush's missile defense agenda and her diligence in coordinating the massive amount of information coming into the National Security Council about the war on terrorism, Condi has struck a balance as an NSA who is both a highly visible policy operator and a manager. There are moments when familiar voices remind her of the effect that the constant threat of terrorism is having on everyone, such as the day she got a call from a friend in Birmingham. "Tell Aunt Condi what you've been saying," she heard Deborah Carson say to someone near the phone. Deborah's three-year-old son then got on the line and said, "Bin Laden is a bad man. You and the president are going to put Bin Laden in jail." Condi laughed and said, "Joe, I'm going to tell President Bush first thing in the morning that you said that he was going to put Bin Laden in jail."

As the search for Bin Laden continued, a congressional investigation began in Washington to try to uncover where the intelligence processing went wrong. When reports emerged in May 2002 that the Bush administration knew about a possible al Qaeda hijacking plot before it occurred in September 2001, Condi addressed the press to clarify what the government knew. "In the period starting in December 2000, the intelligence community started reporting increase in traffic concerning terrorist activities," she said on May 16, 2002. "There was specific threat reporting about al Qaeda attacks against U.S. targets or interests that might be in the works." She added that the possibility of hijackings were also included in the reports. "At the end of July," she said, "the FAA issued another [communication] which said, 'There's no specific target, no credible info of attack to U.S. civil aviation interests, but terror groups are known to be planning and training for hijackings, and we ask you therefore to use caution.'" She stressed that the consensus of the intelligence community was that an attack might occur against an American interest in a foreign country such as an embassy, but that they did not anticipate an incident on U.S. soil. "I want to reiterate," she said, "that during this time the overwhelming bulk of the evidence was that this was an attack that was likely to take place overseas." She also stated that no one expected American airliners to be used as suicide bombs. "I don't think that anybody could have predicted that these people would take an airplane and slam it into the World Trade Center, take another one and slam it into the Pentagon," she said.

In addition to the ongoing investigation into the administration's analysis of terrorist activities and the day-to-day events in the war on terrorism, the National Security Council held discussions on crises such as potential war between India and Pakistan, suicide attacks and escalating tensions in the Middle East, and a possible U.S. attack on Iraq during the first half of 2002. Trained as a Sovietologist, Condi had to broaden her knowledge of these regions to coordinate the Council's recommendations on these and other global issues and bring various foreign policy opinions to the president.

After 9/11, the president's weekend getaways at Camp David became primarily working trips. Condi has spent more weekends at Camp David than any other Bush advisor. She has also been a frequent guest at the Bush ranch in Crawford, the "Western White House," for official business as well as socializing. Sometimes the informality of the ranch lends itself to fresh ideas, such as the day Condi sat around the kitchen table with Laura Bush and the president's advisor Karen Hughes discussing the war in Afghanistan. There they came up with the idea of dropping food bundles to help alleviate the severe food shortages in the country. Their brainstorm turned into reality when the first bright yellow packages containing peanut butter, lentils, protein bars, and other items were dropped by American cargo jets in early October 2001.

In a speech given in early 2002, Condi summarized her feelings about the unifying effect of the 9/11 attacks, and her words reveal that her trademark optimism extends to her outlook on the nation's future. They also confirm her parents' influence throughout her life, an influence that strove to empower her to be a positive, driving force in the world:

We are committed to a world of greater trade, of greater democracy and greater human rights for all the world's people wherever they live. September 11th makes this commitment more important, not less. Because . . . America stands for something real. It stands for rights that are inalienable and truths that are self-evident. It stands for compassion and hope. September 11th reintroduced America to a part of itself that some had forgotten or that some thought we no longer had. And we will carry this better part of ourselves out into the wider world.

The attacks of September 11th swept the nation into a new era, took America into a controversial war, and brought laser-like scrutiny to the Bush administration's pre-9/11 terrorism policies. In addition to explaining the president's policies as each event unfolded, Condi went before a historic investigatory commission to explain her own actions in the administration. The controversy surrounding the buildup to her public hearing was a story in itself, and ushered in perhaps the most turbulent phase of her career.

TEN

At War and Under Fire

"I know that, had we thought that there was an attack coming in Washington or New York, we would have moved heaven and earth to try and stop it. And I know that there was no single thing that might have prevented that attack."
—*Condoleezza Rice, testifying before the 9/11 Commission on April 8, 2004*

BY the summer of 2004, Condoleezza Rice's role as President Bush's closest advisor in the White House had elevated her to center stage in both U.S. politics and foreign policy. *Forbes* magazine affirmed this standing in August by naming her number one in its list of "The World's Most Powerful Women." The magazine announced that "advising the leader of the world's largest superpower—and having the ear of leaders around the globe—makes Rice, 49, the most powerful woman in the world."

Although Condi had become well known as one of the most visible national security advisors in history, the primary factor behind her increased global familiarity from 2002 onward has been the war in Iraq. As the Bush administration laid out its plans to continue the war against terrorism by using military force against Iraq, Condi continued to be the White House's lead spokesperson by taking the president's message to the media in news conferences as well as on the political talk show circuit.

President Bush, Vice President Cheney, and other members of the administration had begun to make their case against Iraq in the spring of 2002. At a press conference on March 17, for example, Cheney voiced concerns over Iraq's weapon stockpiles and potential nuclear capabilities:

> The President's made it clear that we are concerned about nations such as Iraq developing weapons of mass destruction. . . . We know they have biological and chemical weapons. . . . And we also have reason to believe they're pursing the acquisition of nuclear weapons. That's a concern to the United States. We think it's of concern to people all over the region. And we think it's important that we find a way to deal with that emerging threat.

The following August, Condi spelled out the president's perspective on Saddam Hussein in a widely quoted BBC interview. Speaking to BBC Radio 4, she stated that the Iraqi leader "is an evil man who, left to his own devices, will wreak havoc again on his own population, his neighbors and, if he gets weapons of mass destruction and the means to deliver them, on all of us." Her argument stressed that there was a "very powerful moral case" for removing Hussein from power, based on lessons from history. The United States was justified in considering a preemptive strike, she explained, in that:

> History is littered with cases of inaction that led to very grave consequences for the world. We just have to look back and ask how many dictators who end up being a tremendous global threat, and killing thousands, and indeed millions of people, should we have stopped in their tracks.

In the interview, part of the BBC's September 11 anniversary radio series entitled "With Us or Against Us," Condi reiterated the administration's message that Hussein had "developed biological weapons [and] lied to the UN repeatedly about the stockpiles."

Among the critics of the administration's preemptive strategy was Condi's mentor Brent Scowcroft, who had served as George H. W. Bush's national security advisor and brought Condi into that administration as an expert in Soviet and Eastern European affairs. In an opinion piece published in the *Wall Street Journal* on the same day of Condi's BBC interview, Scowcroft warned that military action in Iraq would divert the United States from its war on terrorism, isolate us from the global community that did not support such a strike, and destabilize the Middle East. "There is scant evidence to tie Saddam to terrorist organizations, and even less to the September 11 attacks," Scowcroft wrote. By focusing on Iraq, he stated, the president undermined the country's "pre-eminent security priority" of the war on terrorism and unraveled the global support that had developed in the wake of the 9/11 attacks. "An attack on Iraq at this time would seriously jeopardize, if not destroy, the global counter-terrorist campaign we have undertaken," he stated.

Scowcroft believed that launching a war in Iraq would not only divert the country from the war on terrorism but, if undertaken without America's traditional allies, be far too costly:

> There is a virtual consensus in the world against an attack on Iraq at this time. So long as that sentiment persists, it would require the U.S. to pursue a virtual go-it-alone strategy against Iraq, making any military operations correspondingly more difficult and expensive. The most serious cost, however, would

> be to the war on terrorism. Ignoring that clear senti-
> ment would result in a serious degradation in
> international cooperation with us against terrorism.
> And make no mistake, we simply cannot win that
> war without enthusiastic international cooperation,
> especially on intelligence.

In addition, Scowcroft predicted dire consequences
in the region if the United States struck Iraq. The Middle East, which considers the Israeli-Palestinian conflict
the most crucial issue, would interpret such an attack as a
turning away from that conflict. This would ignite, according to Scowcroft, "an explosion of outrage against
us." Rather than contributing to solutions in that
decades-long struggle, "we would be seen as ignoring a
key interest of the Muslim world in order to satisfy what
is seen to be a narrow American interest," he said.

Unlike Scowcroft, Condi's statements echoed the administration's more hawkish policy toward war and its
willingness to go it alone. When France, Germany, and
Russia announced that they would not join the coalition
in the spring of 2003, her reaction was sharp and strident.
She referred to their policy as "non-nein-nyet," and
stated that the U.S. strategy should be to "punish France,
ignore Germany, and forgive Russia." This hard-line position contrasted with the more moderate, Scowcroft-like
foreign policy perspective Condi had spelled out in her
Foreign Affairs article in January 2000. According to her
close associates, the 9/11 attacks transformed her world
view and set her upon a more conservative path. After the
attacks, her foreign policy perspective more closely reflected that of the president and neoconservative
members of his administration. "They believe that September 11 was a wake-up call," said Condi's friend Coit
Blacker, "and that certain things had to be done—

painful, violent, but they had to be done—and let the chips fall where they may. They've shaken up the chessboard, and now no one doubts the ability of the United States to run risks that were unimaginable before September 11."

Condi admitted that her more conservative foreign policy views were not "the orientation out of which I came," but evolved out of the president's focus on universal values and freedom. "This president has a very strong anchor and compass about the direction of foreign policy, about not just what's right and what's wrong, but what might work and what might not work," she said. "I found myself seeing the value of that."

One strong characteristic of Condi and George W. Bush's connection to each other is their deep religious faith, and the values that Bush expressed in speeches during the first anniversary of the terrorist attacks revealed the religious undertones of his foreign policy. The moral compass that Condi noted was clear in Bush's comments about America's duty to spread its ideals throughout the world. On September 11, 2002, he stated that the "attack on our nation was also an attack on the ideals that make us a nation. . . . Our deepest national conviction is that every life is precious because every life is the gift of a Creator who intended us to live in liberty and equality. More than anything else this separates us from the enemy we fight." The enemy, he added, is "any terrorist or tyrant [who means] to threaten civilization with weapons of mass murder."

Continuing his description of the nation's "sacred promise," Bush stated that "our cause is even larger than our country. Ours is the cause of human dignity, freedom guided by conscience and guarded by peace. This ideal of America is the hope of all mankind. . . . That hope still lights our way, and the light shines in the darkness, and the darkness will not overcome it."

In a radio address a few days later, the president reiterated his argument that Hussein posed a threat to the world that must be addressed by U.S. and global intervention:

> Congress must make it unmistakably clear, when it comes to confronting the growing danger posed by Iraq's efforts to develop or acquire weapons of mass destruction, that the status quo is totally unacceptable. The issue is straightforward—we must choose between a world of fear or a world of progress. We must stand up for our security and for the demands of human dignity. By heritage and choice the United States will make that stand. The world community must do so as well.

A few weeks after the president made these remarks, Condi presented a speech at the Waldorf Astoria Hotel in New York that outlined Bush's national security strategy. While she had acknowledged the role of values in making foreign policy decisions in her 2000 *Foreign Affairs* article, here she emphasized the need to integrate idealistic concerns with issues of power. "In real life, power and values are married completely," she said. "Great powers matter a great deal—they have the ability to influence the lives of millions and change history. . . . And the values of great powers matter as well." Like the president, Condi now focused on a more idealistic view of foreign policy as an instrument of defining the nation's values: "Foreign policy is ultimately about security—about defending our people, our society, and our values, such as freedom, tolerance, openness, and diversity." And also like the president, she described foreign policy in terms of a new, grandiose struggle that divided the world: "Since September 11th all the world's great powers see themselves

as falling on the same side of a profound divide between
the forces of chaos and order."

The U.S. House and Senate passed a measure that allowed the president to use military force against Iraq in
October 2002, and the next month the United Nations
Security Council passed resolution 1441 that called for
new weapons inspections in Iraq. In January 2003, Condi
published an editorial in *The New York Times* entitled
"Why We Know Iraq Is Lying," in which she summarized
Hussein's non-compliance with the new inspections. Inspectors had not been given the full access demanded by
Resolution 1441, she stated, and Iraq's "recent promises
to do better can only be seen as an attempt to stall for
time." She concluded that Iraq treated the inspections as
a game, and warned that the country "should know that
time is running out."

In the *Times* editorial, Condi also discussed an issue
that would become a hot-button crisis in the administration. Writing about the 12,200-page declaration that Iraq
had submitted to the United Nations about its weapons
program, Condi stated that the document "fails to account for or explain Iraq's efforts to get uranium from
abroad." The question of Iraq's purchase of uranium
from Niger had been investigated by the CIA and the
State Department, both of which concluded that the attempts to buy this material could not be confirmed. The
evidence was so scant that the CIA urged Great Britain to
drop references to this alleged event in a dossier it published in the fall of 2002. In spite of the CIA and State
Department's reports, President Bush announced in his
January 2003 State of the Union address that "the British
government has learned that Saddam Hussein recently
sought significant quantities of uranium from Africa."
Secretary of Defense Donald Rumsfeld repeated the

statement at a press briefing at the Pentagon the following day. Secretary of State Colin Powell, however, omitted the uranium story from his presentation to the United Nations in February 2003, explaining later that he did not think the evidence was substantial enough to announce. When the British report was found to be a forgery, Condi was forced to admit on *ABC News This Week* on June 8, 2003, that "clearly, that particular report, we learned subsequently, subsequently, was not credible."

On February 24, the Bush administration and two allies, Great Britain and Spain, attempted to make this urgency official by proposing a U.N. resolution that stated that "Iraq has failed to take the final opportunity afforded to it in resolution 1441." In response, France, Germany, and Russia drafted their own resolution calling for more inspection time. "The military option should only be a last resort," stated the draft, which argued that the conditions for using force against Iraq "are not fulfilled."

The day that both of these draft resolutions were submitted, Condi reiterated the president's call for swift action in dealing with Hussein. In a news conference at the White House, she outlined the Iraqi threat and reminded the press corps of the president's timetable. "We all continue to live under the threat of continued programs of weapons of mass destruction linked to someone who's got links to terrorism," she said. "It's time to deal with this problem. And so it should be very clear by now that when the President said, weeks, not months, he really did mean, weeks, not months." Condi also reminded the press that the president was willing to act alone: "The President has made very clear that the Security Council needs to act and that, if the Security Council is unable to act, then we will have to act with a coalition of the willing."

The proposed U.N. resolution from the United States, Great Britain, and Spain found only one supporter at the Security Council, Bulgaria, and the sponsors did not call for a vote. On March 20, 2003, the administration followed through on its plan to act alone and launched its attack on Iraq with Operation Iraqi Freedom. On April 9, U.S. forces took control of Baghdad, and millions of television viewers watched the symbolic toppling of a statue of Saddam Hussein.

The following month, President Bush announced from the aircraft carrier *Abraham Lincoln* off the coast of San Diego, California, that major combat operations in Iraq were over, and that the U.S. and its allies had prevailed. Awaiting the president's S-3 Viking jet on deck were Condi, Chief of Staff Andy Card, and White House spokesman Ari Fleischer, all of whom had flown in earlier on a less glamorous C-2 Greyhound delivery plane. Passengers on the Greyhound are seated backward in a dark interior, and jolted unexpectedly by air currents and during landing. Condi, sporting goggles and ear protectors, looked unfazed when she stepped out of the plane. She explained that it was her second trip in a Greyhound and that "the weather was better this time." The image of the president on the deck of the carrier, with a "Mission Accomplished" sign in the background, became fodder for Bush's critics in coming weeks and months as the war in Iraq continued to escalate.

Another carefully orchestrated presidential appearance in 2003 reestablished the fact that Condi is the president's closest advisor and confidante. When President Bush began planning his top-secret, morale-boosting Thanksgiving trip to Baghdad in October, Condi was one of only a handful of staff who knew about the plan, and the only staffer selected to join him. Secrecy, the number-one priority among the many challenges of safely flying the president into a war zone, went into every detail of the plan. First Lady Laura Bush was aware that the trip was a possibility, but was not told it would actually happen until a few hours before Air Force One flew. Bush's daughters learned about the trip that day, too, but Bush's parents were not informed until the president landed in Baghdad. The word from the White House was that the Bush family would spend Thanksgiving at the ranch in Crawford.

At about 8 P.M. Wednesday night, November 26, the president and Condi slipped away from the Crawford ranch in an unmarked car, both dressed casually with baseball caps pulled over their eyes. "We looked like a normal couple," Bush told reporters later. The trip on Air Force One was unusually quiet, as they were accompanied by only a small press pool and the usual security. The plane flew in radio silence with its call sign disguised from all air-traffic controllers, and all cell phones and other electronic devices were packed away in manila envelopes during the flight. Baghdad International Airport, which had been the site of a missile attack on a cargo jet just five days earlier, was blacked out when the plane approached, and Air Force One, also totally dark, was virtually invisible upon landing.

The president stunned the six hundred troops who were having Thanksgiving dinner in the mess tent at the airport, and was met with "Hoo-ah" shouts and wild, stamping applause. After a two-and-a-half-hour visit, the president, Condi, and their small pool of journalists boarded Air Force One for the flight home.

When critics charged that Bush made the dangerous trip for political gain, Condi defended the president's motivations. "Let the chips fall where they may," she said. "But for the American people, I don't care what your party, they know that the president of the United States, as commander in chief, going to see these troops is an important step."

Bush's decision to bring Condi along on this dangerous, top-secret trip revealed the enormously close working relationship they share. Bush's father developed a deep admiration for and trust in his national security advisor, Brent Scowcroft, but George W. appears to put even more confidence in his NSA. Spending so much time with the president in the White House, at Camp David and at the Crawford ranch, Condi was prompted to make a slip during a dinner party in the spring of 2004. At one point she said, "As I was telling my husb—As I was telling President Bush . . ."

Eager to uncover the facts about what the administration knew about potential terrorist attacks prior to 9/11, families of the victims pressed for an official investigation. The ten-member September 11 Commission was created by Congress in November 2002, and charged with the job of "providing the nation the most comprehensive examination of the vulnerabilities that made the attacks possible." The independent, bi-partisan commission was "intended to be unflinching in assigning blame for specific government failures."

Condi testified before the members in private sessions after the hearings were underway. In the spring of 2004, however, public opinion demanded that she testify in public, which set off a cascade of events that once again put the spotlight on her role as national security advisor. The panel unanimously called for her public appearance, but Condi refused on the grounds that the constitutional powers of the executive branch legally forbade her from doing so. "Nothing would be better, from my point of view, than to be able to testify," she stated on CBS' *60 Minutes*. "I would really like to do that," she added, "but there is an important principle here—it is a longstanding principle—that sitting national security advisors do not testify before the Congress."

The issue of Condi's public testimony were spurred by the testimony of Richard A. Clarke, a former counterterrorism official in the Bush and Clinton administrations. Clarke had recently published an exposé of the Bush administration's actions and inactions regarding al Qaeda leading up to the attacks. In *Against All Enemies: Inside America's War on Terror,* Clarke charged that the administration ignored critical intelligence about the terrorist threat and ultimately inflamed the al Qaeda cause by attacking Iraq. Clarke wrote:

> George W. Bush . . . failed to act prior to September 11 on the threat for al Qaeda despite repeated warnings and then harvested a political windfall for taking obvious yet insufficient steps after the attacks; and . . . launched an unnecessary and costly war in Iraq that strengthened the fundamentalist, radical Islamic terrorist movement worldwide.

Following his testimony before the 9/11 Commission, Clarke called for the declassification of government documents from before the attacks as well as other materials. These documents should include, he stressed, Condi's private testimony before the 9/11 Commission and correspondence that Clarke had had with her and her deputy, Stephen Hadley, while he was serving in the administration.

Pressure mounted for Condi to appear before the commission in public, and on March 30, 2004, White

House counsel Alberto R. Gonzales sent a letter to the commission agreeing to her appearance, pending two conditions. Gonzales required that Condi's testimony would not set a precedent for future commission requests for testimony by a national security advisor or any other White House official, and that the commission agree in writing that it will not request additional public testimony from any White House official, including Rice. To some observers, Condi's actions during the controversy forced the administration's hand to allow her to testify. "Rice herself weakened the administration's argument against public testimony by granting numerous interviews and stating her own desire to testify," noted one editorial. Regardless of Condi's repeated statements on television and in the press that she had nothing to hide, the administration's claim of executive privilege did not sit well with the public. Bush allowed her to testify before the political damage could go any further.

On April 8, Condi was sworn in before the 9/11 Commission, standing behind the center of a large table that faced the panel. At the beginning of her opening statement, she admitted that the United States had been slow to react to a long-developing terrorist threat before the 9/11 attacks. "The terrorists were at war with us but we were not yet at war with them," she said. She overviewed several events in history in which the United States was slow to act to looming danger, such as "the growing threat from Imperial Japan until it became all too evident at Pearl Harbor." She defended the administration's strategy on terrorism, citing the president's briefing schedule and her own meetings with intelligence officials, and outlined various initiatives such as bolstering the Treasury Department's power to track and seize terrorist assets.

The highlight of the testimony surrounded the con-

tent of an intelligence memo given to the president on
August 6, 2001, which contained information about
Osama bin Laden's plans to attack on U.S. soil. Condi
stressed that the memo did not contain new warnings
about an impending attack, but was based on "historical
information based on old reporting." She summarized the
memo as follows:

> The briefing team reviewed past intelligence re-
> porting, mostly dating from the 1990s, regarding
> possible Al Qaeda plans to attack inside the United
> States. It referred to uncorroborated reporting
> that—from 1998—that a terrorist might attempt to
> hijack a U.S. aircraft in an attempt to blackmail the
> government into releasing U.S. held terrorists who
> had participated in the 1993 World Trade Center
> bombing. This briefing item was not prompted by
> any specific threat information. And it did not raise
> the possibility that terrorists might use airplanes as
> missiles.

During the question-and-answer period, Condi
stressed that the administration did not anticipate any
strikes within the country, but was focused on terrorist activities in other parts of the world. Commission member
Richard Ben-Veniste brought the subject back to the
memo, however, to point out that its very title pointed to
a domestic attack. The sharp exchange began as follows:

> BEN-VENISTE: Isn't it a fact, Dr. Rice, that the Aug.
> 6 P.D.B. warned against possible attacks in this
> country? And I ask you whether you recall the title
> of that P.D.B.
>
> RICE: I believe the title was "Bin Laden Deter-
> mined To Attack Inside the United States." Now,
> the P.D.B. —

BEN-VENISTE: Thank you.

RICE: No, Mr. Ben-Veniste —

BEN-VENISTE: I will get into the —

RICE: I would like to finish my point here.

BEN-VENISTE: I didn't know there was a point.

RICE: Given that—you asked me whether or not it warned of attacks.

BEN-VENISTE: I asked you what the title was.

RICE: You said did it not warn of attacks. It did not warn of attacks inside the United States. It was historical information based on old reporting. There was no new threat information. And it did not, in fact, warn of any coming attacks inside the United States.

Throughout her testimony, including the heated exchange above, Condi remained calm and steady, just as she had in every other public appearance when discussing the president's controversial policy on Iraq. Viewers did not witness any attitude or behavior that contrasted with Condi's previous appearances on television talk shows. And as one reporter observed, war continued to rage in Iraq during her testimony, a reality that concerned Americans as much, if not more, than the dramatic televised hearings. "Although Rice's testimony produced no bombshells, there were plenty exploding in Iraq even as she spoke," wrote Tony Karon in *Time* magazine. "The uprising among both Sunni and Shiite Iraqis that has shaken Coalition forces there and thrown U.S. transition plans into crisis may be a more immediate concern on the minds of the American electorate than the increasingly partisan post-mortem over 9/11."

In June 2004, the 9/11 Commission released a statement that refuted the administration's argument that the terrorist threat—which president Bush had acknowledged as specifically a threat from al-Qaeda—lay in Iraq. "We have no credible evidence that Iraq and al-Qaeda co-operated on attacks against the United States," stated the report. Critics of the president's decision to go to war in Iraq found new fuel for their case in this dramatic statement. The commission's declaration supported the view of those like Scowcroft who did not believe that the war on terrorism should be fought in Iraq, but by that time the war had gone on for fifteen months. As of this writing in January 2005, American casualties in Iraq numbered 1,340, with total coalition deaths numbering 1,491.

During the presidential campaign of 2004, Condi accompanied Bush to several cities, such as a September 2 trip to Columbus in the battleground state of Ohio. In the following weeks leading up to the November 2 election, she made speeches in key states including Oregon, Washington, North Carolina, Pennsylvania, Michigan, and Florida. "The frequency and location of her speeches differ sharply from those before this election year," reported the *Washington Post*, "and appear to break with the long-standing precedent that the national security advisor try to avoid overt involvement in the presidential campaign." A *New York Times* editorial complained that Condi appeared so often "on the campaign trail that she sometimes seemed more like a press secretary than a national security advisor." Condi refuted these charges, however, stating on the National Public Radio, for example, that she had not stepped across the line in her job. "Of course not," she told Tavis Smiley. "I'm the national security advisor. I take it as part of my role to talk to the American people. We're at war. This is a time for those of us who have responsible positions to get out of Washington."

Although Condi stepped up her speech schedule during the campaign, she did not participate in political events as she had done during the 2000 campaign when she served as Bush's foreign affairs tutor. In contrast to her 2000 appearances in the "W Is for Women" campaign and as a keynote speaker at the Republican National Convention, she was absent from the 2004 convention in New York City. "By tradition and custom," explained Sean McCormick, a National Security Council spokesman, "the national security advisor does not actively participate in campaign or political events."

Two weeks after Bush won the November 2004 election, he expressed his trust in his national security advisor's competence and admiration of her qualifications by nominating Condi as his next Secretary of State. She would succeed Colin Powell, who had announced his retirement from the cabinet post.

At the White House announcement on November 16, two days after Condi's fiftieth birthday, she was nearly moved to tears by the president's proud, heartfelt description of her career and personal background. "During the last four years I've relied on her counsel, benefited from her great experience, and appreciated her sound and steady judgment," Bush said. "And now I'm honored that she has agreed to serve in my Cabinet. The Secretary of State is America's face to the world. And in Dr. Rice, the world will see the strength, the grace, and the decency of our country." Referring to Condi's childhood in Birmingham during the violent era of the Civil Rights struggle, Bush added, "Above all, Dr. Rice has a deep, abiding belief in the value and power of liberty, because she has seen freedom denied and freedom reborn."

In her remarks, Condi said that it was "humbling" to consider succeeding Colin Powell, and that she would greatly miss working with everyone in the White House. Those comments followed her words of praise for the president:

> Thank you, Mr. President. It has been an honor and a privilege to work for you these past four years, in times of crisis, decision and opportunity for our nation. Under your leadership, America is fighting and winning the war on terror. You have marshaled great coalitions that have liberated millions from tyranny, coalitions that are now helping the Iraqi and Afghan people build democracies in the heart of the Muslim world. And you have worked to widen the circle of prosperity and progress in every corner of the world.

Bush also announced that day that Condi's deputy, Stephen Hadley, would be promoted to national security advisor. Condi's nomination was part of a flurry of changes in Bush's cabinet following the election, including resignations from Commerce Secretary Don Evans, Attorney General John Ashcroft, and Homeland Security Secretary Tom Ridge.

Prior to Condi's nomination, there has been one woman (Madeleine Albright) and one black (Colin Powell) Secretary of State in American history. Several European countries weighed in on the prospects of future relations with the United States under Condi's watch at the State Department. An editorial in Germany's weekly magazine *Die Zeit* remarked that relations with the United States would probably get better because they couldn't get worse than they were in the two previous years. Eberhard Sandschneider, director of the German council on Foreign Relations, noted that Condi's background as an academic rather than as a professional politician were positives, and that her close relationship with the president would be an important change. "With Powell you never knew whether his policies would have influence with the president," Sandschneider said, "but if Ms. Rice says 'x,' you know that the president will also say 'x.'"

Writing in *The New York Times*, Richard Bernstein explained that Europe held two general views about Condi's potential influence there. "One is that she will strengthen further the hard-line views" of the neoconservatives in the administration, and the other that "her sophisticated understanding of international affairs, particularly of Russia and Germany, will prove to be both . . . sympathetic to, or at least, cognizant of, European views."

On November 19, three days after her nomination as the next secretary of state, Condi was admitted to Georgetown University Hospital in Washington, D.C., for minor surgery to treat non-cancerous, uterine fibroid tumors. She chose a low-invasive procedure, uterine fibroid embolisation, which is performed in about one-and-a-half hours under local anesthesia and involves an overnight stay. In this procedure, the surgeon injects tiny particles into the uterine artery, which block the blood supply to the tumors. Traditionally, most women who undergo treatment for this condition undergo a hysterectomy, a much more complex surgery that requires general anesthesia and a long recovery period. "Having someone like her choose [embolisation] means more women will hear about this option," said a Boston surgeon.

Embolisation has been available for about ten years, but only 13,000 to 14,000 American women choose this alternative each year, as opposed to approximately 200,000 women who choose to have a hysterectomy. "Dr. Jacob Cynamon, director of interventional radiology at Montefiore Medical Center in the Bronx, said many patients say their gynecologists did not present the option of the less invasive procedure," reported New York *Newsday*. According to Cynamon, hysterectomies have long been the "bread and butter" of gynecologists.

Condi was released the day after the procedure and returned to work the following Monday. Her high profile brought this medical topic to the front pages of newspapers around the world, revealing the powerful effect that a world figure can have on a single issue.

Condi will have many options when she finishes her service in the White House. Some speculate that she's got all the attributes of a successful presidential candidate. "The first viable female candidate for president, whatever her party, must demonstrate deep military knowledge to win the confidence of the electorate," said social scientist Camille Paglia. She described a frequently repeated chorus that broke out whenever a group of women caught a glimpse of Condi on TV—"That woman should be president!"

In California, polls conducted in the summer of 2002 indicated she was a top pick as the Republican candidate for governor. Some of her closest colleagues see her in international banking or consulting, fields she toyed with when she left Stanford in 1999. There's always the NFL, which she would love to run one day. Her former job as provost of Stanford gives her perfect entrée to the presidency of a major university. And the door to Stanford's political science department, where she has tenure, is always open. Most of those options could also include a return to corporate boards, all of which she left when she was appointed national security advisor.

Condi will cross that bridge when she comes to it. "I am not a very good long-term planner," she said. "I tend to take things on one at a time and worry about getting that job done and doing a good job at that." Whatever she decides, she will undoubtedly delve into it with the same enthusiasm and drive with which she has approached everything else. "I'd like to think of myself as passionate about life," she said. "I'm certainly passionate about music and I'm passionate about my work, passionate about family and about my faith."

Her relatives and friends in Birmingham, including everyone at the church Granddaddy Rice founded nearly sixty years ago, are behind her every step of the way. "We look at her as one of our own who has gone on to high service because of her ability," said Reverend Jones. "We pray for her every day."

Condi's appointment as NSA was a monumental stride for both women and blacks, coming nine years after Carol Moseley-Braun became the first black woman elected to the U.S. Senate. With the scarcity of blacks in upper levels of foreign policy (Colin Powell was the first black NSA, appointed by President Reagan), her rise to this position was as important as Marian Anderson becoming the first black to become a regular member of an American opera company and Jackie Robinson breaking the color barrier in baseball. The NAACP recognized her achievement in 2002 by giving her that year's President's Award. This honor recognizes those who, through leadership or by example, have promoted the cause of minorities. According to then–NAACP President

Kweisi Mfume, Condi has been breaking new ground her entire life. "There were no role models for her to follow," he said, "because there was no one like Condoleezza Rice."

Condi's career has come a long way from her first assistant professorship, in which she gave students insights into the Soviet Union during the Cold War. In the first Bush administration she stood at the front lines of policy-making, helping the president and the National Security Council staff outline new policies toward the newly mapped regions of Europe. In the first term of George W. Bush's administration, she was at the forefront of policy-making once again, providing the president with the Security Council's views—and her own, if asked—on the war on terrorism and other international crises. Rather than researching political history, she was creating it.

Her job as NSA was gratifying on many levels, allowing her to utilize her expertise in her chosen field in the most exciting capacity possible. As a member of the president's staff she performed a public service, something that her parents practiced in many ways and ingrained in her as a virtue. And she traveled throughout the world, often finding common threads that bind people to each other. During a visit to the Holocaust Museum in Jerusalem, for example, she was moved by a photograph of a well-dressed, impeccably groomed couple who contrasted with the bleak surroundings of their Warsaw ghetto. She heard others comment that it seemed odd for the couple to pay so much attention to their appearance when their lives were at stake. "I had a different reaction," said Condi. "I said immediately, 'I understand that photograph. These people are saying, I'm still in control, I still have my dignity.' They are saying, 'You can take everything from us, including life itself. But you cannot take away our pride.'" In that couple, Condi saw the pride and dignity with which her mother always dressed in Birmingham, crisp and tailored and beautiful.

Her journeys throughout the world have given her greater appreciation for her own country, in spite of its faults and snail-paced social progress. "As I travel with [President Bush] around the world and as we meet with leaders from around the world," she told an audience in 2002, "I see America through other people's eyes. I see a country that still struggles with the true meaning of multiethnic democracy, that still struggles with how to accommodate, and indeed, how to celebrate diversity. But it's a country that is admired because . . . it does struggle to become better. It is not perfect but it is a long, long way from where we were."

She may be far from Titusville on the southwest side of Birmingham, but Condi is not a long way from who she was as an individual when she was growing up there. She is still working hard (and probably not playing enough), still taking her piano seriously (even though summer music workshops in Montana are canceled or cut short by White House obligations), still utterly self-confident and optimistic that things are always moving forward and getting better (she *did* get a job inside the White House that was closed to her when she was ten), and still strong in her faith. She did not have the same challenges as less-privileged black children of Birmingham, but she had her share of the struggle. The darkness of that time has been a springboard in her life, propelling her to the farthest reaches of her talents and intellect. Like her father before her, she understands that without a struggle there would be no incentive to grow. And like three generations of Rices and Rays before her, she finds glory in that revelation:

We do not choose our circumstances or trials, but we do choose how we respond to them. Too often when all is well, we slip into the false joy and satisfaction of the material and a complacent pride and faith in ourselves. Yet it is through struggle that we find redemption and self-knowledge. This is what the slaves of Exodus learned. And it is what slaves in America meant when they sang: "Nobody knows the trouble I've seen—Glory Hallelujah!"

When Condi's parents instilled in her the belief that she could one day be president of the United States, they prepared her to become a person who could make a mark on the world. Did John Rice ever imagine that his "little star" would one day be dubbed "the most powerful woman in the world," or did Angelena Rice foresee that her musical prodigy would play at the Kennedy Center, introduced by the First Lady of the United States? They may not have imagined these specific events, but John and Angelena Rice did not put limits on their own dreams, nor on those of their daughter.

In fifty years, Condi has become a Renaissance woman in the truest sense of the word, accomplished in more than one field as artist and academic, writer and university provost, foreign policy czarina and presidential advisor. There is undoubtedly much more to come from her, and the world is watching.

APPENDIX I

National Security Advisors, 1950–2005

Stephen Hadley	2005–
Condoleezza Rice	2001–2005
Samuel L. Berger	1997–2001
W. Anthony Lake	1993–1997
Brent Scowcroft	1989–1993
Colin L. Powell	1987–1989
Frank C. Carlucci	1986–1987
John M. Poindexter	1985–1986
Robert C. McFarlane	1983–1985
William P. Clark	1982–1983
Richard V. Allen	1981–1982
Zbigniew Brzezinski	1977–1981
Brent Scowcroft	1975–1977
Henry A. Kissinger	1968–1975
Walt W. Rostow	1966–1968
McGeorge Bundy	1961–1966
Gordon Gray	1958–1961
Robert Cutler	1957–1958
Dillon Anderson	1955–1956
Robert Cutler	1953–1955
James L. Lay*	1950–1953
Sidney Souers*	1947–1949

*Executive Secretary of the National Security Council

APPENDIX II

Major Events in the Life of Condoleezza Rice

November 14, 1954	Born in Birmingham, Alabama
1965	First black student to attend music classes at Birmingham Southern Conservatory of Music
1969	Moves to Denver, Colorado, and attends an integrated school for the first time
1971	Graduates from high school; finishes first year of university
1974	Graduates *cum laude* from the University of Denver
1975	Receives M.A. in government from the University of Notre Dame
1981	Receives Ph.D. in international studies from the University of Denver
1981	Assistant professor of political science at Stanford University

1984	Publishes *Uncertain Allegiance: The Soviet Union and the Czechoslovak Army, 1948-1963* (Princeton University Press)
1986	Publishes *The Gorbachev Era* (with Alexander Dallin; Stanford Alumni Press)
1986–1987	Special assistant to the director–Joint Chiefs of Staff position at the Pentagon through Council on Foreign Relations Fellowship
1987	Promoted to associate professor of political science at Stanford
1989–1991	Bush administration posts as director of Soviet and East European affairs, special assistant to the president for national security affairs, and senior director for Soviet affairs at the National Security Council
1991	Joins Boards of Directors at Chevron, TransAmerica Corporation, Hewlett-Packard
1992	Gives address at the Republican National Convention
May 1993	Promoted to full professor at Stanford
September 1993	Named provost of Stanford University
1994	Elected to the Board of Trustees at the University of Notre Dame
1995	Publishes *Germany Unified and Europe Transformed: A Study in Statecraft* (with Philip Zelikow; Harvard University Press)

1995	Joins Board of Directors at J. P. Morgan
1999	Joins Board of Directors at Charles Schwab
July 1999	Steps down as provost of Stanford; foreign policy advisor for George W. Bush's presidential campaign
2000	Gives address at the Republican National Convention
December 2000	Named national security advisor by President-elect George W. Bush
January 2001	Sworn in as national security advisor
April 2004	Testifies before 9/11 Commission
January 2005	Sworn in as Secretary of State

SOURCES

ARTICLES

"Academic Style: Stanford's New Provost Brings a Different Perspective to Campus," *Chicago Tribune*, August 15, 1993

"Academics Start to Line up Behind Presidential Candidates," *Chronicle of Higher Education*, May 28, 1999

"Adviser Condi Rice," *Denver Post*, August 2, 2000

AFRO-American Almanac web site (toptags.com/aama/docs/jcrow.htm)

"American Dream Must be Delivered to All People, Rice says," Stanford University *Campus Report*, June 19, 1985

"August 1: Bush's Secret Weapon," ABCnews.com web site, August 1, 2000 (abcnews.go.com)

"Aunt G.'s Favorite Niece: Condoleezza Rice," *Virginian-Pilot*, March 14, 2002

"Beyond the ABM Treaty," *The Wall Street Journal*, June 14, 2002

"Bush Advisor Speaks of Faith's Deep Roots," *Denver Post*, May 5, 2000

"Bush Campaign Turns to Big Gun—His Mom Barbara Bush Leads W is for Women Tour," *Baltimore Sun*, October 20, 2000

"Bush, Gorbachev Hold Malta Shipboard Summit," *World News Digest*, December 8, 1989

"Bush Look, The," Salon.com, February 28, 2001 (www.salon.com)

"Bush on a Revenge Mission," *The Independent* (London), April 26, 2003

"Bush's Foreign Policy Guru," ABCnews.com web site (abcnews.go.com)

"Bush's Foreign Policy Tutor," *The New York Times*, June 16, 2000

"Bush's Secret Weapon," Salon.com, March 20, 2000 (www.salon.com)

"Bush's Tutor and Disciple—Condoleezza Rice," *New York Times*, November 17, 2004

"Bush's 'Vulcans' Iron Out Foreign Policy," *Birmingham News*, June 30, 2000

"Can't Testify, Condi Insists," *Daily News*, March 29, 2004

"Casper Selects Condoleezza Rice to be Next Stanford Provost," Stanford University News Service press release, May 19, 1993

"Chevron redubs ship named for Bush aide," *San Francisco Chronicle*, May 5, 2001

College Acquaintance Recruitment Experience (CARE) brochure, University of Denver

"Commander in Chief's Visit Sets Aircraft Carrier's Crew Abuzz, *Seattle Post-Intelligencer*, May 2, 2003, (seattlepi.nwsource.com/local/120279_lincolnsub.html)

"Compulsion to Achieve," *The New York Times*, December 18, 2000

"Condi Rice a rare woman in world affairs," *Denver Rocky Mountain News*, December 18, 2000

"Condi Rice Can't Lose," *Time*, September 20, 1999

"'Condi' Rice: Presbyterian with faith, political mettle," *The Presbyterian Layman*, November 22, 2000

"Condoleezza Rice," BusinessWeek online, February 11, 2002 (www.businessweek.com)

"Condoleezza Rice: Defying the Stereotypes," *Birmingham News*, January 22, 2001

"Condoleezza Rice: George W.'s Realist," *World Policy Journal*, Winter 1999

"Condoleezza Rice Farewell," *Stanford Report*, June 16, 1999

"Condoleezza Rice Interview," About.com web site (uspolitics.about.com)

"Connor Behind Bill Banning 'Rides,'" *Birmingham Post-Herald*, August 25, 1961

"Containment," *New Republic*, February 5, 2001

"Contributing to CREES," Center for Russian and Eastern
      European Studies web site
      (www.stanford.edu/dept/CREES/giving.html)

"Dean's Awards for Distinguished Teaching, 1992–93," Stanford
      University News Service, undated press release

"Dogs, Water Used to Halt Negro March," *Montgomery Advertiser*,
      May 4, 1963

"Don't Attack Saddam," *Wall Street Journal*, August 15, 2002,
      (www.opinionjournal.com/forms/printThis.html?id=11000
      2133)

"Dr. Condoleezza Rice Discusses President's National Security
      Strategy," October 1, 2002, White House online,
      (www.whitehouse.gov/news/releases/2002/10/print/200210
      01-6.html)

"Dr. Condoleezza Rice Talks About her Career as Assistant to
      the President for National Security Affairs," National
      Public Radio, "Tavis Smiley," October 28, 2004

"Dream Job for Rice: N.F.L. Commissioner," *The New York Times*,
      April 17, 2002

"Dream's Focus Fundamental for Leadership in 21st Century," edi-
      torial by Condoleezza Rice, *Birmingham News*, April 23, 2000

"Dysgenics, Geneticity, Raceology" by William Shockley, *Phi
      Delta Kappan*, January 1972

"End of the Cold War: Challenge for U.S. Policy," *The Common-
      wealth*, December 6, 1991

"Excerpts from White House Letter on Rice's Testimony," *New
      York Times*, March 31, 2004

Fifty Years in the Gospel Ministry, by T. G. Goud, online text at
      University of North Carolina at Chapel Hill Libraries
      "Documenting the American South"
      (docsouth.unc.edu/church/steward/steward.html)

"For Condoleezza Rice, National Security by Day and Brahms by
      Night," *The Wall Street Journal*, April 24, 2002

"For Rice, A Daunting Challenge Ahead," *Washington Post*, De-
      cember 18, 2000

"Forces: U.S. & Coalition/Casualties," CNN.com, December 8, 2004,
      (www.cnn.com/SPECIALS/2003/iraq/forces/casualties/)

"Fox News Sunday" August 27, 2000, online transcript from eMe-
    diaMillWorks

"The Friends of George," *New York Times*, November 17, 2004

"From 'Not College Material' to Stanford's No. 2 Job," *The New
    York Times*, June 23, 1993

"From 'Splendid Isolation' to 'Fruitful Cooperation': The Harri-
    man Institute in the Post-Soviet Era," *Columbia Magazine*,
    Summer 1996

"Gender Politics, " Chicagomag.com web site (chicagomag.com)

"GOP Star to Skip Convention," *Washington Post*, August 7, 2004

"Gorbachev Era, The," *The Commonwealth*, June 13, 1988

"Honored to Have the Chance," *The Boston Globe*, December 21,
    2000

"How Many Heads Does the Prime Minister Have?" *New Presence:
    The Prague Journal of Central European Affairs*, Spring 2002

"How White House Planners Kept High-risk Journey Secret to
    the End," *Ottawa Citizen*, November 28, 2003

"In Race for White House, the 'Cult of Condi' Plays Growing
    Role," *Los Angeles Times*, May 28, 2000

"Iraq: US/UK/Spain Draft Resolution," February 24, 2003,"
    posted on The United States Mission to the European
    Union site, (www.useu.be/Categories/GlobalAffairs/Iraq/
    Feb2403ResolutionIraq.html).

"Is There Anything This Woman Can't Do?," *George* magazine,
    June 2000

"Josef Korbel's Enduring Foreign Policy Legacy," *Washington Post*,
    December 28, 2000

"Leaders for a New Millennium," *Financial Times*, December 28, 1995

"Lessons of Might and Right," *Washington Post*, September 9, 2001

"Mad About Music," transcript of the WNYC radio program aired
    on September 7, 2001

"Memorandum Submitted by France, Germany & Russia on Iraq
    Weapons Inspections," February 24, 2003, posted on C-
    Span.org, (c-span.org/resources/fyi/frenchresolution. asp)

"Messenger to Moscow," *Time*, August 6, 2001

Minutes of Stanford University's Senate of the Academic Council,
    May 13, 1999 (www.stanford.edu)

"'Moral case' for deposing Saddam," BBC News online, August 15, 2002, (news.bbc.co.uk/1/hi/world/americas/2193426.stm)

"National Security Advisor Condoleezza Rice Chosen for Special NAACP Image Award," Associated Press web site, February 24, 2002 (http://wire.ap.org)

Naval War College announcement posted on web site (nwc.navy.mil)

"New Army for a New State, A," *Time*, September 16, 1991

"New Faces of U.S. to the World, The," *Christian Science Monitor*, December 18, 2000

"New Leadership on National Security," speech by George W. Bush, posted on the Nuclear Age Peace Foundation web site May 23, 2000 (nuclearfiles.org/docs/2000/0523newleadershipbush.html)

"Oprah Talks to Condoleezza Rice," *O: The Oprah Magazine*, February 2002

"Overview of the Enemy: Staff Statement No. 15," National Commission on Terrorist Attacks on the United States, June 16, 2004, (www.9-11commission.gov/staff_statements/index.htm)

"Partnership: A History of the *Apollo-Soyuz* Test Project, The," NASA web site (hq.nasa.gov/office/pao/History)

"People in the News Profile: Condoleezza Rice," CNN.com web site (www.cnn.com/CNN/programs/people/shows/rice/profile.html)

"Perspectives," *Newsweek*, May 3, 2004, as posted on MSNBC.com, (msnbc.msn.com/id/4824766/)

"Pick for National Security Adviser has DU Ties," *Denver Rocky Mountain News*, December 17, 2000

"Political Punch in a Package of Charm," *Financial Times*, February 26, 2000

"President Discusses Growing Danger Posed by Saddam Hussein's Regime," September 14, 2002, White House online, (www.whitehouse.gov/news/releases/2002/09/)

"President Nominates Condoleezza Rice as Secretary of State," White House press release, November 16, 2004, (www.whitehouse.gov/news/releases/2004/11/20041116-3.html)

"President's Prodigy, The," *Vogue*, October 2001

"President's Remarks to the Nation," September 11, 2002, White House online, (www.whitehouse.gov/news/releases/2002/09/)

"Press Briefing by Dr. Condoleezza Rice," February 24, 2003, White House online, (www.whitehouse.gov/news/releases/2003/02/20030224-14.html)

"Press Conference by Vice President Dick Cheney," White House online, March 17, 2002, (www.whitehouse.gov/vicepresident/news-speeches/speeches/vp20020317.html)

"Profile: Condoleezza Rice," BBC News Online, September 25, 2001 (news.bbc.co.uk)

"Promoting the National Interest," *Foreign Affairs* magazine, January/February 2000

"Remarks by the National Security Advisor, Condoleezza Rice, to the Conservative Political Action Conference, February 1, 2002, as posted on the NATO web site, February 1, 2002 (nato.int)

"Report of the Federal Advisory Committee on Gender-Integrated Training and Related Issues to the Secretary of Defense," December 16,1997 (www.defenselink.mil/pubs/git/report.html)

"Rice: A Russophile with Bush's Ear," MSNBC web site (www.msnbc.com)

"Rice Appointed to Urban Renewal Authority," *Intermountain Jewish News*, May 26, 1978

"Rice called a Good Fit for Foreign Policy Post," USATODAY.com web site, December 18, 2000 (www.usatoday.com)

"Rice Hitting the Road to Speak," *Washington Post*, October 20, 2004

"Rice Holds the Line," *Time*, April 8, 2004, online edition, (www.time.com/time/nation/article/0%2C8599%2C609491%2C00.html)

"Rice on Front Lines as Adviser to Bush," *The New York Times*, August 16, 2001

"Rice on Students, Tough Decisions and her Oil Tanker," *Stanford Magazine*, May/June 1999

"Rice Quits Post," *Stanford Daily*, March 14, 1991

"Rice Says Bush, Putin 'Moved Forward,'" U.S. Department of State International Information Programs web site, July 22, 2001 (usinfo.state.gov/topical/pol/arms/stories/01072209.htm)

"Rice Shapes Bush's View of the World," Cox Newspapers On-line, November 15, 2001 (coxnews.com)

"Rice to Step Down in June after Six Years as Provost," *Stanford Report*, December 9, 1998

"Rice Turns her Focus to Family," *Birmingham News*, March 19, 2001

"Rice: War Stories No Teaching Tool, But Role Playing Works," Stanford University *Campus Report*, October 28, 1998

"Russia's Bold Challenge," *Time*, January 14, 1980

"Sawislak to appeal denial of tenure to Advisory Board," *Stanford Report*, April 1, 1998

"See George. See George Learn Foreign Policy," *Newsweek*, June 18, 2001

"Sharon smitten with Rice," *Denver Post*, February 5, 2001

"Soviets Face Hard Choices in Arms Control, Rice Says," Stanford University News Service, December 2, 1983

"Stanford Cuts Budget Third Straight Year," *San Francisco Chronicle*, November 11, 1993

"Stanford Provost Condoleezza Rice Appointed Hoover Senior Fellow," *Hoover Institution Newsletter*, Summer 1999

Stanford University *Campus Report*, April 1, 1992

Stanford University News Service press release, December 2, 1983

Stanford University News Service press release, June 18, 1984

Stanford University News Service press release, May 10, 1996

"Star in Waiting," *National Review*, August 30, 1999

"State Black Codes," National Parks Service web site (www.nps.gov/malu/documents/jim_crow_laws.htm)

"Status of Women in International Affairs Professions, The," Women's Foreign Policy Group web site (wfpg.org)

"Steely Southerner, A," *Newsweek*, August 6, 2001

"Stillman College: A Glance at the Past," Stillman College Archives, 1974

"Take Small Classes, Experiment, College Frosh Told," Stanford News Service bulletin, October 1993

"Testimony of Condoleezza Rice Before 9/11 Commission," *New York Times*, April 8, 2004, transcript posted on nytimes.com,

(www.nytimes.com/2004/04/08/politics/ 08RICE-TEXT.html?ex=1102050000&en=787702147 cceca23&ei=5070)

"Thanksgiving Surprise Raises Stakes for Bush," *Seattle Times*, November 29, 2003

"There IS a Doctor in the House," *In the Black*, Summer 2001

"Timeline of the Iraq Uranium Allegations," ABC News online, (abcnews.go.com/International/story?id=79455)

Title 5 U.S. Code 3331, Oath of Office, U.S. Code as of 01/23/01

"To Europeans, Rice Brings Mitigated Hope of Harmony," *New York Times*, November 20, 2004

"Transform America, One by One," editorial by Condoleezza Rice, *Birmingham News*, May 22, 1994

University of Denver *Clarion*, October 9, 1972

University of Denver Graduate School of International Studies brochure

"Uphill Battle to Improve Status of Women on the Faculty," Stanford University News Service press release, March 12, 1997

"U.S. Intelligence and the End of the Cold War," a speech given by George Bush at Texas A&M on November 19, 1999

"Uterine Fibroid Surgery; Rice to Undergo Procedure," *Newsday*, November 19, 2004

"Velvet-glove Forcefulness," *Stanford Report*, June 9, 1999

Washington's Famous Atlanta Address of 1895, as posted on the Booker T. Washington National Monument web site (nps.gov/bowa/tuskin.html)

"Welcome Back, Professor Rice," REES Center for Russian & East European Studies Newsletter, Spring 1991

"West Wing Story: America's Favorite Bushie," *Newsweek*, August 1, 2001

"The White House Blinks," *Buffalo News*, March 31, 2004

"Why We Know Iraq Is Lying," *New York Times*, January 23, 2003

"The World's 100 Most Powerful Women," *Forbes*, August 20, 2004, (www.forbes.com/2004/08/18/04powomland.html)

BOOKS

Blackman, Ann, *Seasons of Her Life: A Biography of Madeleine Korbel Albright* (New York: Scribners, 1998)

Bush, George, *All the Best, George Bush: My Life and Other Writings* (New York: Scribners, 1999)

Bush, George and Brent Scowcroft, *A World Transformed* (New York: Knopf, 1998)

Clarke, Richard A., *Against All Enemies* (New York: Free Press, 2004)

Dobbs, Michael, *Madeleine Albright: Twentieth Century Odyssey* (New York: Holt, 1999)

Eskew, Glenn T., *But for Birmingham* (Chapel Hill: University of North Carolina Press, 1997)

Kean, Thomas H. and Lee H. Hamilton, *The 9/11 Report* (New York: St. Martin's Press, August 2004)

Kegley, Charles W. and Eugene Wittkopf, *American Foreign Policy* (New York: St. Martin's Press, 1996)

Montview Centennial Book Committee, *The Spirit of Montview: 1902–2002*, 2001

Morgenthau, Hans, *Politics Among Nations: The Struggle for Peace and Power* (New York: WCB/McGraw-Hill, 1985)

Parmet, Herbert S., *George Bush: The Life of a Lone Star Yankee* (New Brunswick: Transaction Publishers, 2001)

Prados, John, *Keepers of the Keys: A History of the National Security Council from Truman to Bush* (New York: Morrow, 1991)

Rice, Condoleezza, *The Soviet Union and the Czechoslovak Army, 1948–1983* (Princeton: Princeton University Press, 1984)

Rosenthal, Joel H., *Righteous Realists* (Baton Rouge: Louisiana State University Press, 1991)

Rotundo, Anthony E., *American Manhood: Transformations in Masculinity from the Revolution to the Modern Era* (New York: Basic Books, 1994)

White, Deborah Gray, *Ar'n't I a Woman? Female Slaves in the Plantation South* (New York: Norton, 1999)

Zelikow, Philip and Condoleezza Rice, *Germany Unified and Europe Transformed: A Study in Statecraft* (Cambridge: Harvard University Press, 1997)

INTERVIEWS

George Barth
Paul Brest
George Brinkley
Albert Cannella
Deborah Carson
Margaret Cheatham
Jim Copland
Jack Davis
John Ferejohn
Karen Feste
Jason Galie
Dmitri Gerasamenko
Rev. Richard Hutchison

Rev. William Jones
Pam King
Robby Laitos
Gail Lapidus
Mark Wateska
Sr. Sylvia Pautler
John Raisian
Clara Bailey Rice
Betty Richardson
Therese Saracino
Juliemma Smith
Darcy Taylor
Margaret and Russ Wehner

NOTES

vi *"Henry, sorry to tell you this . . ."* "The Status of Women in International Affairs Professions," Women's Foreign Policy Group web site (wfpg.org)

PRELUDE

1 *"education evangelists"* "Lessons of Might and Right," *Washington Post*, September 9, 2001

1 *"Daddy, I'm barred out of there now . . ."* "Is There Anything This Woman Can't Do?" *George* magazine, June 2000

2 *"rock-star big . . ."* "Star in Waiting," *National Review*, August 30, 1999

3 *"She is, all agree, an immensely appealing person . . ."* Ibid.

3 *"Condi is one of those happy-go-lucky kinds of people . . ."* Interview with Karen Feste

3 *"I'm a really religious person . . ."* "Oprah Talks to Condoleezza Rice," *O: The Oprah Magazine*, February 2002

3 *"I think I'm above average . . ."* Ibid.

One: COACHING THE CANDIDATE

5 *"The presidency is not just . . ."* "Condi Rice Can't Lose," *Time*, September 20, 1999

6 *"Here was this slip of a girl . . ."* "Condoleezza Rice: George W.'s Realist," *World Policy Journal*, Winter 1999

6 *"One of my first phone calls . . ."* Ibid.

For further information on the book titles, please see the Sources section on page 245.

7 *"tells me everything I know about the Soviet Union"* "Rice: A Russophile with Bush's Ear," MSNBC web site (www.msnbc.com)

7 *"Some of the most dramatic and epochal events . . ."* *A World Transformed*, by George Bush and Brent Scowcroft

8 *"Governor Bush was very impressed"* "Bush's Foreign Policy Tutor," *The New York Times*, June 16, 2000

8 *"He's really smart—and he's also disciplined . . ."* "Oprah Talks to Condoleezza Rice," *O: The Oprah Magazine*, February 2002

9 *"I don't get seasick . . ."* "Bush's Secret Weapon," Salon.com, March 20, 2000 (www.salon.com)

9 *"What about relations with Russia . . ."* Ibid.

10 *"When we talked about it . . ."* Interview with Deborah Carson

10 *"I like to be around her . . ."* "Bush's Foreign Policy Tutor," *The New York Times*, June 16, 2000

11 *"a close confidant . . ."* "Compulsion to Achieve," *The New York Times*, December 18, 2000

11 *"I've respected him from the first time we talked . . ."* "Oprah Talks to Condoleezza Rice," *O: The Oprah Magazine*, February 2002

11 *"I grew up right there in Birmingham with Vulcan . . ."* "Bush's 'Vulcans' Iron Out Foreign Policy," *Birmingham News*, June 30, 2000

12 *"I don't try to do it all myself . . ."* Ibid.

12 *"can explain to me foreign policy matters . . ."* "Compulsion to Achieve," *The New York Times*, December 18, 2000

12 *"She has an extraordinary ability to be clear,"* "The President's Prodigy," *Vogue*, October 2001

12 *"One of the things that is appealing . . ."* Ibid.

12 *"She is a novel commodity . . ."* "People in the News Profile: Condoleezza Rice," CNN.com web site (www.cnn.com/CNN/programs/people/shows/rice/profile.html)

13 *"I may not be able to tell you exactly . . ."* "Condoleezza Rice: George W.'s Realist," *World Policy Journal*, Winter 1999

13 *"As an executive . . ."* "Academics Start to Line up Behind Presidential Candidates," *Chronicle of Higher Education*, May 28, 1999

14 *"Governor Bush has not spent . . ."* "Condi Rice Can't Lose," *Time*, September 20, 1999

14 *"I've been pressed to understand . . ."* "Compulsion to Achieve," *The New York Times*, December 18, 2000

15 *"America must build effective missile defenses . . ."* "New Leadership on National Security," speech by George W. Bush, posted on the Nuclear Age Peace Foundation web site May 23, 2000 (nuclearfiles.org/docs/2000/0523newleadershipbush.html)

16 *"He's always been surrounded by strong, smart women . . ."* "Bush Campaign Turns to Big Gun—His Mom Barbara Bush Leads W is for Women Tour," *Baltimore Sun*, October 20, 2000

17 *"George W. Bush . . ."* Rice's Speech at the Republican National Convention, August 1, 2000

17 *"Anybody who really knows me . . ."* "Condoleezza Rice Interview," About.com web site (uspolitics.about.com)

17 *"I actually think . . ."* "Dream Job for Rice: N.F.L. Commissioner," *The New York Times*, April 17, 2002

18 *"'You make me sound like a tyrant!' . . ."* "Compulsion to Achieve," *The New York Times*, December 18, 2000

18 *"She's got this quiet demeanor . . ."* "The President's Prodigy," *Vogue*, October 2001

18 *"both very upbeat and very down to business . . ."* Interview with Paul Brest

19 *"I am a very deeply religious person . . ."* "The President's Prodigy, *Vogue*, October 2001

19 *"Dr. Rice is not only . . ."* "Rice called a Good Fit for Foreign Policy Post," USATODAY.com website, December 18, 2000 (www.usatoday.com)

20 *"This is an extraordinary time . . ."* "Compulsion to Achieve," *The New York Times*, December 18, 2000

20 *"I, Condoleezza . . ."* Title 5 U.S. Code 3331, Oath of Office, U.S. Code as of 01/23/01

21 *"Advisors such as Rice and Kissinger . . ."* "How Many Heads Does the Prime Minister Have?" *New Presence: The Prague Journal of Central European Affairs*, Spring 2002

21 *"I will remember the sound advice . . ."* All the Best, George Bush: My Life and Other Writings, by George Bush

22 *"one of the single most important positions . . ." Keepers of the Keys: A History of the National Security Council from Truman to Bush,* by John Prados

Two: AN AMERICAN LEGACY

23 *"The multiethnic part [of American society] . . ."* "Dream's Focus Fundamental for Leadership in 21st Century," editorial by Condoleezza Rice, *Birmingham News*, April 23, 2000

24 *It could be the opening moments . . .* "Condoleezza Rice: Defying the Stereotypes," *Birmingham News*, January 22, 2001

25 *"Knowledge must be acquired . . ."* Fifty Years in the Gospel Ministry, by T. G. Goud, online text at University of North Carolina at Chapel Hill Libraries "Documenting the American South" (docsouth.unc.edu/church/ steward/steward.html)

25 *"Around 1918 . . ."* Rice's speech at the Republican National Convention, August 1, 2000

26 *"My grandfather asked . . ."* "The President's Prodigy," *Vogue*, October 2001

26 *"My family has been Presbyterian . . ."* Ibid.

27 *"I can see him even now . . ."* "Lessons of Might and Right," *Washington Post*, September 9, 2001

27 *"He really was a person who believed . . ."* "Rice Turns her Focus to Family," *Birmingham News*, March 19, 2001

27 *Strong parallels run between Condi's paternal . . .* "Lessons of Might and Right," *Washington Post*, September 9, 2001

28 *"civilizing agent . . ."* Washington's Famous Atlanta Address of 1895, as posted on the Booker T. Washington National Monument web site (nps.gov/bowa/tuskin.html)

28 *"habits of thrift . . ."* Ibid.

28 *"Albert Ray worked three jobs . . ."* "Transform America, One by One," editorial by Condoleezza Rice, *Birmingham News*, May 22, 1994

29 *"As a matter of fact . . ."* "Lessons of Might and Right," *Washington Post*, September 9, 2001

29 The term Jim Crow . . . AFRO-American Almanac web site (toptags.com/aama/docs/jcrow.htm)

30 *Nurses: No person or corporation . . .* "State Black Codes National Parks Service," web site (www.nps.gov/malu/documents/jim_crow_laws.htm)

31 *"Always remember . . ."* "Lessons of Might and Right," *Washington Post*, September 9, 2001

31 *"They had broken the code . . ."* Ibid.

31 *"If you take the time to learn . . ."* "Transform America, One by One," editorial by Condoleezza Rice, *Birmingham News*, May 22, 1994

32 *"Our grandfathers had this indomitable outlook . . ."* Ibid.

33 *"Dr. Love was absolutely committed . . ."* Interview with Betty Richardson

34 *"Angelena was very beautiful . . ."* "The President's Prodigy," *Vogue*, October 2001

34 *"the very picture . . ."* "Star in Waiting," *National Review*, August 30, 1999

34 *"So I should have . . ."* "Political Punch in a Package of Charm," *Financial Times*, February 26, 2000

34 *"I don't know too many American families . . ."* "People in the News Profile: Condoleezza Rice," CNN.com web site (www. cnn.com/CNN/programs/people/shows/rice/profile.html)

34 *"They wanted the world . . ."* Ibid.

Three: TWICE AS GOOD

36 *"My parents . . ."* "Profile: Condoleezza Rice," BBC News Online, September 25, 2001 (news.bbc.co.uk)

37 *"They simply ignored . . ."* "People in the News Profile: Condoleezza Rice," CNN.com web site (www.cnn.com/CNN/programs/people/shows/rice/profile.html)

37 *"I had parents who gave me . . ."* "The President's Prodigy," *Vogue*, October 2001

37 *"It was a very controlled . . ."* "A Steely Southerner," *Newsweek*, August 6, 2001

38 *"My mother played . . ."* "Mad About Music," transcript of the WNYC radio program aired on September 7, 2001

38 *"So she said . . ."* Ibid.

38 *"Condi's always been so focused . . ."* "Aunt G.'s Favorite Niece: Condoleezza Rice," *Virginian-Pilot*, March 14, 2002

39 *"They didn't play . . ."* Interview with Juliemma Smith

39 *"Condi learned how . . ."* Ibid.

39 *"My mother was stunningly beautiful . . ."* "Honored to Have the Chance," *Boston Globe*, December 21, 2000

40 *"My sister always knew that . . ."* "Aunt G.'s Favorite Niece: Condoleezza Rice," *Virginian-Pilot*, March 14, 2002

40 *"I knew my baby . . ."* Ibid.

41 *"waiting for what seemed like hours . . ."* "Lessons of Might and Right," *Washington Post*, September 9, 2001

41 *"[She] wasn't an outdoors child . . ."* Ibid.

41 *"What in the world . . ."* "Condoleezza Rice: Defying the Stereotypes," *Birmingham News*, January 22, 2001

41 *"Condi doesn't belong to us . . ."* "Honored to Have the Chance," *Boston Globe*, December 21, 2000

42 *"I'm waiting for my instructions . . ."* "A Steely Southerner," *Newsweek*, August 6, 2001

42 *"John and Angelena were the perfect parents . . ."* "There IS a Doctor in the House," *In the Black*, Summer 2001

42 *"I remember when I was about ten . . ."* "Mad About Music," transcript of the WNYC radio program aired on September 7, 2001

42 *"I think I was the first black student . . ."* Ibid.

43 *"I grew up in a family in which . . ."* "Compulsion to Achieve," *The New York Times*, December 18, 2000

43 *"It wasn't as if someone said . . ."* "A Steely Southerner," *Newsweek*, August 6, 2001

43 *"My parents were very strategic . . ."* "Lessons of Might and Right," *Washington Post*, September 9, 2001

44 *"I remember the woman standing there . . ."* Ibid.

44 *"She just could not understand"* "Condoleezza Rice: Defying the Stereotypes," *Birmingham News*, January 22, 2001

45 *"I don't remember . . ."* "Lessons of Might and Right," *Washington Post*, September 9, 2001

45 *"You don't want to go to Kiddieland . . ."* Ibid.

45 *"My parents had to try to explain . . ."* "Academic Style: Stanford's New Provost Brings a Different Perspective to Campus," *Chicago Tribune*, August 15, 1993

45 *"The Rices were kind of joyless . . ."* "Lessons of Might and Right," *Washington Post*, September 9, 2001

46 *"He was a big man . . ."* Interview with Margaret Cheatham

46 *"John's scouts made up one . . ."* Interview with Reverend William Jones

47 *"this fine young man . . ."* "Lessons of Might and Right," *Washington Post*, September 9, 2001

47 *"My dad was a football coach . . ."* "Oprah Talks to Condoleezza Rice," *O: The Oprah Magazine*, February 2002

47 *"When I grow up I'm going to marry . . ."* "Lessons of Might and Right," *Washington Post*, September 9, 2001

48 *"It was music with my mother . . ."* University of Denver Graduate School of International Studies brochure

48 *"Condi was always interested in politics . . ."* Interview with Juliemma Smith

48 *"We almost always stopped on college campuses . . ."* "Honored to Have the Chance," *Boston Globe*, December 21, 2000

48 *"Figure skating was . . ."* "West Wing Story: America's Favorite Bushie," *Newsweek*, August 1, 2001

49 *"the year of all the bombings . . ."* "Honored to Have the Chance," *Boston Globe*, December 21, 2000

50 *"The police would show up . . ."* Interview with Pam King

50 *"I have a sort of pure . . ."* "The President's Prodigy," *Vogue*, October 2001

51 *"Those terrible events . . ."* "Soviets Face Hard Choices in Arms Control, Rice Says," Stanford University News Service, December 2, 1983

51 *"It's too hard to get there . . ."* Interview with Pam King

51 *"When integration occurred . . ."* Ibid.

52 *"We all lived within range . . ."* "The President's Prodigy," *Vogue*, October 2001

53 *"The white power structure . . ."* Interview with Jack Davis

53 *"My father worked downtown . . ."* Ibid.

53 *"challenging our way of life"* "Connor Behind Bill Banning 'Rides,'" *Birmingham Post-Herald*, August 25, 1961

54 *"With firemen brandishing their hoses . . ."* "Dogs, Water Used to Halt Negro March," *Montgomery Advertiser*, May 4, 1963

55 *"My father was not a march-in-the-street preacher . . ."* "Lessons of Might and Right," *Washington Post*, September 9, 2001

56 *"I remember a slight sensation . . ."* "In Race for White House, the 'Cult of Condi' Plays Growing Role," *Los Angeles Times*, May 28, 2000

56 *"I remember more than anything the coffins . . ."* "Honored to Have the Chance," *Boston Globe*, December 21, 2000

57 *"In 1952, John Rice himself went to vote . . ."* Ibid.

57 *"The first Republican I knew . . ."* Rice's Speech at the Republican National Convention, August 1, 2000

58 *"The people there stopped eating . . ."* "Oprah Talks to Condoleezza Rice," *O: The Oprah Magazine,* February 2002

58 *"a revered figure"* "Lessons of Might and Right," *Washington Post,* September 9, 2001

58 *"The legal changes made a tremendous difference . . ."* "Lessons of Might and Right," *Washington Post,* September 9, 2001

58 *"I am so grateful to my parents . . ."* Stanford University News Service bulletin, December 2, 1983

59 *By the time John arrived as the new dean . . .* "Stillman College: A Glance at the Past," Stillman College Archives, 1974

Four: CHOPIN, SHAKESPEARE, OR SOVIETS

60 *"I don't ever remember . . ."* "Oprah Talks to Condoleezza Rice," *O: The Oprah Magazine,* February 2002

61 *"sick and tired . . ."* "Acknowledge that You Have an Obligation to Search for the Truth," *Stanford Report,* June 16, 2002

61 *"I will never forget . . ."* Ibid.

62 *"DU is more aware of minority problems . . ."* University of Denver *Clarion,* October 9, 1972

64 *"That seems to be how . . . In the 1940s . . ."* Interview with Sr. Sylvia Pautler

65 *"All that I remember is focusing . . ."* "The President's Prodigy," *Vogue,* October 2001

65 *"Now once you got out into the larger world . . ."* "People in the News Profile: Condoleezza Rice," CNN.com web site (www.cnn.com/CNN/programs/people/shows/rice/profile.html)

66 *"She was very . . ."* Interview with Sr. Sylvia Pautler

66 *"The Sisters of Loretto . . ."* Interview with Therese Saracino

67 *"I was her math teacher . . ."* Ibid.

67 *"That was a lot of money back then . . ."* Interview with Deborah Carson

68 *"Poor guy. He felt sort of . . ."* "The President's Prodigy," *Vogue,* October 2001

69 *"My father was fundamentally against it . . ."* College Acquaintance Recruitment Experience (CARE) brochure, University of Denver

70 *"I'm the one who speaks French! . . ."* "Lessons of Might and Right," *Washington Post*, September 9, 2001

71 *"That had been my mother and father's strategy . . ."* Ibid.

71 *"The truth is that I was a terrible procrastinator . . ."* "Oprah Talks to Condoleezza Rice," *O: The Oprah Magazine*, February 2002

71 *"I did the reading at the last minute . . ."* "Take Small Classes, Experiment, College Frosh Told," Stanford News Service bulletin, October 1993

72 *"I met eleven-year-olds who could play . . ."* "Mad About Music," transcript of the WNYC radio program aired on September 7, 2001

72 *"We both became disillusioned . . ."* Interview with Darcy Taylor

72 *"We all entered several contests a year . . ."* Ibid.

73 *"murder Beethoven"* "Star in Waiting," *National Review*, August 30, 1999

73 *"I decided . . ."* "Dream's Focus Fundamental for Leadership in 21st Century," editorial by Condoleezza Rice, *Birmingham News*, April 23, 2000

73 *"pretty good but not great . . . Technically, I can play most anything . . ."* "Oprah Talks to Condoleezza Rice," *O: The Oprah Magazine*, February 2002

73 *"I went on a mad search for a major . . ."* Ibid.

74 *"squishy"* "Star in Waiting," *National Review*, August 30, 1999

74 *"It just clicked . . ."* "Oprah Talks to Condoleezza Rice," *O: The Oprah Magazine*, February 2002

74 *"I can still feel the strong sense I had of remorse and regret . . ."* Stanford University News Service bulletin, December 2, 1983

75 *"I really adored him . . ."* "Star in Waiting," *National Review*, August 30, 1999

75 *"Condi is the kind of person who is very sure of herself . . ."* "Is There Anything This Woman Can't Do?" *George* magazine, June 2000

75 *"Design is a way . . ."* Interview with Darcy Taylor

75 *"John Rice was friendly . . ."* Ibid.

76 *"I found my passion in the study of Russia . . ."* "Mad About Music," transcript of the WNYC radio program aired on September 7, 2001

76 *"I don't regret giving up the music career . . ."* Ibid.

76 *"Korbel had a way of encouraging talented people . . ."* *Madeleine Albright: A Twentieth-Century Odyssey,* by Michael Dobbs

77 *"Korbel was one of . . ."* Ibid.

79 *"There is no doubt . . ."* Ibid.

80 *"It helps to have another foreign language under your belt . . ."* Interview with Jason Galie

81 *"The membership of these churches got together . . ."* Interview with Russ Wehner

81 *"church members were asked to sign . . ."* *The Spirit of Montview: 1902–2002,* by the Montview Centennial Book Committee

81 *"He got Martin Luther King . . . "* Interview with Russ Wehner

82 *"He brought an enormous . . ."* Ibid.

82 *"When John came on the staff . . ."* *The Spirit of Montview: 1902–2002,* by the Montview Centennial Book Committee

82 *"John was always forthright, honest, and challenging . . ."* Interview with Richard Hutchison

83 *"She had a beautiful voice . . ."* Interview with Margaret Wehner

83 *"We performed . . . the Beethoven Christ on the Mount of Olives . . ."* "Mad About Music," transcript of the WNYC radio program aired on September 7, 2001

83 *In addition to his work as a university dean . . .* "Rice Appointed to Urban Renewal Authority," *Intermountain Jewish News,* May 26, 1978

83 *"I believe that sports has a place . . ."* "Rice on Students, Tough Decisions and her Oil Tanker," *Stanford Magazine,* May/June 1999

84 *"The University of Denver . . . "* University of Denver Graduate School of International Studies brochure

85 *"Since he didn't tell me precisely how . . ."* *Stanford Campus Report,* June 19, 1985

Five: THE SCHOLAR

86 *"Culture is something you can adopt . . ."* "Political Punch in a Package of Charm," *The Financial Times,* February 26, 2000

87 *"I'm five-foot-eight, black and female . . ."* Ibid.

89 *"Condoleezza came to Notre Dame . . ."* Interview with George Brinkley

90 *"The government gathered all those it could collect . . ."* "From 'Splendid Isolation' to 'Fruitful Cooperation': The Harriman Institute in the Post-Soviet Era," *Columbia Magazine*, Summer 1996

91 *"Well, the job market's a lot better . . ."* "Oprah Talks to Condoleezza Rice," *O: The Oprah Magazine*, February 2002

91 *"Most students had little background . . ."* Interview with George Brinkley

92 *"He understood the dark side of Russia . . ."* "Star in Waiting," *National Review*, August 30, 1999

92 *"Our graduate program . . ."* Interview with George Brinkley

92 *"She was one of those self-driven students . . ."* Ibid.

92 *"She had some Russian . . ."* Ibid.

93 *"It was clear from the beginning . . ."* Ibid.

93 *"I read early on and was influenced . . ."* "Condoleezza Rice: George W.'s Realist," *World Policy Journal*, Winter 1999

94 *"Power is the control . . ."* *Politics Among Nations*, by Hans Morgenthau

94 *"Realists insisted that the national interest could . . ."* *Righteous Realists*, by Joel. H. Rosenthal

95 *"attracted to the Byzantine nature . . ."* Ibid.

95 *"I am a realist. Power matters . . ."* "Star in Waiting," *National Review*, August 30, 1999

95 *"Condi came to see the cold war . . ."* "Is There Anything This Woman Can't Do?," *George* magazine, June 2000

95 *"While she was at Notre Dame . . ."* Interview with George Brinkley

95 *"She and I worked . . ."* Ibid.

96 *"She partied quite a bit there . . ."* Interview with Deborah Carson

97 *"You are very talented, you have to become a professor . . ."* "Josef Korbel's Enduring Foreign Policy Legacy," *Washington Post*, December 28, 2000

97 *"Thinking broadly about the whole world . . ."* "Soviets Face Hard Choices in Arms Control, Rice Says," Stanford University News Service, December 2, 1983

97 *"I realized that I liked . . ."* Ibid.

97 *"He was nothing but . . ."* Ibid.

98 *"She is one of the few people . . ."* Interview with Robby Laitos

98 *"That day . . ."* Ibid.

98 *"I remember her mother . . ."* Ibid.

99 *"Looking back, the school doesn't seem a lot different . . ."* Interview with Karen Feste

99 *Josef Korbel had not always . . . Madeleine Albright: A Twentieth Century Legacy,* by Michael Dobbs

100 *"He and I were close . . ."* Interview with Karen Feste

101 *"contributions to transatlantic relations . . ."* Naval War College announcement posted on web site (nwc.navy.mil)

102 *"Dear American TV people . . ."* "The Partnership: A History of the *Apollo-Soyuz* Test Project," NASA web site (hq.nasa.gov/office/pao/History)

103 *"a deliberate effort by a powerful atheistic government . . ."* "Russia's Bold Challenge," *Time,* January 14, 1980

103 *"I remember thinking, What did you think . . ."* "The President's Prodigy," *Vogue,* October 2001

103 *"I was a registered Democrat . . ."* "Honored to Have the Chance," *The Boston Globe,* December 21, 2000

104 *"I admired what Lyndon Johnson did for civil rights . . ."* "Is There Anything This Woman Can't Do?," *George* magazine, June 2000

104 *"all-over-the-map Republican . . ."* "'Condi' Rice: Presbyterian with faith, political mettle," *The Presbyterian Layman,* November 22, 2000

104 *"It was the constitution and foreign policy . . ."* Ibid.

104 *Condi takes a ribbing . . .* "Honored to Get the Chance," *The Boston Globe,* December 21, 2000

104 *"I'm in the G.O.P. for the right reasons . . ."* Ibid.

105 *"Korbel liked Condi because . . ."* Interview with Karen Feste

106 *"research ability"* Stanford University News Service

106 *"He expected a lot out of people . . ."* Interview with Karen Feste

106 *"He was as proud of [Madeleine] . . ."* Madeleine Albright: A Twentieth Century Legacy,* by Michael Dobbs

106 *"It was Josef Korbel who taught her . . ."* Seasons of Her Life: A Biography of Madeleine Korbel Albright,* by Ann Blackman

106 *"probably more liberal . . ."* "Josef Korbel's Enduring Foreign Policy Legacy," *Washington Post,* December 28, 2000

107 *"Our program works best for students . . ."* Interview with Karen Feste

107 *"There wasn't a lot written about the subject . . ."* "Pick for National security Adviser has DU Ties," *Denver Rocky Mountain News,* December 17, 2000

108 *"The General Staff [of the USSR] was my life . . ."* "Is There Anything This Woman Can't Do?" *George* magazine, June 2000

108 *She had estimated that there were about 5,000 . . .* Ibid.

109 *"The majority of Soviets . . ."* Interview with Dmitri Gerasamenko

109 *"Foreigners saw . . ."* Ibid.

109 *"A black student . . ."* Ibid.

110 *"a very major player. . . . She was seriously going to marry him . . ."* Interview with Deborah Carson

111 *"He died of stomach cancer . . ."* Interview with Karen Feste

111 *On his sickbed, Korbel continued working . . . Madeleine Albright: A Twentieth-Century Odyssey,* by Michael Dobbs

111 *"Because of the small . . ."* Graduate School of International Studies brochure

112 *"I tell students, 'If you don't know what you want . . ."* Ibid.

112 *"[For years] I structured my life to be a concert musician . . ."* "Star in Waiting," *National Review,* August 30, 1999

112 *"I think we all knew . . ."* "Adviser Condi Rice," *Denver Post,* August 2, 2000

112 *"We always thought . . ."* Interview with Karen Feste

Six: PROFESSOR RICE

113 *"The understanding of arms control . . ."* "Soviets Face Hard Choices in Arms Control, Rice Says," Stanford University News Service, December 2, 1983

114 *"tells me everything . . . I hope you know a lot."* "Rice: A Russophile with Bush's Ear" MSNBC web site (msnbc.com)

114 *"[The] characteristics of the Cold War . . ."* "Bush, Gorbachev Hold Malta Shipboard Summit," *World News Digest,* December 8, 1989

116 *"They didn't need another Soviet specialist . . ."* "The President's Prodigy," *Vogue,* October 2001

116 *"I think what struck people . . ."* Stanford Report, December 9, 1998

116 *"She got along well with everybody . . ."* Interview with John Ferejohn

118 *"It is increasingly difficult . . ."* Stanford Report, October 28, 1998

118 *"orderly, post hoc recreations we teach . . ."* Ibid.

118 *It's interesting to watch students . . ."* Ibid.

118 *"It is still the most . . ."* "Dean's Awards for Distinguished Teaching, 1992–93," Stanford University News Service, undated press release

119 *"wasn't a surprise, it was commonly known . . ."* Interview with John Ferejohn

119 *"Condi heard about it . . ."* Interview with Paul Brest

119 *Condi is not the first to make this analogy . . . American Manhood: Transformations in Masculinity from the Revolution to the Modern Era,* by E. Anthony Rotundo

120 *"It was a large lecture class . . ."* Interview with anonymous

120 *"Anyone who has had the good fortune . . ."* "Dean's Awards for Distinguished Teaching, 1992–93," Stanford University News Service

121 *"I will always remember . . ."* Ibid.

121 *"a marvelous facilitator . . ."* Ibid.

121 *"She treated us . . ."* Ibid.

121 *"for bringing enthusiasm . . ."* Stanford University News Service press release, June 18, 1984

122 *"her intellect and charm—charm in the profound sense . . ."* "Lessons of Might and Right," Washington Post, September 9, 2001

123 *"I was affiliated . . ."* Interview with George Brinkley

124 *"ill understood . . . I found them welcoming . . ."* "The Gorbachev Era," The Commonwealth, June 13, 1988

124 *"I realized then . . ."* "Bush Advisor Speaks of Faith's Deep Roots," Denver Post, May 5, 2000

125 *"We walked in the door . . ."* Interview with Deborah Carson

125 *"They were a real couple . . ."* Ibid.

126 *"The opening of the Berlin Wall was as electrifying . . ." Germany Unified and Europe Transformed: A Study in Statecraft,* by Philip Zelikow and Condoleezza Rice

Seven: BUSH I

128 *"Condi was brilliant . . ."* "Is There Anything This Woman Can't Do?" *George* magazine, June 2000

128 *"All you have to do with the large, huge, and very frightening problems . . ."* Stanford University *Campus Report*, June 19, 1985

130 *"Television and radio play a major . . ."* KQED legal department document supplied by Counsel Margaret Berry

131 *"I think of people as being one of two types . . ."* Interview with John Raisian

133 *"a distinguished scholar . . ."* "Contributing to CREES," Center for Russian and Eastern European Studies web site (www.stanford.edu/dept/CREES/giving.html)

133 *"The Stanford Alumni Association had asked Alex . . ."* Interview with Gail W. Lapidus

134 *"Clearly they approached . . ."* Ibid.

134 *"I never shall forget the day we returned . . ."* "Honored to Have the Chance," *The Boston Globe*, December 21, 2000

138 *"Scowcroft and Baker placed a premium on cooperation . . ."* *Germany Unified and Europe Transformed: A Study in Statecraft*, by Philip Zelikow and Condoleezza Rice

138 *"I had chosen Condi . . ."* *A World Transformed*, by George Bush and Brent Scowcroft

139 *"We went to the meetings . . ."* "Welcome Back, Professor Rice," Stanford REES Newsletter, Spring 1991

141 *"Condi's memo laid out the premises . . ."* Ibid.

141 *"aggressively to promote . . ."* Ibid.

141 *"setting our sights . . ."* Ibid.

142 *"it had a high concentration of families with ties to Eastern Europe . . ."* Ibid.

143 *"Németh presented President Bush with a plaque . . ."* Ibid.

143 *"beacon of light . . ."* Ibid.

144 *"This isn't the door you go in . . ."* "Is There Anything This Woman Can't Do?" *George* magazine, June 2000

145 *"I think the Russians . . ."* "Political Punch in a Package of Charm," *Financial Times*, February 26, 2000

145 *"I never have felt lonely or stressed in these environments . . ."* "Honored to Have the Chance," *The Boston Globe*, December 21, 2000

146 *"He was right in my face in a confrontational way . . ."* "Academic Style: Stanford's New Provost Brings a Different Perspective to Campus," *Chicago Tribune*, August 15, 1993

146 *"I have to confess, it was hard for me to concentrate . . ."* "Sharon smitten with Rice," *Denver Post*, February 5, 2001

147 *"would rip the heart out . . ."* Germany Unified and Europe Transformed: A Study in Statecraft, by Philip Zelikow and Condoleezza Rice

147 *"peaceful, gradual . . ."* Ibid.

147 *"It was a risky move . . ."* "Is There Anything This Woman Can't Do?" *George* magazine, June 2000

149 *"Condi was brilliant, but she never tried to flaunt it . . ."* Ibid.

149 *"She's not only a person with extraordinary ambition . . ."* Interview with George Brinkley

149 *"It was an exciting time . . ."* "Political Punch in a Package of Charm," *The Financial Times*, February 26, 2000

149 *"Was it inevitable that Germany unified . . ."* "Star in Waiting," *National Review*, August 30, 1999

150 *"My colleagues were the smartest people I had ever met . . ."* "Leaders for a New Millennium," *The Financial Times*, December 28, 1995

150 *"The most personally satisfying was working . . ."* "Welcome Back, Professor Rice," Stanford REES Newsletter, Spring 1991

150 *"Excellence describes the people that I had . . ."* "U.S. Intelligence and the End of the Cold War," a speech given by George Bush at Texas A&M on November 19, 1999

Eight: ROOM AT THE TOP

152 *"I tell my students . . ."* "From 'Not College Material' to Stanford's No. 2 Job," *The New York Times*, June 23, 1993

152 *according to Scowcroft . . .* "Bush's Foreign Policy Tutor," *The New York Times*, June 16, 2000

152 *"It wasn't an easy decision . . ."* "Welcome Back, Professor Rice," REES Center for Russian & East European Studies Newsletter, Spring 1991

153 *"I wanted a life . . ."* Ibid.

154 *"I've always tried to teach some of the decision-making . . ."* Ibid.

154 *"The events in the Soviet Union will unfold . . ."* "Rice Quits Post," *Stanford Daily*, March 14, 1991

154 *"All the assumptions that I started out with as a student . . ."* "End of the Cold War: Challenge for U.S. Policy," *The Commonwealth*, December 6, 1991

155 *"The Soviet Army still has as chance . . ."* "A New Army for a New State," *Time*, September 16, 1991.

155 *"People in the Soviet Union associate Gorbachev . . ."* "End of the Cold War: Challenge for U.S. Policy," *The Commonwealth*, December 16, 1991

157 *"assess the current training programs . . ."* "Report of the Federal Advisory Committee on Gender-Integrated Training and Related Issues to the Secretary of Defense," December 16,1997 (www.defenselink.mil/pubs/git/report.html)

157 *"I was a principal at Menlo Oaks Middle School . . ."* Interview with Clara Rice

158 *"He really didn't like . . ."* Ibid.

158 *"The three of us . . ."* Ibid.

159 *"He was retired . . ."* Ibid.

160 *"Those are sort of my kids . . ."* "Lessons of Might and Right," *Washington Post*, September 9, 2001

160 *"Ever since I've been out of school . . ."* "The President's Prodigy, *Vogue*, October 2001

160 *"I have never accepted this notion . . ."* Ibid.

160 *"Dr. Rice has participated . . ."* Stanford University *Campus Report*, April 1, 1992

162 *"White men prove . . ."* Interview with Albert A. Cannella

162 *"She's very well connected . . ."* Ibid.

163 *"business experts . . ."* Ibid.

165 *"American oil companies are important . . ."* "Fox News Sunday" August 27, 2000, online transcript from eMediaMillWorks

165 *"Oil companies have come a long way . . ."* Ibid.

166 *"We made the change to eliminate the unnecessary attention . . ."* "Chevron redubs ship named for Bush aide," *San Francisco Chronicle*, May 5, 2001

169 *"Condi's greatest expertise was on the international side . . ."* Interview with Paul Brest

171 *"I was greatly impressed . . ."* "People in the News Profile: Condoleezza Rice," CNN.com web site (www.cnn.com/ CNN/programs/people/shows/rice/profile.html)

172 *"I did not beat around the bush . . ."* Ibid.

172 *"I knew it would be somewhat controversial . . ."* Ibid.

173 *"Stanford—like all universities—is in a maelstrom . . ."* "Casper Selects Condoleezza Rice to be Next Stanford Provost," Stanford News Service press release, May 19, 1993

173 *With her new appointment, Condi changed . . .* "From 'Not College Material' to Stanford's No. 2 Job," *The New York Times*, June 23, 1993

174 *"I tell my students, 'If you find yourself . . .'"* Ibid.

174 *"I actually don't think of this as a budgetary crisis . . ."* "Stanford Cuts Budget Third Straight Year," *San Francisco Chronicle*, November 11, 1993

174 *"There was a sort of conventional wisdom . . ."* "Velvet-glove Forcefulness," *Stanford Report*, June 9, 1999

174 *"I always feel bad for the dislocation . . ."* "Oprah Talks to Condoleezza Rice," *O: The Oprah Magazine*, February 2002

175 *"In the first couple of years . . ."* *Stanford Magazine*, May/June 1999

176 *"Obviously this is slow, steady progress . . ."* "Uphill Battle to Improve Status of Women on the Faculty," Stanford University News Service press release, March 12, 1997

176 *"You see 1 to 2 percent turnover rates . . ."* "Velvet-glove Forcefulness," *Stanford Report*, June 9, 1999

177 *"is more than outweighed by the downside . . ."* "Uphill Battle to Improve Status of Women on the Faculty," Stanford University News Service press release, March 12, 1997

177 *"Done in the right way . . ."* Minutes of Stanford University's Senate of the Academic Council, May 13, 1999 (www.stanford.edu)

178 *"Tenure is granted to those who have achieved . . ."* "Sawislak to appeal denial of tenure to Advisory Board," *Stanford Report*, April 1, 1998

179 *"The argument that I have never bought . . ."* "Velvet-glove Forcefulness," *Stanford Report*, June 9, 1999

179 *"I think the experience . . ."* Ibid.

180 *"This is something the entire university . . ."* Stanford University News Service press release, May 10, 1996

180 *"I'm very proud we're fiscally sound now . . ."* "Velvet-glove Forcefulness," *Stanford Report,* June 9, 1999

180 *"Condi was the provost when I was dean of the law school . . ."* Interview with Paul Brest

181 *"There's always a lot of give and take . . ."* Ibid.

182 *"When we began working I didn't know . . ."* Interview with George Barth

182 *"If she got a call . . ."* Ibid.

182 *"She played it very well . . ."* Ibid.

183 *"Most of my students are . . ."* Ibid.

183 *"We worked on that . . ."* Ibid.

184 *"I now play almost exclusively chamber music . . ."* "Mad About Music," transcript of the WNYC radio program aired on September 7, 2001

184 *"I played with orchestras . . ."* Ibid.

184 *"She would pay attention . . ."* Interview with George Barth

185 *"Condi is very self-disciplined . . ."* Ibid.

185 *"I put her through . . ."* Interview with Mark Wateska

186 *"If you don't have children who are a break . . ."* "Condoleezza Rice: Driven to Achieve," *The New York Times,* December 18, 2000

186 *"I get very caught up in what's going on with the music . . ."* "Mad About Music," transcript of the WNYC radio program aired on September 7, 2001

186 *"She's very goal-oriented . . ."* Interview with Mark Wateska

186 *"As a strength coach I guess I was the low man . . ."* Ibid.

187 *"He said, 'you know . . .'"* "Mad About Music," transcript of the WNYC radio program aired on September 7, 2001

187 *"I . . . tell them that I've been to Europe . . ."* "Academic Style: Stanford's New Provost Brings a Different Perspective to Campus," *Chicago Tribune,* August 15, 1993

187 *"I don't suffer from Potomac fever . . ."* "Leaders for a New Millennium," *Financial Times,* December 28, 1995

188 *"The most important thing became to get back . . ."* *Stanford Magazine,* May-June 1999

188 *"I'm going to take a leave from the university . . ."* "Rice to Step

Down in June after Six Years as Provost," *Stanford Report*, December 9, 1998

188 *"We all know her real passion . . ."* "Condoleezza Rice Farewell," *Stanford Report*, June 16, 1999

189 *"To Condoleezza Rice . . ."* Ibid.

189 *"warm grace . . ."* Ibid.

189 *"She has this incredible reputation . . ."* Interview with John Raisian

190 *"She has had other . . ."* Ibid.

190 *"Condi is one of the brightest people . . ."* "Stanford Provost Condoleezza Rice Appointed Hoover Senior Fellow," *Hoover Institution Newsletter*, Summer 1999

Nine: PORTALS OF POWER: BUSH II

193 *"If there is any lesson from history . . ."* "Promoting the National Interest," *Foreign Affairs* magazine, January/February 2000

193 *"What a weird accident"* "Oprah Talks to Condoleezza Rice," *O: The Oprah Magazine*, February 2002

195 *"Since I was a girl I have relied on faith . . ."* Ibid.

196 *"If she's doing her job well . . ."* "West Wing Story: America's Favorite Bushie," *Newsweek*, August 1, 2001

196 *"I try very hard to remember that I have to be very disciplined . . ."* "The President's Prodigy," *Vogue*, October 2001

197 *"I am responsible for making sure that I've checked things . . ."* "Oprah Talks to Condoleezza Rice," *O: The Oprah Magazine*, February 2002

197 *"We had gotten off on the wrong foot . . ."* "See George. See George Learn Foreign Policy," *Newsweek*, June 18, 2001

197 *"Using the American armed forces as the world's '911' . . ."* "Promoting the National Interest," *Foreign Affairs* magazine, January/February 2000

198 *"lightning brained"* "For Rice, A Daunting Challenge Ahead," *Washington Post*, December 18, 2000

198 *"rare ability . . . When you see her giving talks . . ."* Interview with John Raisian

198 *"On a scale of one to ten in degree of difficulty . . ."* "Rice Shapes Bush's View of the World," Cox Newspapers Online, November 15, 2001 (coxnews.com)

200 *"A poker-playing crony of the president's . . ."* *Keepers of the Keys: A History of the National Security Council from Truman to Bush*, by John Prados

200 *"He should be a non-political confidant . . ."* Ibid.

200 *The nation's twentieth national security advisor . . .* The first two in that position were classified as "executive secretaries"; the title "National Security Advisor" was first given in the Eisenhower administration. See the Appendix for a complete list of all former advisors.

201 *"Foreign policy is dominated by bald, graying white men . . ."* "Condi Rice a rare woman in world affairs," *Denver Rocky Mountain News*, December 18, 2000

201 *"The foreign policy establishment, comprised primarily by males . . ."* "The Status of Women in International Affairs Professions," Women's Foreign Policy Group web site (wfpg.org)

201 *"The appointment of Madeleine Albright . . ."* Ibid.

202 *"High self-esteem and confidence went . . ."* Ibid.

202 *"I tried to pattern myself after him . . ."* *Madeleine Albright: Twentieth Century Odyssey*, by Michael Dobbs

203 *"He corrected her essays . . ."* Ibid.

203 *"spent a lot of time . . ."* Ibid.

204 *"Madeleine, I don't know how to tell you . . ."* "Lessons of Might and Right," Washington Post, September 9, 2001

204 *"I know and like Madeleine very much . . ."* "Political Punch in a Package of Charm," *Financial Times*, February 26, 2000

206 *"Her touch was authoritative . . ."* "For Condoleezza Rice, National Security by Day and Brahms by Night," *The Wall Street Journal*, April 24, 2002

206 *"to help make sure . . ."* "Condoleezza Rice," BusinessWeek online, February 11, 2002

207 *"a bureaucratic infighter without equal . . ."* "Containment," *New Republic*, February 5, 2001

208 *"According to several Bush advisers . . ."* Ibid.

208 *"They have a very nice, easy, friendly style . . ."* "The New Faces of U.S. to the World," *Christian Science Monitor*, December 18, 2000

208 *"keeping the trains running . . ."* "Containment," *New Republic*, February 5, 2001

208 *"She not only spends the most time . . ."* "Condoleezza Rice,"

BusinessWeek online, February 11, 2002
(www.businessweek.com)

209 *"Her mission to Moscow was unprecedented . . ."* "Rice on Front
Lines as Adviser to Bush," *The New York Times*, August 16, 2001

209 *"We've always said that we believe . . ."* "Rice Says Bush, Putin
'Moved Forward,'" U.S. Department of State International Information Programs, July 22, 2001 (online posting)

210 *"I've been in lots of meetings . . ."* "Messenger to Moscow,"
Time, August 6, 2001

211 *"As a result of hard work and determination . . ."* "Beyond the
ABM Treaty," *The Wall Street Journal*, June 14, 2002

211 *"Tell Aunt Condi . . ."* Interview with Deborah Carson

212 *"In the period starting in December 2000 . . ."* "Rice: 'No specific time, place or method mentioned,'" CNN.com/Inside
Politics, posted May 17, 2002 (CNN.com)

214 *"We are committed to a world . . ."* "Remarks by the National
Security Advisor, Condoleezza Rice, to the Conservative Polit-
ical Action Conference," February 1, 2002, as posted on the
NATO web site, February 1, 2002 (nato.int)

Ten: AT WAR AND UNDER FIRE

215 *"advising the leader of the world's..."* "The World's 100 Most
Powerful Women," *Forbes*, August 20, 2004,
(www.forbes.com/2004/08/18/04powomland.html)

216 *"The President's made it clear..."* "Press Conference by Vice
President Dick Cheney," White House online, March 17,
2002, (www.whitehouse.gov/vicepresident/news-
speeches/speeches/vp20020317.html)

216 the Iraqi leader *"is an evil man..."* "'Moral case' for deposing
Saddam," BBC News online, August 15, 2002,
(news.bbc.co.uk/1/hi/world/americas/2193426.stm)

216 *"History is littered..."* "'Moral case' for deposing Saddam,"
BBC News online, August 15, 2002,
(news.bbc.co.uk/1/hi/world/americas/2193426.stm)

217 *"There is a virtual consensus..."* Brent Scowcroft, "Don't Attack
Saddam," *Wall Street Journal*, August 15, 2002, (www.opinion-
journal.com/forms/printThis.html?id=110002133)

218 *"an explosion of outrage..."* Ibid.

218 *"punish France…"* "Bush on a Revenge Mission," *The Independent* (London), April 26, 2003, p. 1

218 *"They believe that September 11 was…"* "Bush's Tutor and Disciple—Condoleezza Rice," *New York Times*, November 17, 2004, p. A1

219 *"the orientation out of which I came…"* Ibid.

219 he stated that the *"attack on our nation was also…"* "President's Remarks to the Nation," September 11, 2002, White House online, (www.whitehouse.gov/news/releases/2002/09/)

220 *"Congress must make it…"* "President Discusses Growing Danger Posed by Saddam Hussein's Regime," September 14, 2002, White House online, (www.whitehouse.gov/news/releases/2002/09/)

220 *"In real life, power and values…"* "Dr. Condoleezza Rice Discusses President's National Security Strategy," October 1, 2002, White House online, (www.whitehouse.gov/news/releases/2002/10/print/20021001-6.html)

221 *"Inspectors had not been given…"* Condoleezza Rice, "Why We Know Iraq Is Lying," *New York Times*, January 23, 2003, p. A25

221 the document *"fails to account for…"* Ibid.

222 *"clearly, that particular report…."* "Timeline of the Iraq Uranium Allegations," ABC News online, (abcnews.go.com/International/story?id=79455)

222 *"Iraq has failed to take…"* "Iraq: US/UK/Spain Draft Resolution," February 24, 2003," posted on The United States Mission to the European Union site, (www.useu.be/Categories/GlobalAffairs/Iraq/ Feb2403ResolutionIraq.html)

222 *"The military option should…"* "Memorandum Submitted by France, Germany & Russia on Iraq Weapons Inspections," February 24, 2003, posted on C-Span.org, (c-span.org/resources/fyi/frenchresolution. asp)

222 *"We all continue to live under…"* "Press Briefing by Dr. Condoleezza Rice," February 24, 2003, White House online, (www.whitehouse.gov/news/releases/2003/02/20030224-14.html)

223 *"the weather was better this time"* "Commander in Chief's Visit Sets Aircraft Carrier's Crew Abuzz, *Seattle Post-Intelligencer*,

May 2, 2003, (seattlepi.nwsource.com/local/120279_lincolnsub.html)

224 *"We looked like a normal couple"* "How White House Planners Kept High-risk Journey Secret to the End," *Ottawa Citizen*, November 28, 2003, p. A1

225 *"Let the chips fall…"* "Thanksgiving Surprise Raises Stakes for Bush," *Seattle Times*, November 29, 2003, p. A1

225 *"As I was telling…"* "Perspectives," *Newsweek*, May 3, 2004, as posted on MSNBC.com, (msnbc.msn.com/id/4824766/)

225 *"providing the nation…"* Thomas H. Kean and Lee H. Hamilton, *The 9/11 Report* (New York: St. Martin's Press, August 2004), p. ix

226 *"Nothing would be better…"* "Can't Testify, Condi Insists," *Daily News*, March 29, 2004, p.2

226 *"George W. Bush…failed to act…"* Richard A. Clarke, *Against All Enemies* (New York: Free Press, 2004), p. x

227 *White House counsel Alberto R. Gonzales sent…* "Excerpts from White House Letter on Rice's Testimony," *New York Times*, March 31, 2004, p. A20

227 *"Rice herself weakened…"* "The White House Blinks," *Buffalo News*, March 31, 2004, p. B8

227 *"The terrorists were at war with us…"* "Testimony of Condoleezza Rice Before 9/11 Commission," *New York Times*, April 8, 2004, transcript posted on nytimes.com, (www.nytimes.com/2004/04/08/politics/ 08RICETEXT.html?ex=1102050000&en=787702147cceca23&ei=5070)

228 *"Isn't it a fact, Dr. Rice…"* Ibid.

229 *"Although Rice's testimony produced…"* "Rice Holds the Line," *Time*, April 8, 2004, online edition, (www.time.com/time/nation/article/0%2C8599%2C609491%2C00.html)

230 *"We have no credible evidence…"* "Overview of the Enemy: Staff Statement No. 15," National Commission on Terrorist Attacks on the United States, June 16, 2004 (www.9-11commission.gov/staff_statements/index.htm)

230 *American casualties…* "Forces: U.S. & Coalition/Casualties," CNN.com, December 8, 2004, (www.cnn.com/SPECIALS/2003/iraq/forces/casualties/)

230 *"The frequency and location…"* "Rice Hitting the Road to Speak," *Washington Post*, October 20, 2004, p. A2.

230 *Condi appeared so often "on the campaign trail…"* "The Friends of George," *New York Times*, November 17, 2004, p. A1

231 *"Of course not…"* "Dr. Condoleezza Rice Talks About her Career as Assistant to the President for National Security Affairs," National Public Radio, "Tavis Smiley," October 28, 2004.

231 *"By tradition and custom…"* "GOP Star to Skip Convention," *Washington Post*, August 7, 2004, p. A7

231 *"During the last four years…"* "President Nominates Condoleezza Rice as Secretary of State," White House press release, November 16, 2004, (www.whitehouse.gov/news/releases/2004/11/20041116-3.html)

232 *"Thank you, Mr. President…."* Ibid.

233 *"One is that she will…"* "To Europeans, Rice Brings Mitigated Hope of Harmony," *New York Times*, November 20, 2004, p. A1

233 *"Having someone like her choose…"* "Uterine Fibroid Surgery; Rice to Undergo Procedure," *Newsday*, November 19, 2004, p. A44

234 *"Dr. Jacob Cynamon…"* Ibid.

234 *"The first viable female candidate …"* "The Bush Look" Salon.com web site, February 28, 2001 (www.salon.com)

235 *"I am not a very good long-term planner …"* "Academic Style: Stanford's New Provost Brings a Different Perspective to Campus," *Chicago Tribune*, August 15, 1993

235 *"I'd like to think of myself as passionate …"* "Mad About Music," transcript of the WNYC radio program aired on September 7, 2001

235 *"We look at her as …"* Interview with Reverend William Jones

236 *"There were no role models for her …"* "National Security Advisor Condoleezza Rice Chosen for Special NAACP Image Award," Associated Press web site, February 24, 2002 (http://wire.ap.org)

236 *"I had a different reaction …"* Public speech given at the Capital Rotunda at the 2002 National Commemoration of the Days of Remembrance

237 *"As I travel . . ."* Ibid.
238 *"We do not choose our circumstances . . ."* Ibid.

INDEX

About the Author

Antonia Felix is the author of fourteen nonfiction books, including *Wesley K. Clark: A Biography;* the national best-seller *Laura: America's First Lady, First Mother; Andrea Bocelli: A Celebration*; and *Silent Soul: The Miracles and Mysteries of Audrey Santo.* She has also edited a number of movie books including *Windtalkers: The Making of the Film About the Navajo Code Talkers of World War II* and *Pearl Harbor: The Movie and the Moment.* In addition to her writing career, she is an operatic soprano who performs throughout the United States and Europe. She lives with her husband, Stanford Felix, in Lawrence, Kansas.